MW01098414

Engineered Transparency

Published by
Princeton Architectural Press
37 East Seventh Street
New York, New York 10003

For a free catalog of books, call 1.800.722.6657.
Visit our website at www.papress.com.

Printed and bound in China
11 10 09 08 4 3 2 1 First edition

This book was made possible by the generous sponsorship of Oldcastle Glass®, the leading North American supplier of architectural glass and aluminum glazing systems, including custom-engineered curtain and window walls, architectural windows, storefront systems, doors, and skylights.

Editor: Laurie Manfra
Designer: Jan Haux

Special thanks to: Nettie Aljian, Sara Bader, Dorothy Ball, Nicola Bednarek, Janet Behning, Becca Casbon, Carina Cha, Penny (Yuen Pik) Chu, Russell Fernandez, Pete Fitzpatrick, Wendy Fuller, Clare Jacobson, Aileen Kwun, Nancy Eklund Later, Linda Lee, Aaron Lim, Katharine Myers, Ceara O'Leary, Lauren Nelson Packard, Jennifer Thompson, Arnoud Verhaeghe, Paul Wagner, Joseph Weston, and Deb Wood of Princeton Architectural Press
—Kevin C. Lippert, publisher

Library of Congress Cataloging-in-Publication Data
Engineered transparency : the technical, visual, and spatial effects of glass / Michael Bell and Jeannie Kim, editors ; preface by Mark Wigley.—1st ed.
p. cm.
Includes bibliographical references and index.
ISBN 978-1-56898-798-9 (hardcover : alk. paper)
1. Glass construction—Congresses. 2. Architecture, Modern—21st century—Congresses. 3. Architectural glass—Congresses. I. Bell, Michael, 1960– II. Kim, Jeannie, 1974–
NA4140.E46 2008
721'.04496—dc22

2008024927

Engineered Transparency— The Technical, Visual, and Spatial Effects of Glass

Michael Bell and
Jeannie Kim, editors

Princeton Architectural Press
New York

Contents

Foreword

Architects have created buildings using glass in inspiring ways for hundreds of years. Today, the designers and creators of our modern world continually push the limits of what a building can be. As a result, major advances in glass engineering and architecture have expanded the imaginations of visionary design professionals around the world. In addition to the beauty, majesty, and functional versatility of glass architecture, glass technologies have led to significant structural innovations and measurable energy efficiencies. The result has spawned a re-emergence of glass as a visually and culturally accepted material in modern architecture.

In September 2007, a three-day symposium, "Engineering Transparency: Glass in Architecture and Structural Engineering" held at Columbia University in New York City, brought together some of the world's most extraordinary minds in modern architecture to discuss their ideas and experiences in glass design and engineering. After a stimulating keynote address by Japanese architect Kazuyo Sejima of SANAA, participants explored a wide range of topics relating to glass architecture in sessions led by forty experts.

As part of an ongoing commitment to architecture and the arts, Oldcastle Glass served as the proud sponsor of this initiative, in collaboration with the leadership of Columbia University's Graduate School of Architecture, Planning, and Preservation and the Department of Civil Engineering and Engineering Mechanics, in partnership with the Technische Universität, Dresden's Institute of Building Construction.

This book presents highlights from the symposium, showcasing key insights gained from the collective wisdom, talents, and passion of more than 300 architects, engineers, scholars, and industry experts who participated in this interdisciplinary conference. With the dissemination of this publication, Oldcastle Glass seeks to share the impact of this pivotal conference, inspiring others toward a better understanding and appreciation of major innovations and opportunities in glass architecture.

—Edwin B. Hathaway, Chief Executive Officer, Oldcastle Glass

Preface

Why would a school, dedicated to radical experimentation and potential futures of the built environment, launch a series of intense investigations into materials? Why would it collaborate so closely with individuals who specialize in manufacturing materials as ubiquitous as glass? And furthermore, why would an institution so devoted to tomorrow concentrate on the details of practice today?

The economic and cultural forces now shaping global architecture—complex flows of resources driven by precise material performances—have led to the current state in which leaders in the field and in the research community increasingly find themselves side by side, facing the same questions and learning from each other. When the properties of materials can be custom designed to address an extraordinarily wide range of parameters, there is no longer such a thing as an ordinary material. Even the most routine practices harbor extraordinary potential, and envisioning a radical new future is no longer a specialized speculative venture undertaken at the most advanced schools and labs; it is ever present in the field.

When a school operates as a laboratory on the future of the built environment, it joins forces with new kinds of ventures. The deeper one delves into our design studios, history and theory classes, visual studies workshops, building technology classes, and research units, the more one encounters the same urgent questions being tested at leading design offices, consultancies, technical laboratories, manufacturers, and building sites. In the new paradigm of multitasking and parallel processing, teachers and students are re-engaging with materials at every level, testing them in exciting and important ways. Similarly, the current generation of architects is developing entirely new expectations and forms of experience. It is crucial that we bring together the world's leading designers, scientists, historians, theorists, artists, educators, and engineers to reassess the state of the art in material practice.

—Mark Wigley, Dean, Columbia Graduate School of Architecture, Planning, and Preservation

Introduction

In his essay, "Aldo Rossi: The Idea of Architecture and the Modena Cemetery," Rafael Moneo wrote that, to secure the authority and foundations of architecture in the postwar city, Rossi had adopted an "evasive" and self-imposed amnesia to technology. As Moneo wrote, Rossi's architecture was "deliberately forgetting the framework of the real, even at levels as evident and compromised as the technological one." In contrast, aspirations for architecture today are increasingly based on highly engineered forms of design; more often than not, they are situated within economic and political imperatives that are otherwise understood as fortunate links to high-end production and research techniques. At its most advanced, this intricate work is deeply organized, and its relation to production follows systemic coordination and control factors. Yet, architectural goals that run counter to these factors persist. Counterintuitive to the efficiency of new technologies (and to the abatement of risk), we often see design strategies destined to aggravate the stability and resolve of these new controls. As technologies allow for new levels of risk amelioration, we also see new levels of ambition and a renewed fusion of design with technological potential. One is not possible without the other. This is not design aided by technology; it is design made possible by it. By that I mean, it is the redefinition of technological intervention: a fusion of design and technology as completely integral.

The Glass Pavilion at the Toledo Museum of Art exemplifies the role that constraints play when architects engage engineers in the coordination of spatial possibilities with thermal or structural potentials. The SANAA building is also an example of a kind of architectural transcription, where otherwise well-understood building forms or experiences are rewritten in the context of engineered systems of control and management. SANAA routinely states that their work should not be seen as an extension of that of Mies van der Rohe. Given the differences in how each manages energy, solar gain, and structure—as well as the fundamental contributions of the engineering team of Guy Nordenson, Matthias Schuler, and Mark Malekshahi—it is clear that the Glass Pavilion is not a Miesian project. In fact, new technologies are rewriting architecture in ways that sever it from the linguistic and semiotic familiarities of the past, and in ways that increasingly allow work on architecture to occur in exactly those areas of amnesia, the cordoned-off quarters of a previous generation's work.

Glass is unique in the place it takes in the spectrum of building materials, in part because its use has often been conflated with aesthetic and technical issues. From its origins, its fragility, coupled with its clarity, has always demanded our attention. It has always been impossible to take glass for granted. When we look through it, it begs us to discount its presence. Yet, it is suffused with qualities that compel us to notice it and to manage its fragility. Glass is never perfectly transparent; rather, its complex surface characteristics are reflective. A less obvious aspect of it forms the foundation for the work assembled here. Glass has an overt and demonstrative relationship spanning multiple observers and histories. That is, it has a precise array of historical, as well as actual, subjects. The history of the glass building traces a precise trajectory. Any student of architecture has willingly (or unwillingly) occupied this history, usually without having seen the works firsthand. More often, they are recorded in textual analyses or photography. At the level of day-to-day use, however, these viewers become their own form of users. Their role, as visual subjects, accounts for a kind of occupation, where the more essential or professional terms, such as owner or resident, are replaced with that of temporal or visual occupant. These occupations and their subjects constitute experiences at one end of the spectrum. At the other end, the material scientists, engineers, and designers bring the material to its final implementation. The work included here ranges from the visual aspects of glass and the historically premised experience of the end user (in all of its forms) to a far wider examination of material performance and viewing subjects. The optical/visual project is one of discrete examination and calculation. It creates a fine gradient of effects and situates glass in a host of new systems of adjacencies and armatures. This book offers subtle visualizations of the properties of glass as a material, and it shows what these properties allow architecturally, thereby raising expectations for climate engineering, building design, new forms of structure and sealants, and, ultimately, for a new consideration of the political implications of architectural design. But what is most important are the ways in which glass is rewriting its surroundings: in literal ways, by changing its own framing or suspension systems; and in not so literal ways, by revising the cultural or social experiences that define space. Glass has become less about abetting observation; it is something to be observed in itself. Which aspects of glass do we most often refer to when speaking about glass today, and what new and unforeseen aspects do we casually refer to when we speak of glass in contemporary architecture and engineering? And how have these aspects already changed the meaning of the material?

Staging Its Own Disappearance

Glass is increasingly considered a renewed, radical material but there is an equally strong counterargument that the ubiquity of glass architecture also carries a lack of shock value in its implementation. The commodity of the spectacle—in what appears to be quasi-innovative, market-driven architecture—is apparent in the flush of new glass curtain-wall apartment buildings in Manhattan and worldwide.

As much as these issues are present and worthy of inquiry, there is a sense that glass, even in its most advanced applications, no longer provides an extraordinary starting point for understanding metropolitan life. Not to diminish the achievements featured in the context of this book, but even in its most advanced installations, glass is setting the stage for its own disappearance. In an idealized realm without reflection or surface complexity, glass has always strived to disappear. But now, as a component embedded in an ensemble of correlated procedures, glass has a newly enhanced scope and an ability to manage performance and moderate risk in ways that no building system ever has. This process is far better at anticipating risk and modeling a reaction that outperforms any prior abilities, and it places glass in the unique position of having benefited in countless ways from current advances in computation and materials technology. It means that glass is not a study in isolation but an integral component within a wide array of literal and extended computational systems. Glass is still glass, but only if you examine it in isolation. Beyond that, its identity has been deeply reengineered; its historical evolution, and that of its subjects, has changed dramatically.

Material aspects of glass have also withstood scrutiny. If its brittleness and low ductility urged attempts to isolate it from its supporting frames, its lack of self-sustenance has afforded it more attention with respect to preservation than any other building material. What other material has undergone such relentless analyses of its own framing systems? The isolation of glass from force, coupled with a long history of adhesives and gasket systems, has led to perimeters becoming so sophisticated that the glass itself is less visible. We notice it less because we do not fear its fragility. In this regard, glass is less full of tension, as well as free from outside forces. This being the case, does the role of glass in "desecrating privacy," to quote Massimo Cacciari, still apply? Is there a role for glass that, either as fact or metaphor, still approaches its early role as participant in upheaval and instigator of radical change? Do we notice it less because we have so fully engineered its transparency? Or are we so unaware of its technical performance that we have overlooked its new cultural and political role? The qualities and political aspects of the work assembled here are being discovered, rather than planned. It is important to see this period of experimentation as tied to the idea of glass as flat, as opposed to visually deep or literally transparent, and to consider the larger subset of controls, networks, and material systems that result in glass becoming a membrane or surface, as well as a tool for producing new forms of social and cultural visualization. From lamination and tempering to the use of filters, films, and low-E coatings—not to mention installation by means of structural silicone and its corollary double-glass panel—an insulated glazing unit (IGU) is both literally flatter and physically flattened into its sustaining systems. That is, glass and the IGU have become equal to, rather than suspended within, its peripheral systems. It is engineered at chemical and optical levels, and observed in hundreds of ways, before anyone ever looks through it or sets it into a system. In early curtain-wall design and normative windows, glass was held in place by an applied exterior force. With the use of structural silicone, it is now pulled into place. The "bite" of silicone adhesion originates from inside the building and from an interior-framing surface. Recent work on adhesives, featured in this book, gives new depth to the quest for flatness.

Glass may have found a new role in architecture and engineering, in part because of how much we have observed it. Methods of observation, once understood at the scale of window or room, are now increasingly applied at the microscopic scale to the material itself. We have also examined its frames, adhesives, installations, and how it is shipped. In the end, a glass curtain wall may carry a more significant warranty than a concrete one, and, as such, its financial relevance is newly situated in practice, development, and urbanism. We continue to install glass walls as a way to see and to distance ourselves from that which we observe—to manage visual depth. But as a visual and financial mechanism, what does the future of glass offer? Is glass forecasted to be a more fully engineered product? As a brittle material, no longer overtly isolated from disturbance? As the management, rather than erasure, of risk?

Our professions are more closely interconnected than ever before. New means of measurement, calibration, and modeling are now essential to our work. Optimization, performance-based work, and parameters are newly common in architectural discourse. In many ways, the question "what does a building mean?" has been replaced by "what can a building do?" In the course of this body of work, one sees a persistence in the question of "what does it mean" or perhaps, more accurately, "what will it mean?" We are all doing more to calculate the future for our projects and to situate our work ahead of its own moment. From geographic information systems (GIS) and ray-tracing to the simple use of census data for analyzing demographics, the coordination of tool paths, and the programming of simulations for modeling thermal behaviors, our designs are increasingly data-dependent. Our new comfort with data is very real, but there is also a demand to integrate systems and correlate behaviors. We are decades beyond any idea that the architect and engineer are segregate species, that one simply fulfills the lack of the other. This book seeks to reveal the timbre of this new relationship. The abundance of calculation and control is certainly producing value, including added equity to owners, but one might ask, what is being preserved? Can we replace it with a new material that carries the properties of glass, but is not glass?

The Preemptive Strike

The avant-garde of the early twentieth century imagined a preemptive response to a city that had yet to fully emerge: a set of city-building machines not yet fully capable. Today, we form a reflexive, after-the-fact, and increasingly real-time response. Our site is global. It is rife with distance and inequity, and it is simultaneously and profoundly imbricated with near instantaneous forms of financial and personal communication. *Engineered Transparency*, in this regard, constitutes a new form of practice; it is a response to a city of calculation, filled with specificity. Despite outward appearances of randomness and misfortune, it is a city and world full of purpose that is as likely to manifest distance as proximity. Does glass architecture form itself as just one of many materials organized and demonstrated as business plans, as visual adjacencies for actual human eyes and financial adjacencies for real estate? If that is the case, what we are seeing in evolved forms of construction is not chaotic, nor is it completely organized. The material assemblies are certainly not self-aware, even as they are formed by an array of calculated and instrumental practices of very narrow focus.

Included in *Engineered Transparency* are observations on a range of new forms of urban life. The occupant, whose modes of observation may be focused or distracted, imprecise or trained, may not be aware of the extent to which engineering has supplied the moment they occupy. Glass is tied to the window, tied to the eye, and ultimately tied to observation.

Engineered Transparency is an impetus to discuss the state of the art in glass architecture and engineering. We believe that we are experiencing a watershed moment in technologies that are part of both glass and industry itself, as well as in the ways that products are being deployed and managed within this myriad of new strains. While this is a segregate aspect of what we see in glass technologies and production, it is also an aspect of the wider urban world. It is a world in which observation increasingly forms the generative engine for producing the spaces we occupy, with all of its distractions and forms of amnesia. It is an engineered transparency that runs well beyond glass, forming a new horizon against which social life emerges.

—Michael Bell

Portfolio

Much has been said about the understated quietude of SANAA's work. The collaboration between Kazuyo Sejima and Ryue Nishizawa has produced projects with universally admired exactitude and clarity. While their work pursues a consistent ethos of transparency, this transparency is not merely visual, material, or literal. Since the beginning of their practice, Sejima and Nishizawa have stated, their pursuit of transparency is more than physical; it's about the clarity of programmatic relations and explicitness of spatial organizations. In this sense, the stacked floors of the New Museum of Contemporary Art, in New York, are more transparent than the opaquely layered surfaces of the Glass Pavilion at the Toledo Museum of Art. Similarly, glass is deployed in layered vertical planes in the Christian Dior Omotesando Building, in Tokyo, as a way to obfuscate the slab.

By challenging our understanding of transparency, horizon, and gravity, they produce a palpable tension that is dependent on the observer's position. The atmospheric effects of the firm's deployed materials—apparent in the Toledo Museum of Art, as well as in the Flower House and the Okurayama Apartments—often belie the sophistication of mechanical and structural systems. Even in the renderings and models, the expected clarity of Plexiglas is undone by an overwhelming whiteness that hides edges and boundaries. Beyond the blurring of inside and outside, floor and ceiling, the observer is often left wondering how the columns could possibly be so thin, or whether the walls are really made of glass (or acrylic, which appears even thinner). The projects represented in this portfolio focus on SANAA's work with glass and on their understanding of it as a non-neutral surface. Glass can be transparent, translucent, or nearly opaque. In each instance, its deployment is meticulously specific and its meaning always charged.

—Jeannie Kim

Christian Dior Omotesando

Kazuyo Sejima + Ryue Nishizawa, SANAA

←

View of Christian Dior Omotesando, Tokyo, Japan, 2003

Christian Dior Omotesando

Kazuyo Sejima + Ryue Nishizawa, SANAA

→

Detailed view of facade

↓

Detail of vertical wall section

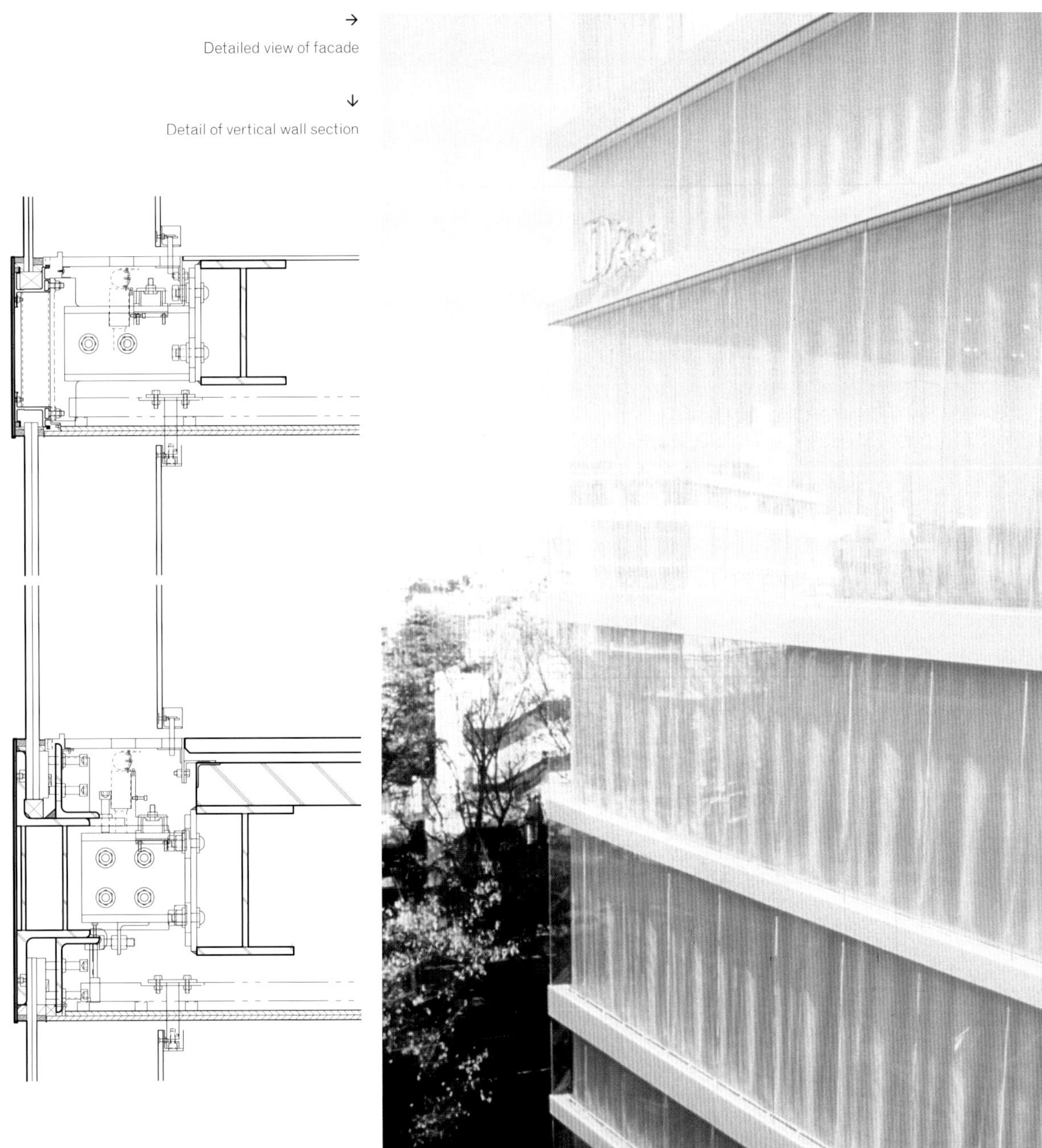

Christian Dior Omotesando

Kazuyo Sejima + Ryue Nishizawa, SANAA

↓

Omotesando street elevations

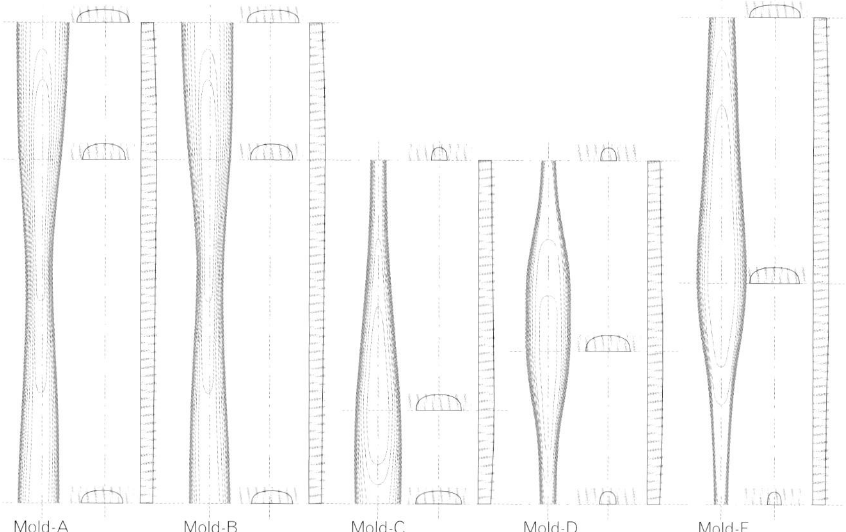

←

Interior cladding of half-transparent curved acrylic screens

Flower House

Kazuyo Sejima + Ryue Nishizawa, SANAA

→
Model view of Flower House showing relationship between interior and exterior spaces, 2006

↙
Plan of Flower House, 2006

↓
↓
Model views of Flower House showing relationship of landscape to interior and exterior

Okurayama Apartments

Kazuyo Sejima + Ryue Nishizawa, SANAA

→
Model view of Okurayama Apartments showing reflective effects of glass, 2006

↘
Planimetric model of Okurayama Apartments, 2006

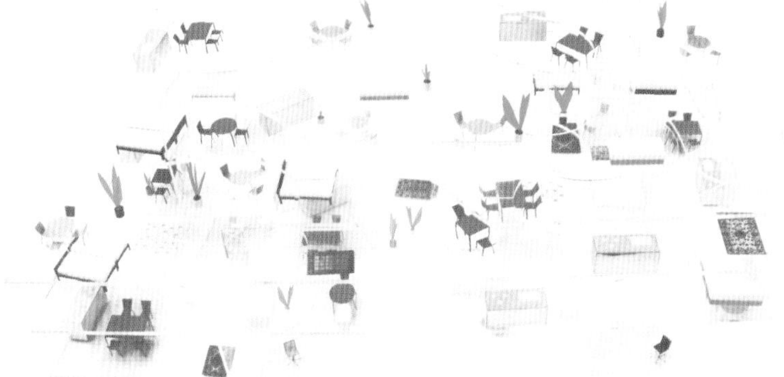

Okurayama Apartments

Kazuyo Sejima + Ryue Nishizawa, SANAA

←

Bird's-eye view of Okurayama Apartments showing relationship of individual courtyards to apartments, 2006

↓

↓

Model views of Okurayama Apartments showing intimate nature of interior and exterior living spaces

→
↘
Views of glass layering within the Glass Pavilion, Toledo Museum of Art, Toledo, Ohio, 2006

↓
Rendering of the Glass Pavilion

↓
Plan of the Glass Pavilion, Toledo Museum of Art, Toledo, Ohio, 2006

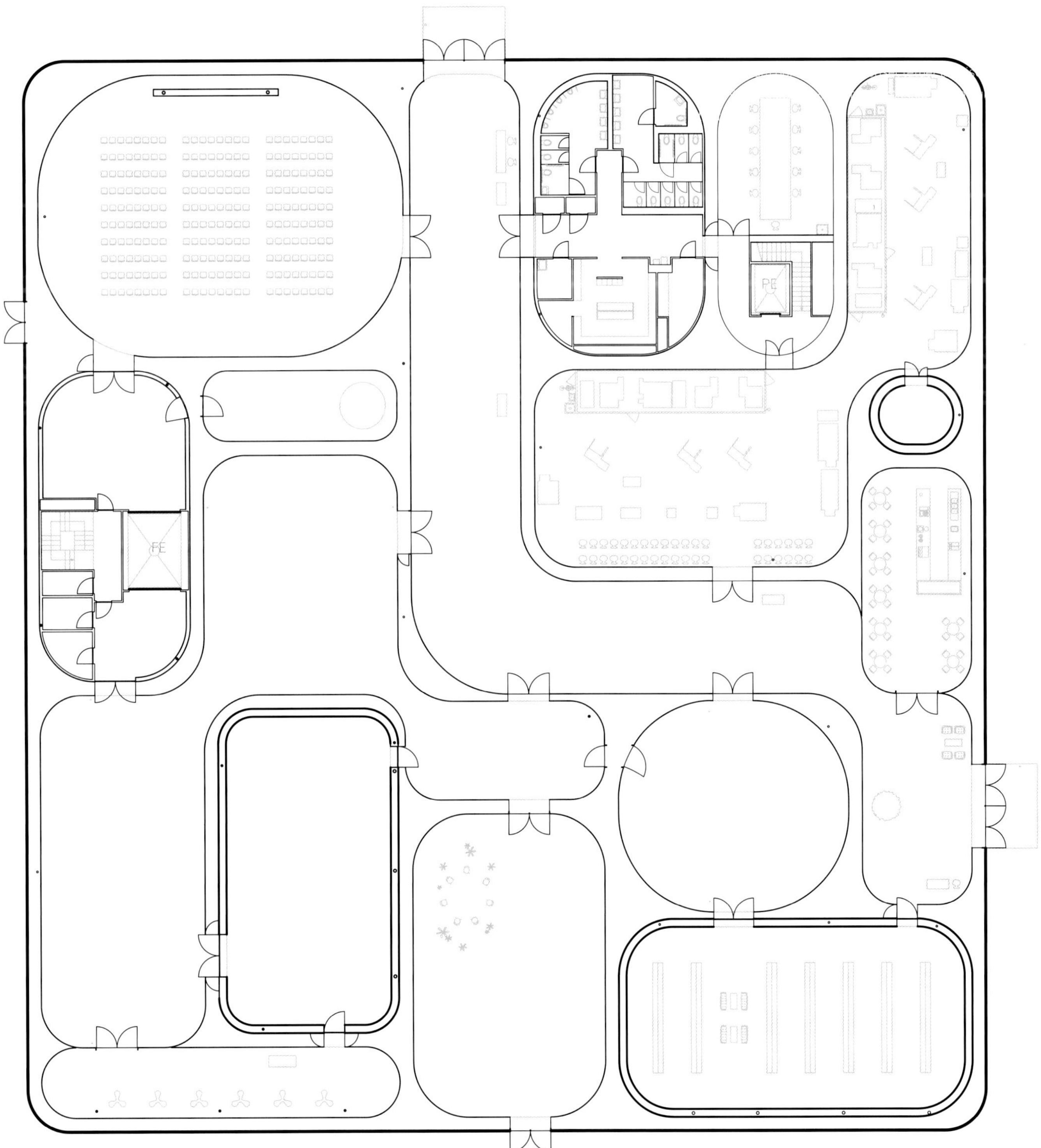

→
↘
Model views of EPFL Rolex Learning Center showing relationship between floor and ceiling planes in the bifurcating section, 2008

EPFL Rolex Learning Center

Kazuyo Sejima + Ryue Nishizawa, SANAA

↓

Plan of EPFL Rolex Learning Center, Lausanne, Switzerland, 2008

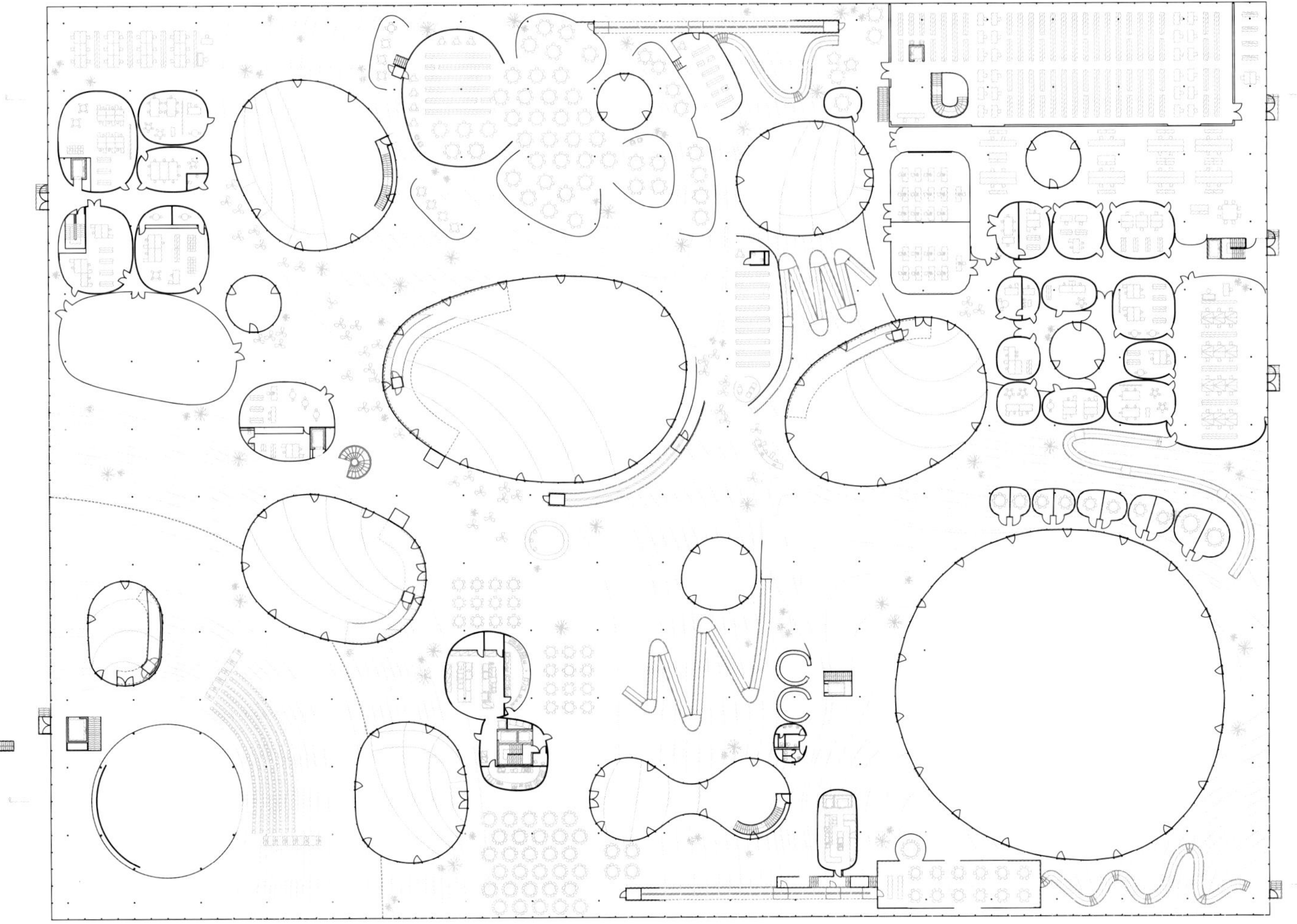

Toyota Aizuma May

Kazuyo Sejima + Ryue Nishizawa, SANAA

→
Model view of first level of Toyota Aizuma May Building, Toyota, Japan, 2006

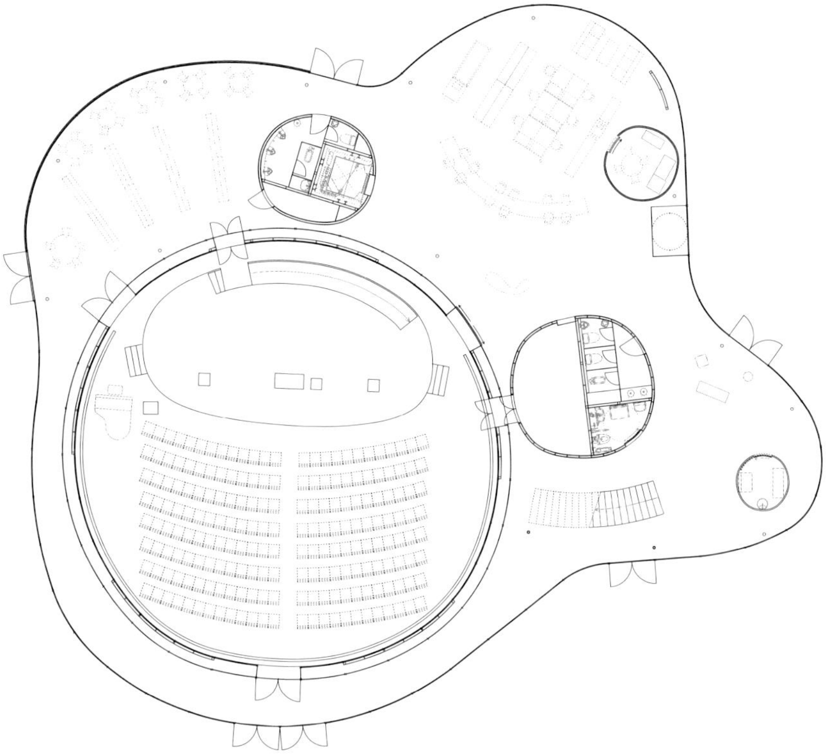

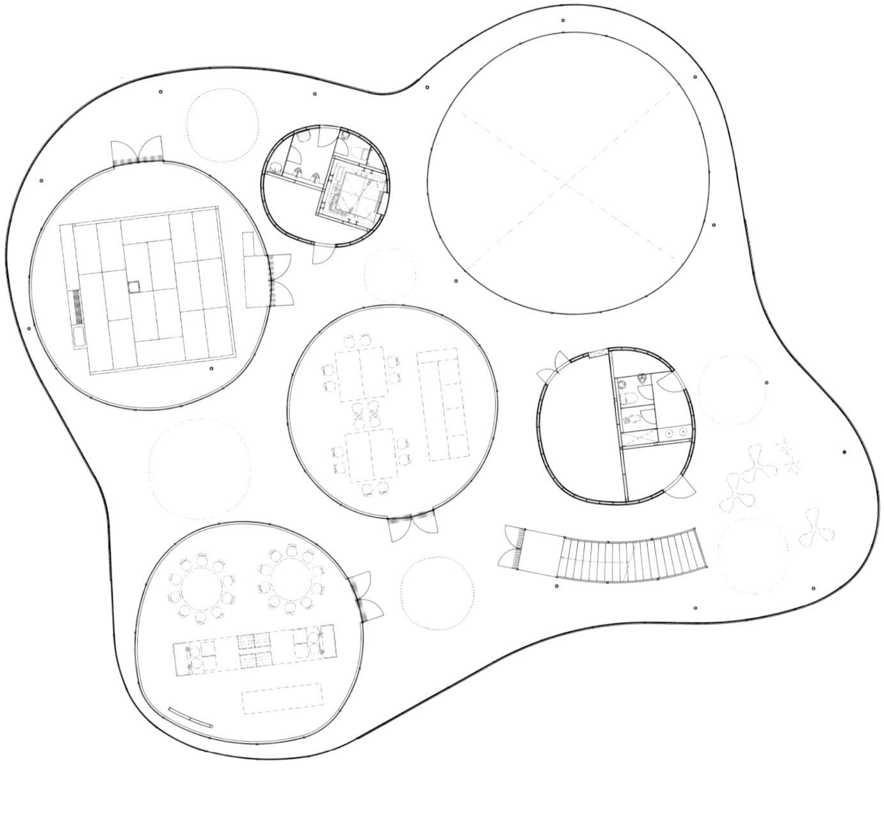

Toyota Aizuma May

Kazuyo Sejima + Ryue Nishizawa, SANAA

←
↙
Plans of levels one and three, Toyota Aizuma May, Toyota, Japan, 2006

↓
↓
Model views of levels two and three

→
↘
Model views with exposed structures, Vitra Factory, Weil am Rhein, Germany, 2009

↓
Bird's-eye view of site plan

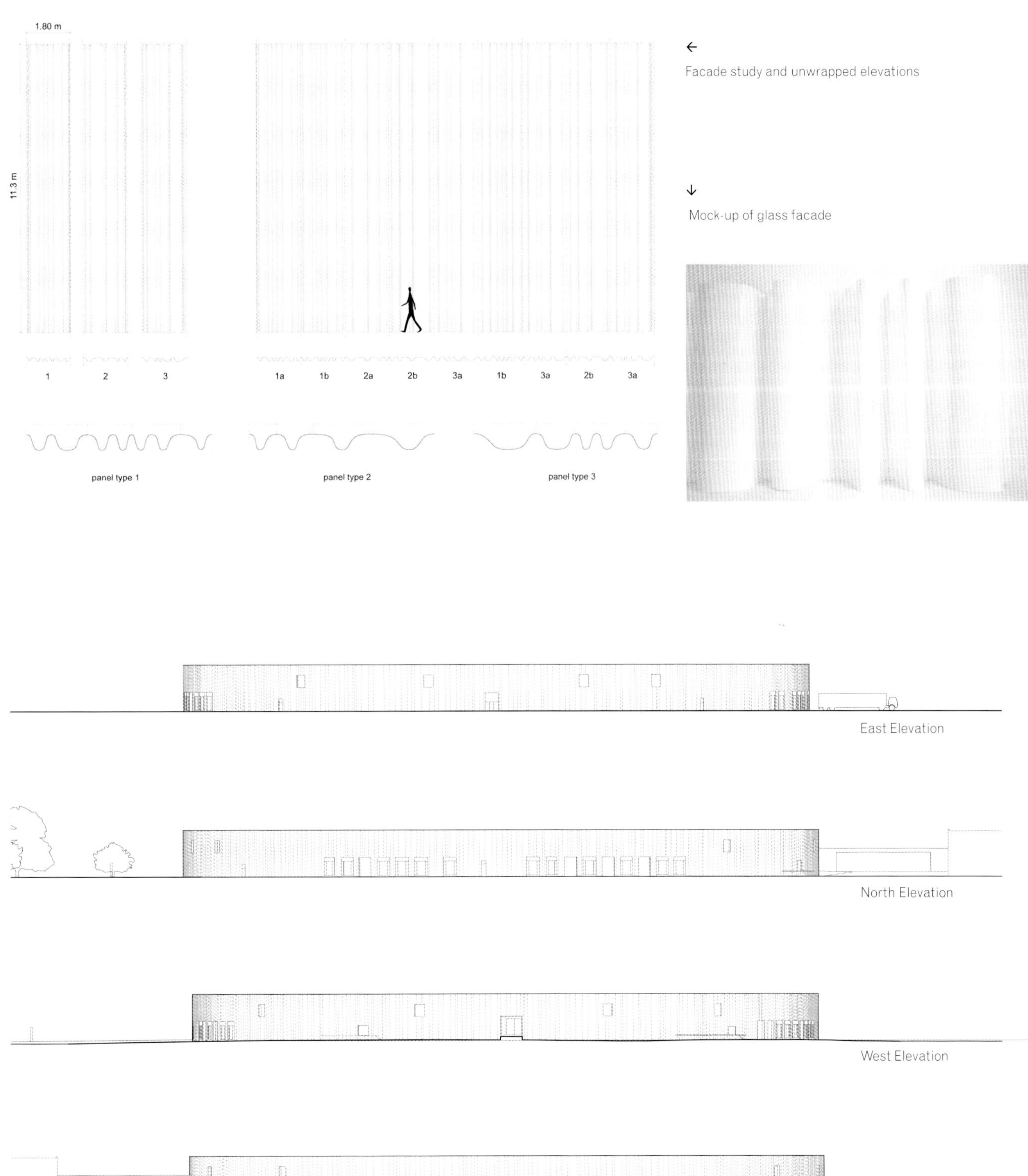

←

Facade study and unwrapped elevations

↓

Mock-up of glass facade

East Elevation

North Elevation

West Elevation

South Elevation

Essays

Bioconstructivisms

Detlef Mertins

Notwithstanding the significant changes that have taken place in technology and culture since the early twentieth century, it can be said that glass is, in fact, still glass because it never was *just glass*. Glass architecture was, and continues to be, both technologically and culturally motivated in the service of aesthetics that have cognitive and socially transformative effects.

The Berlin-based bohemian, poet, and fantasist Paul Scheerbart first launched the notion of glass architecture in his 1914 book, *Glasarchitektur*. In this mock technical treatise, he described many kinds of glass, some old and some new: majolica tiles from 1000 BCE, Gothic stained glass, wired glass, glass blocks, glass fibers, colored Tiffany glass, and even double-glass walls with light and heating in-between.[1] He also described structures with iron skeletons, reinforced concrete, jointless magnesite floor covering, cladding of enameled and porcelain panels, ventilators on the outside of windows, heating and cooling appliances, and even vacuum cleaners for use outside as well as in. In fact, he circumscribed the entire world of modern technology, including electric streetlights, steam and electric trains, and airplanes. For Scheerbart, and many who followed him, glass architecture encompassed the scope of total reconstruction of the world—"remaking the crust of the earth," as he wrote—for the pleasure and comfort of all people. If Scheerbart's prose was, as Walter Benjamin later observed, dry and technical, the world that he envisioned was full of technical wonders, no longer disenchanted by modernization but re-enchanted in a new stage of evolution ushered by the magic of inventors.[2]

Inspired by Scheerbart's scientific fantasies, architect Bruno Taut sought his collaboration on his well-known Glass House, a demonstration pavilion for the glass industry at Werkbund Exhibition, held in 1914 in Cologne, Germany. While he called it the Glass House, its structure was made of reinforced concrete, and none of the glass was, in fact, transparent. Instead, he used hollow glass blocks at the base, as well as for stairs and floors; colored glass lenses for the cupola; and brightly colored mosaics for the walls of the Cascade Room, through which visitors descended toward a large kaleidoscope before being released to the outside. | fig. 1 The cupola had a remarkably fine-ribbed structure in a shape reminiscent of the organic forms of acorns and the microscopic sea creatures known as radiolarians, which biologist Ernst Haeckel discovered in the 1880s and popularized in 1904, in his book, *Art Forms in Nature*. For Taut, as for Scheerbart, glass architecture represented a new stage in the development of technology, which promised to reintegrate humanity with nature. This was not to be a naive return to premodern

fig. 1 | Bruno Taut, Glass House, model view of the cupola, Werkbund Exhibition, Cologne, Germany, 1914

craft but a return forward to a new nature, a second and synthetic nature achieved by humanity, albeit according to nature's laws. It is not insignificant that glass, iron, and concrete are all synthetic materials, not found in nature but fashioned by transforming natural materials. Glass architecture served to designate a compound world—100 percent human and 100 percent natural—resulting from natural evolution and technological development rolled into one. In this world, it was understood that technologies were transparent when their technical forms were perfected and expressed their immanent material, mathematical, and functional logics. The geometric perfection of their morphology gave them the character of a crystal. Their capacity to perform functions and do work gave them the character of living organisms.

Finally, for Scheerbart and Taut, glass architecture created a new environment for new kinds of experiences; in fact, for a new subjectivity. The Glass House provided an immersive artistic environment: a total work of art that integrated glass construction, art, and mosaics, and that induced an altered state of consciousness or delirium as the subject dissolved empathetically to be at one with the world.

After World War I, Taut proposed a visionary *Alpine Architektur* for rehousing the displaced populations of industrial metropolises in new garden cities of glass constructions that would be distributed in clusters in the Alps, in an effort to literally remake the crust of the earth. | **fig. 2** Others in Taut's Crystal Chain circle offered similar fantasies. Artist Wenzel Hablik, for instance, imagined iron and glass towers growing from the ground like living crystals, remarkably similar to the twisted and torqued towers that are springing up all over the world today. | **fig. 3** Drawing on living creatures and plants, Herman Finsterlin dreamed of glass constructions as amorphous growths resembling mollusks and snails, as well as blown glass. | **fig. 4**

The critic Adolf Behne reconceptualized glass architecture in terms of both cubism and biology in *The Return of Art* (*Die Wiederkehr der Kunst*), published in 1919. Behne's book inspired the Hungarian suprematist and self-styled artist-engineer, László Moholy-Nagy to launch his own multiyear exploration of these themes with a painting of 1921–22 titled *Glass Architecture*. At that time, he also introduced constructivist pedagogy at the Bauhaus, mining the potentials of new materials, media, and technologies. From his transparent paintings to his lithographs, photograms, photographs, and stage sets, he constructed effects of transparency through overlapping planes, and he pursued a dynamic and interactive conception of space. He imagined kinetic constructions with which the observer would interact in motion, both physically and perceptually. In 1929, he concluded his book on Bauhaus teaching with a negative photomontage representing a future architecture

fig. 2 | Bruno Taut, *Alpine Architektur*, plate 10, 1919

fig. 3 | Wenzel Hablik, Exhibition Tower, Variation 4A 11, pencil, ink, and watercolor on cardboard, 1921

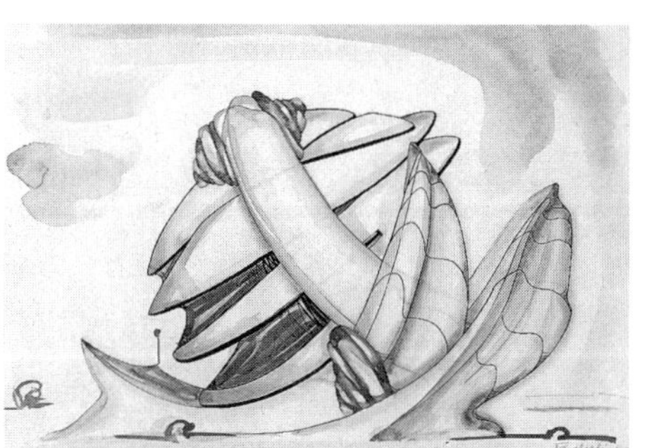

fig. 4 | Herman Finsterlin, Trauma us Glas (Glass Dream) watercolor, graphite, and India ink, 1920

fig. 5 | "Architecture," photomontage by Jan Kamman in László Moholy-Nagy, *Von Material zu Architektur*, 1929

fig. 6 | A spread from El Lissitzky's "Nasci," depicting the seven technical forms of creation and a Proun from his *Kestnermappe* of 1923

of glass that the next generation would be the first to experience. | **fig. 5** That same year, he produced a film, *Light Play*, which simulated the visual effects of a subject floating in a fluid space of light and reflection, moving among the high-tech elements of a rotating apparatus called the "light-space modulator."

In his writings of the late 1920s, Moholy-Nagy referred explicitly to the theories of biotechnics published by botanist Raoul H. Francé. Francé's writings on science and technology came into the art world of Berlin around 1923 and inspired other artists and architects as well, including El Lissitzky, Ludwig Mies van der Rohe, Siegfried Ebeling, and Hannes Meyer.[3] By the mid-1920s, what had begun as future visions of glass culture, architecture, and urbanism had been inflected toward an explicitly biologistic, biocentric, and biotechnic worldview among figures usually associated with international constructivism and thought to be enamored of technology as such. While Scheerbart did not use the term *biotechnics*, it may be apt for any architecture that aspires to the status of a second nature. I have coined the term *bioconstructivism* in order to foreground the biologistic dimension of this strain of constructivist art and architecture and, conversely, to foreground the constructive and generative orientation of biological theories that seek to describe how nature builds living creatures and ecologies. Bioconstructivism is not, I hasten to add, a term that was used at the time.

While the larger field of bioconstructive work is beyond the scope of the present essay, I will focus for a moment on an issue of Kurt Schwitters's journal, *Merz*, coedited by El Lissitzky in 1924, titled "Nasci." | **fig. 6** *Nasci* is Latin for nature; it alludes to becoming and approximates the German term *Gestaltung*, which refers to the process of generating form. Lissitzky begins the text by distancing himself from the ideology of the machine, which had become too reductive:

> We have had enough of perpetually hearing Machine, Machine, Machine when it comes to modern art-production. The machine is no more than a brush and a very primitive one at that... All tools set forces in motion, which are directed to the crystallizing of amorphous nature—which is the aim of nature itself... The machine has not separated us from nature; through it we have discovered a new nature never before surmised... Our work is a limb of nature.[4]

Lissitzky went on to explain that both art and science had managed to reduce form to its basic elements, with which they could be reconstructed according to the universal laws of nature. In so doing, he explained, both had arrived at "the same formula: every form is the frozen instantaneous picture of a process. Thus a work is a stopping-place on the road of becoming and not the fixed goal." Lissitzky expressed an interest in works that "contain a system within themselves," with the understanding that a system evolves over the course of a work, rather than preceding the work. His stated goal was to design "the peace of nature, in which enormous tensions hold the heavenly bodies, rotating uniformly, in equal balance."[5]

Taking a page from Francé's book, *The Plant as Inventor*, Lissitzky explained that all of creation was the result of seven technical forms: the crystal, sphere, plane, rod, ribbon, screw, and cylinder. Everything in the universe—architecture, machine elements, crystals and chemicals, geography and astronomical formations, art and technology—was built up from these fundamental elements. Next to his text, he presented one of his own Proun constructions to demonstrate these principles and goals.

Turning the pages of the journal, we find a diverse array of further examples of biotechnics in modern art and architecture: a neo-plasticist painting by Piet Mondrian; a collage by Kurt Schwitters; a sculpture by Alexander Archipenko; a collage by Hans Arp; Mies's curvilinear glass skyscraper of 1922 juxtaposed with a pavilion by J.J.P. Oud; a human femur bone (redrawn by El Lissitzky after Francé); a lithograph by Fernand Léger; Vladimir Tatlin's design for the Monument to the Third International of 1919 (a structure with large volumes that were to rotate within an open steel framework: a cube, a sphere, and a cylinder); another collage, this time by Georges Braque; and a dark yet luminous photograph of a crystal.

Looking outside the magazine, yet within Lissitzky's work of the same time, his *Wolkenbügel* (Cloud Stirrup) project for major intersections in Moscow of 1924–25 provides further demonstration of Francé's principles and of Lissitzky's idea of architecture participating in a dynamic universe, where structures are momentary stopping places along the way, in endless processes of becoming, through which amorphous nature takes form only to dissolve again into formlessness. | **fig. 7** Lissitzky's well-known 1924–25 self-portrait as a cyborgian constructor is indicative of a conception of the new human subject, whose vision was enhanced by optical instruments like microscopes, telescopes, and X-rays, while the capacity of its body was enhanced by mechanical extensions of limbs and bodily actions. | **fig. 8**

fig. 7 | El Lissitzky, *Der Wolkenbügel* (Cloud Stirrup) 1924–25

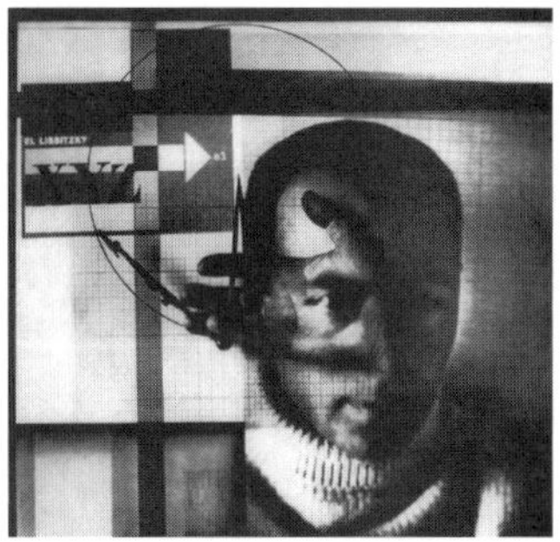

fig. 8 | El Lissitzky, Self-Portrait (Constructor) gelatin silver print collage, 1924–25

Francé's call for a biotechnic rethinking of architecture and engineering became important for architects whose ideologies were as different as those of Mies and Meyer. In 1939, Frederick John Kiesler propounded a theory of "biotechnique" that was more fully ecological and evolutionary than that of either Moholy-Nagy or Lissitzky. Like them, he was interested in formative processes, not just form, as well as in performance and the expansion of the human sensorium through technology.

I hope that this brief rereading of history reveals how avant-garde experiments in engineering and new media in the early twentieth century treated glass as much more than just glass; the glass culture envisioned by the expressionists and constructivists sought to reintegrate humanity in nature, enhance life, and revitalize experience. As we proceed into the twenty-first century, which has been characterized as postindustrial and biotechnic—as the age of genetic engineering, digital media, nanotechnology, alternative energy, and cradle-to-cradle design—it may be helpful to work though this history more thoroughly, as a prehistory of our own aspirations for ecologically benign technologies that enable buildings to perform as if they were alive. Generations before us have left a rich reservoir of work and thought that should be mined, corrected, and updated.

The fact that much of this history was forgotten in the campaign to forge a unified hegemonic modern movement should be salutary for us, a reminder that we no longer need to do that. Insistence on a universal "ism" has thankfully subsided, or largely so. Instead, leading schools of architecture are actively renewing the culture of experimentation as a more heterogeneous, inclusive, and open-ended alternative to monolithic, exclusionary, and dogmatic conceptions of architectural practice. A fuller treatment of the history I have offered here would, of course, need to distinguish between the use of science to legitimate the totalizing visions of modern architects and its role as stimulus for experimentations that need not be assimilated to new totalities. It is in this respect that glass is no longer glass, the commanding signifier of a social utopia. Rather, today's glass architects may be seen as participating in the evolution of the planet through the production of unassimilable diversity, one experiment at a time. Their work is aligned with Charles Darwin, who explained that evolution occurs over many iterations and generations and depends on the production of diversity, as he said, of "endless forms most beautiful and most wonderful."[6]

1 | Paul Scheerbart, *Glasarchitektur* (Berlin: Verlag der Sturm, 1914). Paul Scheerbart, *Glass Architecture*, trans. James Palmes (New York: Praeger, 1972).

2 | For Walter Benjamin's reading of Scheerbart, see Detlef Mertins, "The Enticing and Threatening Face of Prehistory: Walter Benjamin and the Utopia of Glass," *Assemblage* 29 (April 1966): 6-23.

3 | Raoul H. Francé, "Die sieben technischen Grundformen der Natur," *Das Kunstblatt* 7, no. 1 (January 1923): 5–11. The article is excerpted from Francé, *Die Pflanze als Erfinder* (Stuttgart: Kosmos, 1920). English translation as *Plants as Inventors* (Stuttgart: Jung & Sons, 1923). For Francé's reception in the Berlin art world, see Oliver Botar, *Prolegomena to the Study of Biomorphic Modernism: Biocentrism, László Moholy-Nagy's "New Vision," and Ernó Kállai's Bioromantik*, Ph.D. dissertation, University of Toronto, 1998.

4 | El Lissitzky, "Nasci," *Merz* no. 8–9 (April–June 1924).

5 | El Lissitzky, "Nasci."

6 | In concluding *On the Origin of Species* (first published in 1859), Darwin claimed a certain grandeur for his new view that the manifold powers of life had been "originally breathed into a few forms or into one; and that... from so simple a beginning endless forms most beautiful and wonderful have been, and are being, evolved." See Charles Darwin, *On the Origin of Species* (Cambridge & London: Harvard University Press, 1964): 490.

Mirror Glass (A Fragment)

Reinhold Martin

Here is my basic point. I will give it away at the beginning: There are things we are willing to see and things we are not willing to see, regardless of our technological capacity to do so. In its supposed transparency, glass both reveals and conceals, largely because we often have difficulty seeing anything but ourselves in it and through it. This is a special kind of narcissism. At one level it is metaphorical, like the association of optical or conceptual transparency with enlightenment and democracy, but at another level it is very real. Consider, for example, the travesty of enlightenment and democracy in the total vision of the security state—a travesty that is made simultaneously visible and invisible when we talk of such things as blast-resistant glass.

Once upon a time, before it became so fully militarized, transparency carried a more optimistic ring. Still, modern architecture never quite managed to overcome the fact that we cannot see our own eyes, except in a mirror. And the more we look at glass itself, even with the aid of mirrors, the more acute this blindness becomes. What happens, then, when the glass itself is reflective?

As a construction material, glass, of course, is much older than the adhesives used today to bind it together to form insulated panels. It is also older than the scientific and technological knowledge that, in the seventeenth century, made the vacuum possible, enhancing the insulating properties of glass panels by emptying out the air space. Like glass, mirrors are nothing new. The polished metal mirror dates to antiquity, as does its thematization in aesthetic discourse, which is not just a question of first order mimesis, of art imitating or mirroring nature. It also concerns the aesthetic naturalization of technical artifacts through mimetic reversal. Recall, for example, that in Ovid's *Metamorphoses*, the pool of water, the intervening medium that transmits the image of a young Narcissus back to himself, is described as "silvery" (or, in a looser translation, "as smooth as any mirror"). In that sense, the silvery mirror (not the pool of water) serves as a model for the aesthetic and psychic logic of narcissism. This suggests that the narcissistic desire to make the world over in one's own image—a basic precept of humanism, whether of the enlightened or the imperial variety—is technologically mediated from the beginning, rather than being the product of some "natural" human impulse.

Like all materials, mirror glass is fundamentally hybrid, both internally and externally; it is a mix of different objects, forms of knowledge, technical processes, aesthetic projects, economic interests, and so on. While its basic components are much older, it was not until 1962, after modernist ideologies of transparency—and

fig. 1 | Bell Laboratories, Eero Saarinen and Associates, Holmdel, N.J., 1966

its humanist counterpart, rationality—began to give way to a pseudo-humanistic postmodernism that large amounts of mirror glass were used to enclose a building. This occurred in a laboratory designed for Bell Laboratories in Holmdel, New Jersey, by Eero Saarinen and Associates, the second phase of which was completed in 1966, by Saarinen's successor firm, Kevin Roche John Dinkeloo and Associates. | fig. 1 In 1959, one year after Ludwig Mies van der Rohe and Philip Johnson wrapped the Seagram Building in a bronze-tinted metal-and-glass skin, Saarinen's office began working with Kinney Vacuum Coatings, a firm specializing in vacuum-coating glass for use in precision optical instruments. In response to Saarinen's request for a one way mirror, Kinney developed a material made up of two layers of glass, one clear and one vacuum-coated with a combination of aluminum and chromium, laminated together with a clear plastic film. Beyond its optical effects, this hybrid also turned out to have unique thermal properties. In addition to reflecting visible light in one direction, the microscopically thin metal coating blocked out portions of the infrared solar spectrum, significantly enhancing the material's insulating properties.

fig. 2 | Willis Faber and Dumas, Norman Foster and Associates, Ipswich, England, 1975

By the early 1970s, the architectural profession had already begun to notice and evaluate the widespread use of tinted and mirrored glass, particularly on office buildings. Surveys were conducted to assess its suitability for use, and in one case, qualitative data on such factors as "pleasantness" were quantified for different types of glass, adding to the proliferation of charts outlining the material's performance under particular environmental conditions. Thus, in 1975, when Norman Foster used twelve-millimeter-thick "anti-sun bronze toughened [or tempered] glass" in the headquarters of Willis Faber and Dumas in Ipswich, England, he was not using a new material. | fig. 2 Foster was, however, among the first to take advantage of the added strength of tempered glass by suspending it framelessly, with metal clamps only at the corners. Like mirror glass, tinted glass is impure in a chemical sense; though, as in Foster's case, the tint is generally achieved by introducing small amounts of metal into the glass itself during fabrication. When the tint is strong enough, the glass is anything but transparent. Such was the case in Ipswich, where, taking advantage of both the material's structural and optical properties, Foster was able to produce a sinuous, reflective monolith that settled gently into its urban context.

While Saarinen's office built its reflective horizontal monolith during the height of the Cold War, Foster was building during the worldwide energy crisis that erupted following the OPEC oil embargo of 1973. Among other things, this meant that in the discourse surrounding the building, the insulating properties of its single pane of tinted glass were emphasized as a tangible, technological response to the significantly less tangible—though equally real—risks posed by resource depletion at a global scale. The problem, of course, is that resource depletion is difficult to see, as is the environmental destruction that comes with it. This is partly because we tend not to experience these effects directly, at least at first. Rather, as with global warming, we tend to experience its effects statistically and probabilistically—that is, as abstractions captured in charts and graphs produced to quantify risk. Willis Faber and Dumas was an insurance company. Today the organization—now simply called Willis—still occupies Foster's building and advertises itself as "one of the world's largest professional firms specializing in risk management." The architectural fit could not have been better. Why? Because by 1975, the exceedingly uneven global landscape of profit and exploitation had produced a society that revolved around risk.

This idea of a risk society was formulated in the 1980s largely in response to political debates regarding environmental risk that arose in the 1970s.[1] We can take the term to be more or less synonymous with what others might call postindustrial society or, closer to home for architects, postmodernity. In that sense, Foster's building is truly and fully postmodern; Saarinen's is not. Not because of its stylistic properties, but because of its technological properties. Structural gymnastics notwithstanding, the tint of Foster's glass functioned both thermally and rhetorically as an instrument of architectural risk management, as did what I am forced to call the building's invisible invisibility.

In its nonrepresentational, mirrored blankness, Saarinen's building assisted in the becoming-invisible of the network (of networks) that we call the military-industrial complex. What it hides retains something of the brute, mechanical force of a war machine. We know that Bell Laboratories is dangerous, we are just not sure how or why. Whereas, like a pair of 1970s mirrored sunglasses, Foster's building makes itself visible and covers the very invisibility—the "undisclosed location," as it were—of power itself, which has become that much more abstract as it measures its gains and losses in risk and reward calculations laundered through "humane" corporations like Willis. However foreboding its glass curtain wall may be, inside we find a sustainable ecosystem populated by happy workers and palm trees, where the pool of water into which Narcissus gazed is now a swimming pool: the office building as second nature. | **fig. 3**

fig. 3 | Interior of Willis Faber and Dumas, Norman Foster and Associates, Ipswich, England, 1975

The result is second-degree invisibility that in effect blocks out the risks to human life elsewhere—over the horizon, in places where palm trees grow outside, not inside. By the 1970s, such risks were being (quite literally) produced, rather than merely "managed," by the conceptual infrastructures that, for example, guided the Vietnam War's environmental initiative, complete with palm-tree burning materials like napalm. The same is true of today's oil wars, which in so many ways are the result of a structural incapacity to see anyone or anything other than ourselves and our individual or "national" interests when we look at the world—despite, or really because of, the blinding glare of media overexposure. The Foster building, in its thoroughly naturalized techno-fetishism and in its neohumanism, conceals the real risks of environmental and other forms of destruction that corporate capitalism presides over, covering them up with a therapeutic pseudo-solution to a political and economic problem irreducibly mediated through technology and culture.

Here is another mirrored cover-up: PPG Place in downtown Pittsburgh's Golden Triangle, designed by Philip Johnson and John Burgee for the Pittsburgh Plate Glass Company and completed in 1984. | **fig. 4** Almost one million square feet of PPG Solarban 500 Clear Reflective Glass cover its surfaces. Solarban is a low-E glass that reduces heat gain from solar radiation. If we can believe its architects—and this is Philip Johnson—increased energy prices favored this choice. Unfortunately, the blighted urban context in which the complex was situated contained little in the way of buildings found suitable by the architects to be reflected in PPG's mirrors. Their response was to block it out, first by folding the building internally around a mirrored outdoor space called PPG Court, and then by folding the mirrors themselves. As Johnson and Burgee's monograph states,

> In an area awaiting the effect of PPG as a catalyst, the mirror could be expected to have little beyond itself to display. The complex makes the most of this situation by exploring the possibilities inherent in the material, through the use of a jagged facade that offers limitless reflections and re-reflections.[2]

Here at last is a coinage adequate to the problem at hand: not just reflection, but re-reflection. | **fig. 5** A hall of mirrors, a mise en abîme of fragmented imagery that, in principle, reflects only itself to infinity, ending up in a new kind of abstraction that might at last be adequate to the abstractions of neoliberal globalization, urban "revitalization," and the risk society—despite the supposed return to figuration represented by the building's pseudo-Gothic shell. In this building, as in so many others—such as Cesar Pelli's "Blue Whale" Pacific Design Center or the acres of mirrored glass generated by the Roche-Dinkeloo office—we discern a properly postmodern, second-degree abstraction that cannot be seen directly but that, in its very invisibility, corresponds to the utterly abstract reality of the world that it has helped to build.

To conclude, just a few words about a building of more recent vintage. Having arrived at a technique for bending panels of insulated glass into place on

fig. 4 | Pittsburgh Plate Glass Company, Philip Johnson and John Burgee Architects, Pittsburgh, Pa., 1984

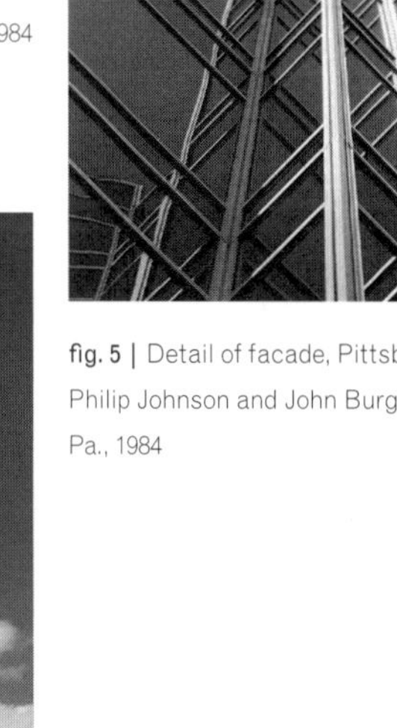

fig. 5 | Detail of facade, Pittsburgh Plate Glass Company, Philip Johnson and John Burgee Architects, Pittsburgh, Pa., 1984

fig. 6 | IAC/InterActiveCorp, Gehry Partners, New York, N.Y., 2006

site—within tolerances dictated by the insulating seal's ability to resist failure—Frank Gehry proposed to his client Barry Diller, the CEO of IAC/InterActiveCorp, that his new headquarters on Manhattan's west side be clad entirely in mirror glass.[3] | fig. 6 According to Gehry, Diller rejected the proposal outright, sending the architect and his model packing. Like the building itself, this decision seems entirely irrational, since the mirrors would have solved two technical problems at once: compliance with energy codes and budget. So why was the mirrored version not built?

We can only speculate, but perhaps because in Gehry's distorting mirrors, Diller saw neither himself nor a benign representation of his company. Instead, he most likely saw nothing, reflections of nothing, and re-reflections of nothing. In other words, it could be that this CEO, who saw himself as a patron of the arts, did not just recoil in horror at the crass commercialism of the now-stereotyped mirror glass office building. Perhaps he also recoiled from the truth of its abstraction. If Gehry had his way, the sixty corporate entities and identities that make up InterActive Corp would have been wrapped up and cancelled out in a feedback loop of re-reflection (invisibility to the second-degree). This may have been too much for a humane patron of the arts to handle. Therefore, in this "global" corporation now reimagined as a world unto itself, with coffee bars throughout, we encounter a narcissism that could not tolerate the truthful sight of its own image as a brittle, empty shell, rather than as a dynamic building full of people. That Diller and Gehry retreated into the decorative and "meaningful" safety of fritted glass—and with it, the clichés of clouds and billowing sails—is therefore understandable, given the alternative.

What was the alternative? To learn to see what cannot be seen, because it hides in plain sight. Just as Saarinen's blank stare, a mirror with nothing in it, led to the self-satisfied smoothness of Foster's ideological curves, Gehry's building, as built, may mark the obsolescence of mirrored glass as a medium of corporate narcissism. But with this obsolescence also comes a kind of half-life, whereby mirrored glass may finally allow us to see and to reflect on its previously invisible invisibility and the silent violence that it conceals.

1 | Ulrich Beck, *Risk Society: Towards a New Modernity*, trans. Mark Ritter (London / New Delhi, 1992), originally published as *Risikogesellschaft: Auf dem Weg in eine andere Moderne* (Frankfurt am Main: Suhrkamp Verlag, 1986).

2 | Nory Miller and Richard Payne, *Johnson/Burgee Architecture: the Buildings and Projects of Philip Johnson and John Burgee* (New York: Random House, 1979), 63.

3 | For a fuller discussion of Gehry's IAC building, on which this section draws, see Reinhold Martin, "The Crystal World: Frank Gehry's IAC," *Harvard Design Magazine* 27 (Fall 2007 / Winter 2008): 1–4.

A Crystal World: Between Reason and Spectacle

Joan Ockman

The most magical of all building materials, glass is a polymorphous substance whose variable states—solid, liquid, and, at least visually, ethereal—make its transmutation from a basic recipe of sand, lime, and sodium carbonate seem almost alchemical. Celebrated as a *super-material* by Frank Lloyd Wright in his essay, "In the Nature of Materials," and as *extraordinary* by Arthur Korn in the opening sentence of his classic survey, *Glas im Bau und als Gebrauchgegenstand,*[1] glass is also one of the defining materials of modern architecture. Its privileged status is due not only to its fascinating and changeling physical nature but also to its history and cultural interpretations.

In its primary identity as a transparent optical surface, glass has, since the nineteenth century, been seen as an embodiment of rationalism, in the sense of both philosophical and technical-instrumental reason. Yet glass architecture has also harbored antirationalist propensities. Joseph Paxton's Crystal Palace is emblematic of this constellation of quintessentially modern but paradoxical meanings. Having its origin in what was little more than a napkin sketch made as an eleventh-hour competition entry, Paxton's building was constructed to house an exhibition conceived in the liberal and progressive spirit of mid-nineteenth-century Britain. | **fig. 1** A polemical statement demonstrating the country's advanced level of industrial production and its enlightened international outlook, the Great Exhibition of the Works of Industry of All Nations was a success, in no small measure, by virtue of the realization of Paxton's visionary building. Celebrated for its lucid plan, its modular prefabrication, its flexible assembly based on a universal system of joints and connectors, its integrated mechanical devices, and its foresighted coordination and management of the construction process, the Crystal Palace was, quite remarkably, constructed in less than six months. | **fig. 2** Its overarching structural rationalism was seen as a metaphor for society's aspiration toward universality and global interconnection; a star-shaped clip used for diagonal bracing appears as a piece of pure, if subliminal, poetry. | **fig. 3**

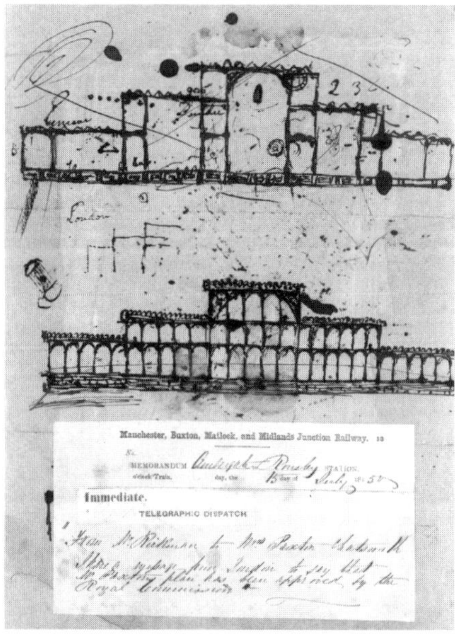

fig. 1 | Joseph Paxton, initial sketch of the Crystal Palace, pen and ink on blotting paper, 1850

At the same time, visitors to this colossal space—with its 900,000 square feet of sheet glass manufactured at the largest size ever attempted, a mere four feet—repeatedly remarked on the dazzling and disorienting experience of being inside it. The Crystal Palace was, in the words of one German visitor, "a spectacle incomparable and fairylike."[2] Not only did the cathedral-like scale and the pale-blue painted lattice of iron girders cause the ceiling to dissolve into the sky, but the atmosphere of evanescence and insubstantiality, which Sigfried Giedion

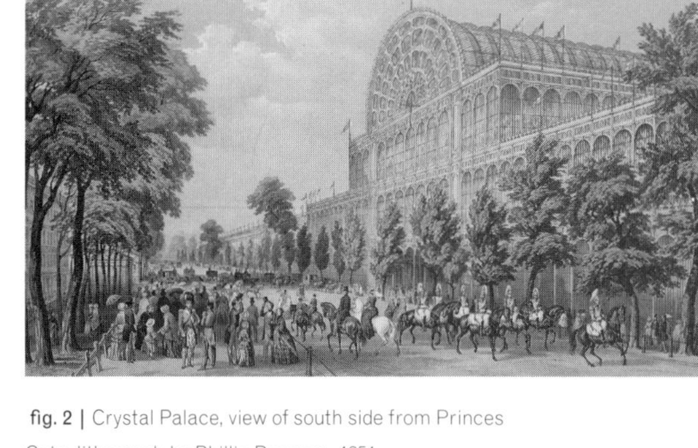

fig. 2 | Crystal Palace, view of south side from Princes Gate, lithograph by Phillip Brannan, 1851

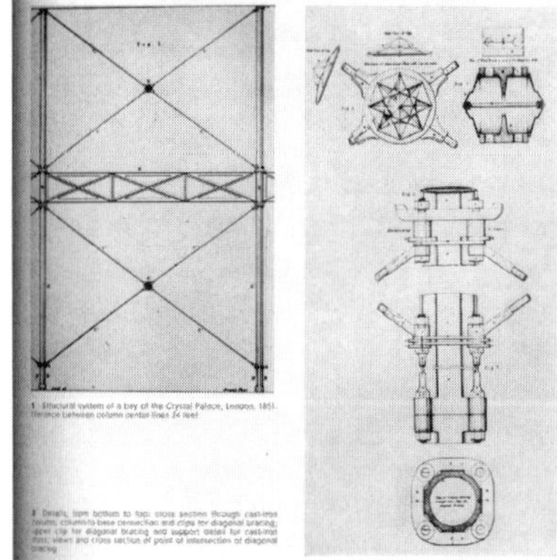

fig. 3 | Crystal Palace, structural system of a twenty-four-foot bay and bracing details, from *The Turning Point of Building* by Konrad Wachsmann, 1961

fig. 4 | Transept of the Grand Entrance to the Crystal Palace, lithograph by J. McNeven, 1851

fig. 5 | Crystal Palace, ridge-and-furrow system of roof, compared to the giant Victoria Regia Water Lily housed in the conservatory at Chatsworth, from *The Turning Point of Building* by Konrad Wachsmann, 1961

likens in *Space, Time and Architecture* to the paintings of J.M.W. Turner, was compounded by an exotic and exorbitant display of goods from every corner of the world. | **fig. 4** Marx's famous prophecy that under conditions of capitalism all that is solid would melt into air—proclaimed in the *Communist Manifesto* and published in London just three years earlier—could not have had a more vivid embodiment than in this glass building, which mixes rationality and spectacle as it inaugurates a new way of seeing.[3]

Notwithstanding his systematic approach, Paxton was neither an architect nor an engineer, but a gardener and conservatory builder. One of his chief inspirations for the ingenious ridge-and-furrow system that he devised for the building's roof was the veining structure of a colossal water lily he had tended in the great hothouse at Chatsworth. | **fig. 5** Paxton's analogy between inorganic and organic systems, between the mechanical and the natural, would become an ongoing dialectic of modern architecture. This same dialectic of reason and nature is evident in the more surreal forms of another iconic nineteenth-century building type, the glass-roofed arcade building.

The great subject of Walter Benjamin's unfinished life-project, the *Passagenwerk,* the arcade is a traditional building type that seems to internalize the contradictions of capitalist development. Its interior urban corridor, which rapidly increased in size over the course of the nineteenth century from modest to gargantuan, sliced through the real estate of old European cities with surgical efficiency. | **fig. 6** It provided a neat shortcut through the maze of medieval streets and a well-lit, weather-protected shelter for the leisurely pursuit of a new type of commerce. At the same time, its phantasmagoric contents and scenes—Benjamin writes about the fashion, circa 1840, of walking turtles in the Paris arcades[4]—stirred new desires in the subjects of early capitalist modernity as it channeled them through an ambiguously demarcated public-private realm of shopping. Rather than ethereal, the atmosphere underneath the glass roofs was immersive, like being in an aqueous medium. In his novel, *Le Paysan de Paris,* the Surrealist writer Louis Aragon describes the new spatiality as resembling an aquarium.[5] (A quarter century later, the same metaphor would describe Edith Farnsworth's sense of confinement and overexposure in her glass house by Mies van der Rohe.)[6]

fig. 6 | Passage Choiseul, Paris, France, 1825–27

The intermingling of rationalist and antirationalist impulses in response to an overwhelming modernity is also evident in the "glass culture" of the years just before and after World War I, as reflected in an extraordinary book by the poet-guru Paul Scheerbart. Scheerbart recommends building in glass for the most practical economic and environmental reasons, while at the same time indulging in wildly imaginative prophecies of a future glass world in which radiant light, streaming through colored-glass surfaces, brings joy and harmony to the planet's inhabitants.[7] This romantic imagery also pervades the glass dreams of Scheerbart's follower Bruno Taut and the architects of the short-lived Crystal Chain, who gathered around Taut just after the war, and it spills over into the projects and pedagogy of the early Bauhaus. In these utopian expressions of longing for a regenerative and socialist future, the essential reference point is not the dour tradition of classicism but the passion and spirituality of the Gothic cathedral, with its jewel-like windows of stained glass. The prismatic forms of Mies van der Rohe's early skyscrapers aspire toward this same sacred-secular sublime, while pursuing the expressive possibilities of translucency rather than color.

In the mid-1920s, during the heyday of the New Objectivity and the celebration of the *esprit nouveau* of the Machine Age, glass was hailed for its see-through properties and the benefits of light, openness, and healthful living that it conferred. The Radiant City was to be climate engineered for *exact respiration*, in Le Corbusier's term.[8] | **figs. 7 + 8** Arthur Korn's 1929 book documents, with pristine photography, the functionality of glass in the widest possible array of architectural uses, from office buildings and shops to hospitals, schools, houses, and interiors. | **fig. 9** Korn also illustrates all kinds of industrial design objects, ranging from light fixtures and chemistry vessels to furniture. In the *beinahe nichts* (almost nothing) of a glass-and-steel coffee table by Marcel Breuer, the structural possibilities of dematerialized form are pushed to the point of fetishization. | **fig. 10** In another metaphoric extension, the transparent environment was interpreted as a necessary training ground for life in a modern society predicated on the enlightened values of democracy, openness, egalitarianism, and freedom. As Benjamin put it in the late 1920s in his essay "Surrealism," "To live in a glass house is a revolutionary virtue par excellence. It is also an intoxication, a moral exhibitionism, that we badly need."[9]

It is no accident that the new abstract aesthetics of interpenetrating space-time were rooted in both cosmic mysticism and the new Einsteinian physics; think of the dalliance of some of the most polemical members of the avant-garde, such as Piet Mondrian and Kazimir Malevich, with spiritualist, esoteric, and *zaumny* (beyond-sense) philosophies. Architects would also quickly discover that glass had the potential to radiate advertising messages just as readily as transcendent social values. If for Le Corbusier, the city of glass heralded a revolutionary clarity by day, for Erich Mendelsohn it conjured dazzlement and seduction by night. Mendelsohn experienced the nocturnal effects of Times Square's illuminated signage in the company of the filmmaker Fritz Lang on his first trip to the United States in 1924. | **fig. 11** He and subsequent architects, such as Oscar Nitzchke in

fig. 7 | Le Corbusier, Genève: Immeuble Wanner, plan, 1928

fig. 8 | Sigfried Giedion, cover of *Befreites Wohnen* (Liberated Living), 1929, with photo by Carl Hubacher of the interior of a house by M. E. Häfeli, Wasserwerkstrasse, Zurich, Switzerland

fig. 9 | Bruno Paul, optics room at a glass exhibition, from Arthur Korn's *Glas im Bau und als Gebrauchsgegenstand*, 1929

fig. 10 | Marcel Breuer, table, from Arthur Korn's *Glas im Bau und als Gebrauchsgegenstand*, 1929

fig. 11 | Fritz Lang, photograph of Times Square at night, from Erich Mendelsohn, *Amerika: Bilderbuch eines Architekten*, 1926

fig. 12 | Erich Mendelsohn, night view of the Petersdorff department store, Breslau, Germany, 1927

fig. 13 | Pierre Chareau with Bernard Bijvoet, Maison de Verre, Paris, France, 1932

fig. 14 | Exterior view of the Glass House by Philip Johnson, New Canaan, Conn., 1949

France, would put glass and electricity in the service of advertising and exhibitionism, inventing a *Reklame Architektur* (publicity architecture) that powerfully and unabashedly expressed the dynamism of modern capitalist society. | **fig. 12**

After World War II, the utopian hopes associated with glass would dim, if not turn thoroughly dystopic. The philosopher Ernst Bloch, who, unlike his friend Walter Benjamin, survived the war's cataclysm, responded to the latter's exhortation about the moral advantages of living in a glass house: "The wide window filled with a noisy outside world needs an outside full of attractive strangers, not full of Nazis; the glass door down to the floor really presupposes sunshine...not the Gestapo."[10] In fact, more threatening at this moment than the ghost of fascism was the escalating Cold War. The precarious nuclear détente between superpowers fostered a climate of suspicion and containment, transforming the earlier faith in radiant openness into fears of Big Brother's intrusive panopticism and the vulnerability of glass buildings to attack. With obstinate if not naïve wishfulness, Lewis Mumford would describe Lever House's fragile curtain wall as a "laughing refutation" of "the threat of being melted into a puddle by an atomic bomb."[11]

The flourishing consumer culture would express its taste for an architecture that placed greater value on privacy, inwardness, and individual expression. While this attitude was already anticipated in the 1930s in Pierre Chareau's extraordinary Maison de Verre in Paris, it was epitomized in the postwar period in Philip Johnson's glass retreat in New Canaan, Connecticut. | **figs. 13 + 14** It was also reflected in desires for a richer and more complex architectonic language. In an influential two-part essay, Colin Rowe and Robert Slutzky, critical of the monotony and banality of the corporate glass box, called for a new architectural aesthetic based on poetics of ambiguity. They preferred a metaphysical or *phenomenal* transparency to see-through or *literal* transparency, looking back to Cubist still-life painting as their model for a richly layered, "retinally intelligent" architecture.[12] Marcel Duchamp's great crazed window, *The Bride Stripped Bare by Her Bachelors, Even,* provided a different iconic reference point. Enigmatic and surreal, it embodied what Duchamp called a delay in glass,[13] a trapping of psychic and erotic meanings within a large glass frame. | **fig. 15**

By the late 1960s, the air-conditioned nightmare and the well-tempered enviro-bubble would increasingly appear as opposite sides of a coin. Whether technologically inspired projects, such as Buckminster Fuller's Dome over Manhattan and Reyner Banham's plug-in "Un-House," should be understood as products of a benevolent neoliberal capitalism or a populist antiestablishment counterculture is ultimately undecidable. | **figs. 16 + 17** Banham's politics remain elusive, while Fuller's career vacillates between that of technocratic designer and maverick prophet.

The "Continuous Monument: An Architectural Model for Total Urbanization," a paper project of 1969–71 by the Florentine group Superstudio, is emblematic of this late-modern moment: it features a limitless glass grid that colonizes the face of the earth. With its imagery of hippies floating blithely on glass icebergs, it, too, embodies the contradiction between emancipation and apocalypse. J. G. Ballard's sci-fi novel *The Crystal World,* in which the earth undergoes a creeping and chilly process of vitrification, pursues a similar theme. Published in 1966, it reads as both a mirror-image parable of global warming and a prognostication of the glass icon-buildings that have been constructed all over the world since the sixties.[14]

Ever since the Crystal Palace inaugurated a modern glass exhibitionism, the architectural imaginary has oscillated between science and objectivity, on the one hand, and sensation and subjectivity, on the other. In our present moment, increasingly sophisticated technologies and smart materials are being put in the service of an architecture that combines environmental mastery with optical titillation. Contemporary architects, in a new spirit of positivism, are hybridizing and re-engineering the materiality of glass to the point that its very identity as glass is sometimes in question. Meanwhile, Guy Debord's prophecy of a society of spectacle holds truer than ever, as a crystalline architecture retains its affinity for ornamental richness and atmospheric effects. Such disparities are in keeping with the historical trajectory of a protean substance that continues to embody both the rational and irrational faces of capitalist society, its most pragmatic impulses and most utopian longings.

1 | See Frank Lloyd Wright, *An Autobiography* (New York: Duell, Sloan and Pearce, 1943), 337–39. "In the Nature of Materials: A Philosophy" is followed by "A New Reality: Glass." Arthur Korn's book, published by Ernst Pollak Verlag in Berlin-Charlottenburg in 1929, was translated into English as *Glass in Modern Architecture* (London: Barrie & Rockliff, 1968).

2 | Sigfried Giedion, *Space, Time and Architecture: The Growth of a New Tradition* (Cambridge, Mass.: Harvard University Press, 3rd ed., 1954), 252. Giedion quotes the phrase from a German visitor, who writes of his experience of the Crystal Palace: "We see a delicate network of lines without any clue by means of which we might judge their distance from the eye or the real size. The sidewalls are too far apart to be embraced in a single glance. Instead of moving from the wall at one end to that at the other, the eye sweeps along an unending perspective, which fades into the horizon. We cannot tell if this structure towers a hundred or a thousand feet above us, or whether the roof is a flat platform or is built up from a succession of ridges, for there is no play of shadows to enable our optic nerves to gauge the measurements. If we let our gaze travel downward it encounters the blue-painted lattice girders. At first these occur only at wide intervals; then they range closer and closer together until they are interrupted by a dazzling band of light—the transept—which dissolves into a distant background where all materiality is blended into the atmosphere.... It is sober economy of language if I call the spectacle incomparable and fairy-like. It is *A Midsummer Night's Dream* seen in the clear light of midday."

3 | On this theme, see also Marshall Berman's seminal *All That Is Solid Melts into Air: The Experience of Modernity* (New York: Simon & Schuster, 1982), 235–48.

fig. 15 | Marcel Duchamp, *The Bride Stripped Bare by Her Bachelors, Even* (The Large Glass) 1915–23

fig. 16 | R. Buckminster Fuller, Dome over Manhattan, photomontage, 1962

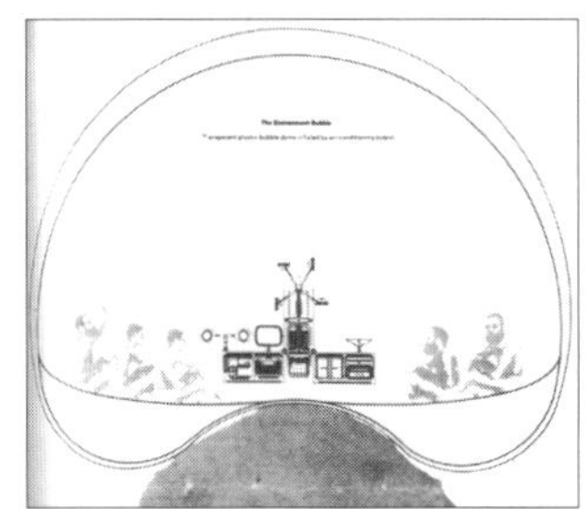

fig. 17 | Reyner Banham, "Un-House," drawing by François Dallegret, 1966

4 | "On Some Motifs in Baudelaire" (1939), in Walter Benjamin, *Illuminations* (New York: Schocken, 1969), 197.

5 | Louis Aragon, *Nightwalker,* trans. Frederick Brown (Englewood Cliffs, N.J.: Prentice-Hall, 1970), 10. Aquatic images pervade this novel, originally published in 1926.

6 | See Joseph Barry, "Report on the Battle between Good and Bad Modern Houses," *House Beautiful,* May 1953, 173.

7 | Scheerbart writes of the advantages of glass architecture for keeping out insects, of the desirability of using double-glass walls for insulation and temperature control, and of the industrial potential of new materials like fiberglass, wire glass, and glass brick. At the same time, he projects no less than "the transformation of the Earth's surface" and of mankind itself through the "miracle" of colored-glass architecture. It is important to emphasize that Scheerbart insists on colored rather than transparent glass. For a translation of this 1914 manifesto, see Dennis Sharp, ed., *Glass Architecture by Paul Scheerbart and Alpine Architecture by Bruno Taut* (New York: Praeger, 1972).

8 | Le Corbusier actually first elaborated the concept of *respiration exacte*—by which he basically meant a hermetically sealed envelope of mechanical ventilation—in relation to his 1932 Salvation Army building in Paris: "We were looking for an opportunity. It came; the shelter of the Salvation Army, the 'Cité de Refuge.' Six hundred poor creatures, men and women, live there. They were given the free and ineffable joy of full light and sun. A sheet of glass more than one thousand square yards in size lights the rooms from floor to ceiling, and from wall to wall ...The sheet of glass was hermetic, since warmed and cleaned air circulated abundantly inside, regulated by the heating plant and the blowers." Le Corbusier, *When the Cathedrals Were White,* trans. Francis E. Hyslop Jr. (New York: Reynal & Hitchcock, 1947 [orig. 1937]), 18. For Le Corbusier's ideas on both optics and climate engineering in glass architecture, see Jules Alazard and Jean-Pierre Hébert (with Le Corbusier), *De la fenêtre au pan de verre dans l'oeuvre de Le Corbusier* (Paris: Dunod, 1961); and Iñaki Abalos and Juan Herreros, *Tower and Office: From Modernist Theory to Contemporary Practice* (Cambridge, Mass.: MIT Press, 2002), 11–40.

9 | "Surrealism: The Last Snapshot of the European Intelligentsia" (1929), in Walter Benjamin, *Selected Writings, Vol. 2, 1927–1934* (Cambridge, Mass.: Harvard University Press, 1999), 209.

10 | "Building in Empty Spaces" (1959), in Ernst Bloch, *The Utopian Function of Art and Literature: Selected Essays* (Cambridge, Mass.: MIT Press, 1988), 187.

11 | "House of Glass" (1952), in Lewis Mumford, *From the Ground Up* (New York: Harcourt, Brace and Company, 1956), 165. Post-9/11, it is impossible to read this statement of Mumford's without a huge sense of irony: "Fragile, exquisite, undaunted by the threat of being melted into a puddle by an atomic bomb, this building is a laughing refutation of 'imperialist warmongering,' and so it becomes an implicit symbol of hope for a peaceful world."

12 | "Transparency: Literal and Phenomenal" was written in 1955–56; Part 1 was published in *Perspecta* 8 (1963), Part 2 in *Perspecta* 13/14 (1971). Apropos of the aqueous qualities of glass space, also see Slutzky's later essay "Aqueous Humor," in *Oppositions* 19/20 (Winter/Spring 1980), 28–51.

13 | Duchamp's instruction that *The Bride Stripped Bare* be understood as a "delay" rather than a "picture" or "painting" appears among the notes in *The Green Box,* a collection of thoughts on scraps of paper about the work that he issued in a limited edition in 1934.

14 | Ballard reveals himself in this novel to be a true (and dystopian) descendant of Scheerbart and the architectural fantasists of the Crystal Chain: "...what most surprised me, Paul, was the extent to which I was prepared for the transformation of the forest—the crystalline trees hanging like icons in those luminous caverns, the jeweled casements of the leaves overhead, fused into a lattice of prisms, through which the sun shone in a thousand rainbows, the birds and crocodiles frozen into grotesque postures like heraldic beasts carved from jade and quartz—what was really remarkable was the extent to which I accepted all these wonders as part of the natural order of thing...." Indeed, the rest of the world seemed drab and inert by contrast, a faded reflection of this bright image, forming a gray penumbral zone like some half-abandoned purgatory." J. G. Ballard, *The Crystal World* (New York: Farrar, Straus and Giroux, 1966), 93.

The Structure of Transparency

Nina Rappaport

Today, the culture of engineering glass—with the creative approaches of engineers integrating structure and skin—has turned design discussions inside out. Moving architecture beyond issues of surface and desired architectural effects toward the consideration of a new holistic paradigm that parallels the ideals expressed in Paul Scheerbart's *Glasarchitektur*, published in 1914, and Bruno Taut's *Alpine Architektur*, published in 1920, the discussion has evolved toward a new philosophy of glass architecture with crystal-like forms, prisms, and shifting spatial effects.

An engineer is an inventor, an innovator, and an artist who combines intuition with technological expertise and applies science to design. The engineer's work is not neutral, and it often takes the lead in a building's design or a project's organizational structure. Today, engineers are involved at the outset, designing alongside the architects, but such work is rarely recognized as creative involvement in designing a structure or three-dimensional model. As structural engineer Peter Rice defined it, "The architect's response is primarily creative, whereas the engineer's is essentially inventive."[1]

The structure of transparency is twofold: the engineering of glass at both the micro and macro scales and the performance of it structurally. Both aspects have technological and phenomenological implications in the effects that glass produces and the spaces that it shapes.

Glass is a dichotomous material. Its structure is both fragile and strong, molten and solid. Like steel, it begins soft and malleable but transforms into hard matter. With composites, it can become even stronger. By studying its behaviors, engineers imbue glass with new potential while taking risks structurally and materially and pushing beyond its known limits. Historically, the engineer's role in working with and structuring glass expanded from designing off-the-shelf products to customizing structural systems and detailing components for integration in what Ove Arup called the "total design" of a building or the synergistic composition of parts to the whole.[2]

Turn-of-the-century engineers such as Gustave Eiffel, Eugène Freyssinet, Robert Maillart, and Moritz Kahn invented construction systems and manufactured products, which they often patented. Engineers also designed manufactured products. For glass systems, a manufacturer typically made the glass plates, the framing, and the mullions, all of which were designed by in-house engineers, as is also the case today. It was common for architects to specify windows by selecting from preexisting products, such as double-hung sash or casement windows with pivoting or hinged fasteners. The builder then installed the windows, which filled the voids in the wall and protected the interior from the natural elements while also providing light and air. At the time, working with traditional materials such as wood or brick, the architect did not need a specialized engineer; it was possible to independently design an entire building.

The use of such products continued into the early twentieth century, as modern architects employed simplified curtain-wall systems made from off-the-shelf parts. Concrete-framed factories, such as the Packard Motor Car Company Plant and the Highland Park Ford Plant designed by Albert Kahn Associates, as well as the Larkin Building, designed by Lockwood and Greene, had wood industrial sashes in multiple groupings to admit light and air to the factory floor. The production of steel window systems, by companies such as Pilkington and Crittall Windows, in England, and Hope's Windows, in the United States, expanded with the modern movement. Large expanses of windows in Walter Gropius and Adolf Meyer's Faguswerk in Alfeld an der Leine, Germany, employed narrow metal mullions to increase illumination in the multistoried stairwell. At the Bauhaus, Gropius employed steel windows manufactured by Crittall, thus helping to define the new industrial aesthetic. After World War I, Albert Kahn developed the Victory sash, replacing steel (an essential wartime material) with wood, but the building industry and codes often limited the architect's choices. | **figs. 1 + 2**

When engineers designed entire buildings, they were able to push the technological potential of materials. For example, Richard Steiff designed a toy factory in Giengen an der Brenz, Germany, using an experimental double-glazed curtain wall that allowed light to permeate the factory floor, which was rare at the time. A frosted-glass facade held in place with interior cross bracing formed a cavity for improved air circulation. | **fig. 3**

Modernist engineers became expert collaborators, having the title *consulting engineer*. As part of the architect's team, they contributed to the structural design, which was and still is foremost in the articulation of a building's form. This is seen in the work of Peter Behrens, who could not have designed the Berlin's AEG Factory without engineer Karl Bernhardt. Another example is the architects of the Van Nelle Factory, Brinkman & Van der Vlugt, who, with the expertise of engineer Jan Gerko Wiebenga, set the concrete columns back from the glass facade, allowing the ribbon windows and slender mullions to form the aesthetic focus. In this way, the consulting engineer became a separate profession but remained connected to the building industry. | **fig. 4**

Through the 1950s, engineers continued to design manufactured facade systems, and many corporate skyscrapers in the United States were constructed

fig. 1 | Highland Park Ford Plant, Albert Kahn Associates, Highland Park, Mich., 1909

fig. 2 | Packard Motor Car Company Plant, Albert Kahn Associates, Detroit, Mich., 1905

fig. 3 | Experimental curtain wall, Richard Steiff, Giengen an der Brenz, Germany, 1903

fig. 4 | Van Nelle Factory, Brinkman & Van der Vlugt, Rotterdam, the Netherlands, 1927 .

out of them. With more sophisticated projects, such as Lever House and the Connecticut General Life Insurance Company Headquarters by Skidmore, Owings & Merrill, architects designed custom windows and wall systems, and the effects they achieved began to symbolize the corporate grandeur of shiny clean surfaces and precision. As noted in a 1955 builder's book, the new corporate office demanded that "the window shall conform completely to the overall architectural conception, and the architect will have to state and maintain his specification with exactitude." [3]

Jean Prouvé, a *constructeur* (combining the knowledge of builder, inventor, and engineer) working on the Center for New Industry and Technology (CNIT) at La Défense in Paris, France (1956–58), proposed an inventive solution for the three facades within the concrete arched volume, incorporating a hung-glass system of tilted panes and articulated steel mullions. He devised a site-specific system for cleaning the wall sections by means of a hanging shelf that functioned as an interior walkway for maintenance access and also braced the facade horizontally.

fig. 5 | Glass installation at La Villette, Peter Rice, RFR (Rice Francis Ritchie), 1986

For innovative projects, this level of design specialization has now become integral to the role of consulting engineer. Engineers such as Peter Rice (RFR), Tim Macfarlane, Werner Sobek, Jörg Schlaich, and Front (facade consultants) design structures that range from transparent to translucent and from solid to reflective in symbiosis with the architect's aesthetic and the building's performative requirements. Creative and inventive engineers work to achieve a specific effect in conjunction with the architect. | **fig. 5** Peter Rice described the role of the engineer working with glass as someone who

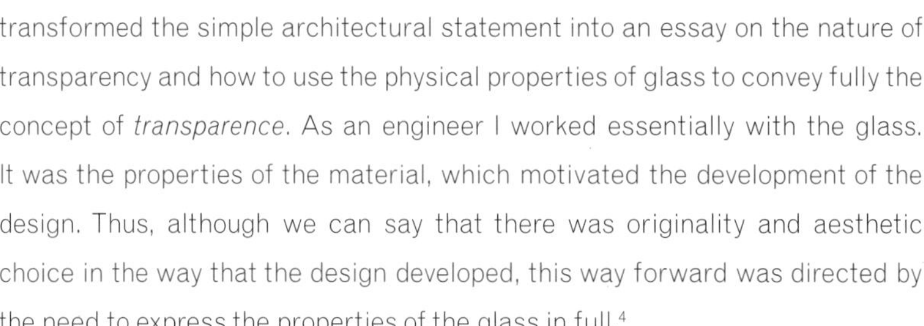

> transformed the simple architectural statement into an essay on the nature of transparency and how to use the physical properties of glass to convey fully the concept of *transparence*. As an engineer I worked essentially with the glass. It was the properties of the material, which motivated the development of the design. Thus, although we can say that there was originality and aesthetic choice in the way that the design developed, this way forward was directed by the need to express the properties of the glass in full.[4]

Thus Rice often focused on making walls of glass by designing the structure for holding glass in place. His systems featured steel clamps or bolts, in point supports, and cable suspension systems that supported the glass, thereby creating a sense of lightness and immateriality. In other projects, he emphasized the presence of the structure, as in the conservatories for the Grandes Serres Cité des Sciences et de l'Industrie at La Villette, which he designed with architect Adrien

Fainsilber in 1981. For this project, stresses were carried by the supports, not by the glass. Rice emphasized that "for a surface to be transparent the presence of the surface must be clearly defined."[5] His team developed a system of suspended two-by-two-meter sheets of glass configured in panels measuring eight-by-eight meters; the panels were suspended from above, with steel point supports inserted at the corners to carry vertical loads. Cable trusses resisted the horizontal wind loads on the glass without blocking visibility. This calibrated system of supports became a patented system and was repeated for many projects.

Rice's work on I.M. Pei's Pyramids for the Louvre—for both the above- and below-ground structures—expressed the limits of the materials. In the Inverted Pyramid, completed in 1991, the glass seems to hang, as in a hanging chain model fastened in place with clips and nodes in a meshlike configuration. As Rice describes it, "the suspended ties and struts, prestressed by the weight of the glass, balance the components of weight between opposite sides, and give geometrical contrast."[6] Transparency is achieved with both the main structure and the interior structure in a filigree of supports. Bernard Tschumi and Gruzen Samton's Alfred J. Lerner Hall at Columbia University in New York is directly influenced by these projects; Hugh Dutton, who worked at RFR, collaborated on the design of the glass facade.[7]

Recently, RFR collaborated with ABP, A+E Architects, and climate engineers Transsolar on the design of a laminated and tempered glass-and-steel walkway with an eight-meter span for Luxembourg's Chamber of Deputies building. A "flying carpet" floor provides a smooth transition between the different elevations of the two historic buildings. The eighty-millimeter-thick surface, built out of curved aluminium extrusions, is hollow, and it houses the ventilation, heating, and cooling systems. The stainless-steel suspension structure is formed out of two compact built-up girders, and a series of suspension rods double as handrails. RFR's fixed-point double-glazed units for the glass envelope perform a structural role. By sealing the lower sheet in a reinforced plastic layer, they minimized the potential risk of the glass falling. | **fig. 6**

fig. 6 | Detail of fixed-point double-glazed units, Peter Rice, RFR

RFR also designed the addition to the Strasbourg TGV train station with the architect of the Société Nationale des Chemins de fer Français (SNCF), Jean-Marie Duthilleul, as well as Transsolar and Seele GmbH & Co.KG. The 140-meter-long, toroidal shelter, which relies on a slender prestressed steel structure and cold-formed curved glass, is transparent so that the historic station remains visible. The new glass structure houses the primary circulation spaces in a complex monolithic roof formed out of a 5,800-square-meter glass bubble, with intermediate temperature control requirements. The toroidal geometry of the constructive

fig. 7 | Alpine House in Kew Gardens, London. Dewhurst Macfarlane with Wilkinson Eyre, 2006

fig. 8 | Facade study of Vakko Building in Istanbul, Turkey, REX with Front, 2007

elements, glass sheets, and structural members is repetitive, and they are contained in planar or conical surfaces, following the torus. The steel structure is organized in elements that are loaded axially, in order to limit their transverse dimensions, providing increased transparency through the structural elements. The primary curved frames are prestressed, as is the surface bracing of the station roof, to maximize the use of slender tension elements, cables, and rods. The cold-forming strategy for shaping of the glass was at RFR's suggestion in order to obtain the curvature during the lamination process.

Alternatively, the approach of engineering firm Dewhurst Macfarlane and Partners often emphasizes the use of glazing in such a way that the glass itself becomes the structure. Macfarlane investigates the "design intelligence" behind the material and its functional processes, considering ways of transforming a historically nonstructural material into a structural one. Macfarlane is interested in glass performing the structural work independently, without the intensity of cables, frames, and bolts. The firm often laminates glass with acrylics and uses annealing to augment performance, making the material composite stronger and seamless.

Within recent structural glass history, perhaps the firm's most pivotal project is the subway station for the Tokyo International Forum (Rafael Viñoly Architects, 1996). Macfarlane designed a cantilevered glass canopy spanning eleven meters. As a load-bearing structure, three laminated glass sheets form parallel beams, which were toughened with Plexiglas panes, and cantilever over the station entrance. The three-quarter-inch glass sheets are bolted together, transferring the forces and preventing high stresses that would otherwise lead to failure.

The replacement Alpine House in Kew Gardens, London, designed by Wilkinson Eyre Architects, in 2006, is a lightweight glass house with a concealed airflow system. The building's shape is derived from two sections of a cylinder, cut and propped up against each other to form parabolic arches, where the cylindrical profile of the wall complements the structural elements. Parallel vertical cables support the glass, as in a harp. Held in place through the joint, long pin fittings support the glass panels at their corners with plate clamps. | **fig. 7**

The integration of structure as decoration exemplifies what I call *deep decoration*, or beyond surface, where the form that the structure takes, whether visible or not, is also decorative. It is inside out: the structure has design emphasis, is visible, or it has a deeper effect in thickening the facade by creating layers.

For the Vakko Building in Istanbul, Turkey, REX architects wanted to "dematerialize the glass, rather than have a strong structure." Working with Front, they folded the glass panels using a bumped-up and indented X-shape to create both a structural system and a facade pattern. To achieve the "X," they worked closely with a local Turkish contractor to develop this system in an innovative way. The glass was heat-slumped to change it from a solid to a softer material, more like its original state. A template was placed below and heated coils were positioned above the areas where they wanted the X-pattern. When it cooled, the rounded lines of the X were formed. Rather than use mullions or cables to support the glass panel, it was designed to be self-reinforcing, similar to the way the ridges in corrugated sheet-metal provide self-reinforcement. The glass is transparent and it distorts at the curves of the bumps, creating the overall effect of a fluctuating glass facade. | **fig. 8**

Engineer Neil Thomas of Atelier One employed an innovative system for Lab Architect's Federation Square, in Melbourne, Australia, using the Penrose pinwheel as the structural diagram. He noted that "when you crumple a piece of paper, or fold it, it can stand. You give it depth, although a single plane. If you then distort the square, you can turn the element and it looks different; then you can place the elements together." The Penrose algorithm allows for the shape of the envelope to change and fold dynamically. The plaza's surface is also defined by this triangulated system. As the triangle turns and shifts, the compositional array organizes into a field. The algorithm provided a way for the architects to break out of the norm of walls, windows, and apertures as a way to integrate surface and structure. The structure of the glazed atrium exemplifies this complex relationship between structure and decoration, exposing the structural form purposefully. In this case, the repetition and distribution of a filigree proposes ideas about patterning by using algorithms to define structure as a form of deep decoration.

Architect Barkow Leibinger, with engineering firm Schlaich Bergermann und Partner, designed the office building Trutec, in Seoul, Korea, (2007) using an optical effect.| **figs. 9 + 10** Like a kaleidoscope, reflective coated glass forms a thickened facade with shifting angular views. As a crystalline structure, from 2-D to 3-D, the fractured glass panels coalesce to form a deep skin. The mass-customized system moves beyond that of structure and form, embracing the phenomenology of light and space with variety beyond a two-dimensional surface. As Barkow has said, "I'm interested in accessing the relatively established technology of CNC-cutting for cutting multiple frames that support standard off-the-shelf mirrored glass to produce this particular effect in this context." [8] The faceted skin of many elements literally extends deep within the surface, modulating and jumping off the single plane and offering numerous readings in a synergy between object, plane, and place. Three hundred self-

fig. 9 | Construction view of Trutec, Seoul, Korea, Barkow Leibinger with Schlaich Bergermann, 2007

fig. 10 | Facade detail of Trutec, Seoul, Korea, Barkow Leibinger with Schlaich Bergermann, 2007

supporting panels, measuring thirteen by nine feet, form a fluctuating array that is prismatic and unified. In a collaborative process, the architects and engineers enabled both the material properties of the glass and its effects to reflect, refract, and shift in holism, filling us with wonderment as it scatters and contains light, returning to those observations of Sheerbart and Taut. Pushing a material to its utmost potential, the structuring of glass—as deep decoration in filigree support systems or as the strengthening and restructuring of the material itself—continues to embody those ideals and aspirations of the modernist architects and engineers who first began to experiment with both the shimmering and clear phenomenology of transparency. With today's technical prowess and increased ability to manipulate materials, the transformative effect must be purposeful, even when unforeseen.

1 | Peter Rice, *An Engineer Imagines* (London: Ellipsis, 1994), 72.

2 | See Ove Arup's "Key Speech," lecture delivered at the Arup Organization, Winchester, England, July 9, 1970.

3 | Michael Rosenauer, *Modern Office Buildings* (London: B.T. Batesford, 1955), 43.

4 | Peter Rice, 72.

5 | Peter Rice, 72.

6 | Rice, image portfolio, no page number.

7 | Hugh Dutton and Peter Rice, *Le Verre Structural, Editions Moniteur,* Paris, 1990.

8 | Barkow Leibinger, *Reflect: Building in the Digital Media City, Seoul, Korea* (Ostfildern: Hatje Cantz, 2007), 68.

Demands on Glass Beyond Pure Transparency

Robert Heintges

There is irony in the notion of climate-engineering glass. Each manipulation for improved energy performance renders glass less like glass and more like other nontransparent materials, such as metal, ceramic, and stone. Engineering glass away from its original state—a transparent, super-cooled liquid—into a selectively opaque material that is coated, tinted, fritted, or etched, is fundamentally at odds with the ultimate goal of pure transparency, suggesting a categorical conflict between the dual modernist goals of technological efficiency and literal transparency. This incongruity fosters the recognition that glass is not, at its essence, exclusively transparent: it is also reflective and material. Any given glass has more or less of each of these three visual attributes: translucency, reflectivity, and materiality.

Nonetheless, we imagine glass to be purely transparent; we *will* it to be transparent; we imbue it with an imagined essence of transparency, even when this is not the physical or visual reality. In pavilion architecture the transparent ideal is perhaps attainable, but in larger projects, it is more difficult, if not impossible, to achieve. Indeed, an imagined transparency is often arrived at by using reflectivity to create the illusion of transparency.

In the context of large curtain-wall buildings, environmental issues and increasingly stringent wind-load and energy codes relegate the modernist obsession with absolute transparency to the same dreamworld that promised unlimited free electricity by mid-century. These considerations, compounded with more recent criteria for security and blast resistance that require thick and composite assemblies, render the goal of pure transparency even more elusive. Considering that physical transparency is inversely proportional to energy efficiency, and adding to this the increasing demands, regulatory and otherwise, on the nonvisual aspects of glass, one might argue that the modernist pursuit of pure transparency is no longer viable.

Out of this impasse, alternate aesthetic possibilities for addressing thermal efficiency have emerged. One can identify three options. The first involves a number of techniques that make glass seem more transparent. With architectural means such as lighting, orientation, and reflectivity control, as well as technical enhancements such as high-transmittance and low-reflectance coatings, we can achieve the appearance or suggestion of transparency while also meeting minimal energy requirements. The second option consists of integrated architectural responses that resolve the tension between transparency and energy efficiency. Le Corbusier understood this opposition and responded to it with the *brise soleil*.

A more contemporary response might be the double-skin facade. The third possibility is an embrace of the material characteristics of glass. Most often, these have been used in the service of transparency rather than as characteristics in themselves. Recently, however, architects have begun to explore and express materiality as a dominant attribute through the use of surface frit, acid etching, and other treatments.

Explorations of these three design responses—technical, architectural, and material—in various combinations with glass's visual attributes of transparency, reflectivity, and materiality are apparent in several of our recent projects.

An elegant example of a simple technical response that employs reflectivity in service of illusional transparency is the Gannett/USA Today Corporate Headquarters in McLean, Virginia, by Kohn Pederson Fox. | **fig. 1** Its unitized curtain wall incorporates a slightly reflective coating and exterior glass fins, with the effect of creating an almost dematerialized facade. The building stands on a landscaped suburban site, making control of reflected surroundings possible.

In contrast to this dematerialization, integrating glass into a context of masonry motivated the facade of the Barnard College Nexus project in New York City, by Weiss/Manfredi. | **fig. 2** The design involved an intense research and development effort by the architects, who explored solutions including combinations of acid etching, ceramic frits, low-iron glass, and low-E coatings. The result is a unique materiality empathetic with the surrounding brick buildings. This won over a skeptical board of trustees, originally partial to brick and mortar, to an all-glass facade. The acid-etched surface of the glass exterior cuts reflections and imparts substance to the glass surface. The design employs the material character of glass as an aesthetic strategy and as a means of attaining energy efficiency.

Similarly, on World Trade Center Tower 4 in downtown Manhattan, Fumihiko Maki and Associates are investigating the use of a ceramic frit on the exterior surface of an insulated glass unit, in conjunction with a reflective coating on the interior of the unit. Hypothetically, this would eliminate reflection wherever there is frit, using the very element that provides energy efficiency to suffuse the glass with a subtle surface materiality, thereby joining a necessary engineering solution and an expression of the material aspect of the glass.

Finally, to consider a current project that may best frame these issues of transparency and performance: the restoration of the facade of the United Nations Secretariat Building, as part of the Capital Master Plan for the campus's next century in New York. Conceived and constructed in the mid-twentieth century, the entire complex is being restored and refurbished for the next fifty or more years of use, with a mandate for sustainability and energy efficiency. The Secretariat's

fig. 1 | Facade detail, Gannett/USA Today Corporate Headquarters, Kohn Pederson Fox and R.A. Heintges and Associates, McLean, Va., 2003

fig. 2 | Facade detail, Barnard College Nexus Project, Weiss/Manfredi and R.A. Heintges and Associates, New York, N.Y., 2008

fig. 3 | United Nations Secretariat Building in its current state, New York, N.Y., 2008

existing curtain wall has deteriorated, and it has increasingly become a significant energy drain on the UN's operating budget. | fig. 3 Various options are being considered, with the overriding premise that the original facade design, proportions, and image are to be maintained and respected.

At the time of the original design, the facade of the Secretariat was somewhat contentious, with Le Corbusier arguing for his *brise soleil* and Wallace K. Harrison arguing for the use of a new green-tinted glass, which at the time was touted as the latest in energy efficiency. In what was, perhaps, one of the earliest examples of value engineering, the design incorporating the new glass was chosen not only because it was more cost effective and easier to maintain but also because it would allow for a symbolic transparency. Unfortunately, this image could not be sustained because heat gain and solar glare were so extreme. Within a few years, the glass was overlaid with a reflective film on the east elevation, and more recently a film was added to the west facade. As a result, most visitors today would have no idea of the appearance of the original facade.

Part of the effort in designing a new facade for the Secretariat, therefore, has been to quantify and model the building's original appearance as a benchmark for evaluating new facade options. Using spectral data of the filmed glass and high-dynamic-range photographs of the building and its surrounding environment taken at 2:30 p.m. and 6:30 p.m. on an April day, a computer model was generated to replicate the exact sky dome, direct and indirect light, surrounding building reflections, and atmospheric conditions in the afternoon and evening. Then, substituting spectral data from the original glass, the model was used to create an accurate image of the original building to assess the implications of new high-performance curtain wall and glass options and to visualize a possible double-skin facade.

After working through the models, cost estimates, and energy calculations; revisiting our research on the history of the design; and considering the UN's current institutional needs, we found that the double-skin facade option holds perhaps the most promise of reconciling the original building with new performance criteria. Such a facade of both sheer glass and *brises soleil* would also, in a sense, reconcile the competing visions of Wallace K. Harrison and Le Corbusier.

One might consider the evolution of glazing attributes in chronological terms and, by extension, in terms of rising energy costs: from clear float glass to tinted glass in the 1960s; to reflective glass in the 1970s; to ever-better-performing low-E coatings in the 1980s and '90s; to ceramics and other surface manipulations in the first decade of the twenty-first century. Despite the compelling advantages of the double-skin facade, however, our recent work suggests that the end of this chronology may evolve toward a new perception of the nature of glass beyond pure transparency.

Glass at the Limits

Antoine Picon

What are the limits of glass? Today, this question may seem paradoxical insofar that recent evolution points toward the removal of many of the material's traditional limits. For instance, glass used to be limited to nonstructural applications given its limited mechanical resistance, but in contemporary uses, it is more often structural. In that respect, the path opened by pioneering engineers and artists such as Peter Rice and James Carpenter is now widely trodden.[1]

Glass used to be transparent, but its transparency was counterbalanced by its poor insulating capacities. Glass can now be both transparent and insulating, and its use on facades is among the fundamental means at the disposal of architects aiming at environmental sustainability. What has happened in the case of glass is a radical redefinition of its properties, and, above all, the possibility for combining characteristics that used to be mutually exclusive. This redefinition presents daunting challenges for the architect, and these challenges are perhaps among the new limits that are emerging. The first of these challenges is the multiplicity of forms and uses; everything, or almost everything, seems feasible in architecture, and the lack of strong constraints is not an easy situation to cope with. This was a problem with the early use of concrete, a material that, contrary to iron, entailed no specific forms or structures.[2] Nowadays, glass has become so protean that it seems to present a similar challenge.

Another way to describe this challenge is in reference to the notion of the tectonic truth of materials. Nineteenth-century rationalism postulated that there was a proper way to use materials, a tectonic truth inherent in their properties and limits. One had to respect this truth in order to avoid major flaws in the design of structures and buildings. In his *Lectures on Architecture*, the preeminent theorist of rationalism, Eugène Emmanuel Viollet-le-Duc, condemned certain uses of iron in the name of tectonic truth.[3]

Modern architecture has generally followed this path, postulating that good and bad uses of materials were linked to the respect or disrespect of their intrinsic strengths and weaknesses. This has been the case with glass, but the same could also be said of concrete or wood. There is no longer a clear-cut truth, but a seamless web of constraints and possibilities that need to be negotiated according to extremely different trajectories. In its current incarnations, glass challenges the traditional distinction between materials and structures. What we call glass today is often a composite that possesses a clear structural quality. Then again, the redefinition of glass is emblematic of a more general evolution. The shift in some of the fundamentals of construction and architecture, such as the opposition between materials, defined as relatively loosely organized, and structures, the organization of which is much more complex. In our contemporary information-driven society, complexity is more and more often to be found at every level, thus blurring traditional distinctions between materials and structures.

As a consequence, our relation to glass and our architectural uses for it are marked by a striking series of inversions. How we make sense of these inversions might represent another limit or battlefront, for limits in technology and architecture are usually productive.

Among these inversions we find a shift in our approach to transparency. Traditionally, transparency was about seeing through. Actually, things were always a bit more complex than that, as Eve Blau has shown in a recent article,[4] but it has become particularly evident with recent evolutions in glass that transparency is as much about concealing as it is about revealing. To be more precise, transparency is now associated with filtering. It is no longer a passive quality; it represents a proactive behavior that is inseparable from energy- and information-based considerations.[5]

Not long ago, glass symbolized the mastery of nature through industrialization and progress. The pairing of those terms dates back to the mid-nineteenth century and Joseph Paxton's Crystal Palace. It is no coincidence that Paxton was a greenhouse specialist. The greenhouse symbolized the possibility for man to master nature, to enclose it in technological ingenuity.

Today, glass has become synonymous with an entirely different set of concerns. Despite its apparent irreducibility to nature, it conveys an ideal of reconciliation between the natural and the technological through the sustainable properties of *green* buildings. Glass no longer encloses but acts as a mediating skin between society and the natural world.

Glass epitomizes a series of fundamental cultural shifts, calling into question distinctions between the natural and the artificial. As sociologist Bruno Latour says in his book *We Have Never Been Modern*, this distinction, to a large extent, is merely a fiction.[6] We are now beginning to systematically explore what, in practical terms, lies beyond this fiction.

It is in this context that we can begin to fully measure the properties of materials, which are not bestowed by an immutable nature but, to a large extent, are constructed or reconstructed. In the past decades, the systematic construction or reconstruction of materials has been greatly enhanced by our more intimate knowledge of the micro-organization of matter. This intimate knowledge has led to the progressive blurring of the distinction of material and structure. As a result, many contemporary uses of glass have rejected the quest for tectonic truth, which once characterized modern architecture. Today, glass is more often linked to complexity, which can be spatial or mechanical, with a multiplication of layers, connecting devices, or activators meant to promote smart behavior and sustainability. Glass is no longer synonymous with tectonic clarity but with the sensation of complexity at every level.

Regarding glass's architectural scope, this complexity might mean a radical departure from the old utopian belief in the value of mere transparency as a means to revealing some hidden truth in need of exposure and thus improve the order of things and the performance of society. This belief has been shared by many utopian thinkers. Jean-Jacques Rousseau, for example, wanted to live in a transparent house. For him, such a way of life was synonymous with a new morality.[7] Perhaps we are definitively abandoning this ideal. If we are still fascinated by transparency, we tend to recognize the notion that it might reveal some previously hidden truth as fallacious. It doesn't mean that we are no longer interested in seeing through, but what we see is far more complex. It is as if the tectonic truth of the material and the truth about ourselves were merely one and the same.

What we see in so many contemporary sustainable buildings is a mix of nature and technology, and complexity has become synonymous with ambiguity. This new vision represents another limit on the contemporary uses of glass in architecture, made possible by the gradual dissolution of our discipline's most established certitudes. But this limit is also a frontier leading to new territories.

1 | See Peter Rice, *An Engineer Imagines* (London: Artemis, 1994); Sandro Marpillero (ed.), *James Carpenter: Environmental Refractions* (New York: Princeton Architectural Press, 2006).

2 | This was a crucial issue for a builder like François Hennebique who tried to promote the new material among architects. See Gwenaël Delhumeau, Jacques Gubler, Réjean Legault, Cyrille Simonnet, *Le Béton en Représentation: La Mémoire Photographique de l'Entreprise Hennebique 1890-1930* (Paris: Hazan, 1993).

3 | Cf. *La Querelle du Fer. Eugène Viollet-le-Duc contre Louis-Auguste Boileau* (Paris: Editions du Linteau, 2002).

4 | See Eve Blau, "Transparency and the Irreconcilable Contradictions of Modernity," in *Praxis: Journal of Writing + Building*, n. 9, 2007, 50–59.

5 | See for instance on that theme Terence Riley (ed.), *Light Construction* (New York: Harry N. Abrams, 1995).

6 | Bruno Latour, *We Have Never Been Modern* (Cambridge, Mass.: Harvard University Press, 1993).

7 | See Jean Starobinski, *Jean-Jacques Rousseau, Transparency and Obstruction* (Chicago: Chicago University Press, 1988).

Infrathin

Guy Nordenson

Working with glass over the years I've come to appreciate how it embodies Marcel Duchamp's *infrathin*, the invisible nuances that exist between objects. This is best seen (or not seen) from the fact that glass is almost not there, that it is the opposite of *poché*. The projects I will highlight range from emphasizing the opportunities that exist with glass as a material, its physical reality, to glass's relation to the self-effacement of structure, the self-effacement of material, and the disappearance of structure in buildings. I am drawn by the relationship of glass to the ephemeral line, the thinness of the line, the thinness of the plane, and the way in which glass has a capacity to communicate that as part of architecture.

The Crystal Palace is a touchstone for the beginning of the modern era and the beginning of a renewed use of glass. It serves as a striking and moving example of the connection between the object, its fate, and the drawing of that object. Here, the concept drawing and the burning ruin become one. | fig. 1

In a more recent case, a diagram that my students at Princeton did a number of years ago—based on construction drawings for the original World Trade Center and using different colors to show the types of steel that structural engineer Leslie Robertson chose for different parts of the perimeter structure—demonstrates the self-effacing brilliance of its conception. An immense amount of creativity went into the development of a structure that uses steel *types* to channel forces away from the strong (and therefore lighter) steels toward the weaker (stiffer) ones, responding to the results of wind tunnel tests and tuning the structure to balance its response. Yet this creativity is completely invisible, and it remained completely invisible until we did the drawing in 2004. There is a strong connection between this creative invisibility or effacement and the way we work and think about glass as a material.

A project that demonstrates not only the concept of *infrathin* but also the extraordinary relationship between the line, the thinness of that line, and the mystery that it holds is the Glass Pavilion at the Toledo Museum of Art in Toledo, Ohio. At the beginning of this project, when I first met Kazuyo Sejima and Ryue Nishizawa (SANAA) in Tokyo with my colleague Mutsuru Sasaki, they presented a drawing I took to be a bubble diagram of the functional relationships of the project. I had a wonderful double take when Sejima said, "No, no, that's it." What I was looking at was actually the plan. Indeed, in the completed building, the joints of the line in the glass can easily be confused with the structural columns. This structure is extremely thin, and the columns are all somewhat randomly placed so that, at first glance, you cannotfind them. Most people assume that the glass is holding up

fig. 1 | Crystal Palace, view of transept, 1851

fig. 2 | Ceiling view of the Glass Pavilion at the Toledo Museum of Art, Toledo, Ohio, 2006

fig. 3 | Chapel designed by Francois de Menil to house the Menil Collection, Houston, Tex., 1997

the roof, which is not the case. | fig. 2 A photo taken during construction points to another aspect of its thinness and demonstrates the intense coordination that went into achieving a twelve-inch-thick sandwich of everything that was needed, structurally and mechanically. That thinness, the quality of the line, and the compression of the *poché* were very much on our minds throughout the building process; all of these ideas resonated with us from the project's conceptual beginning.

The second project that relates a similar idea goes back a number of years to a chapel that Francois de Menil designed for two Byzantine frescoes belonging to the Menil Collection. The building, completed in 1997, is a simple precast concrete box that encloses the chapel, which is a re-creation of the original chapel that housed the frescoes in Cyprus. A defining feature of the glass chapel is the necklace, or web of steel rods, that holds the glass plates. These glass plates were too large to be tempered, so they were made as laminated pieces. They are held with elegant steel and Delrin acetal resin clips conceived by engineer Ignacio Barandiaran in a way that makes the glass-and-rod web into a composite structure. There is a symbiotic structure between these lines and the spider web and plates work together to achieve considerable thinness. | fig. 3

It is the Museum of Modern Art expansion, however, that comes closest to achieving the delicate balance of *infrathin.* When you look at the walls, the extreme thinness of the lines makes them appear to almost vibrate optically, like lines in a Robert Ryman or Agnes Martin painting. There is physicality to the illusion of seeing a line that is distressingly ephemeral. The wall was designed in collaboration with Robert Heintges, Yoshio Taniguchi's office, and Kohn Pedersen Fox Associates; it incorporates two-and-a-half by seven-inch solid-steel-bar mullions to span approximately sixty feet vertically. The mullions are both self-supporting and propped by small struts at mid-height, and they work as a rigid frame for buckling stability and lateral loads. Because of seismic considerations, the wall is not connected to the Museum Tower; it is fully self-reliant. | fig. 4

Even more intriguing is the absence of two primary columns in the second-floor Contemporary Art Galleries of the MoMA expansion. During the design of the building, one of the museum's trustees mentioned that the columns in these galleries were undesirable. Since there was already a truss structure in place above serving as an outrigger for the core bracing of the new tower, it turned out that two of the offending columns could be removed and the floors above could hang from the outrigger truss at a small additional cost. This created an uninterrupted space for showing large-scale contemporary sculptures and installations, such as was done for the Richard Serra exhibition held in 2007. | fig. 5 Our most noteworthy contribution to the MoMA expansion is actually not there.

fig. 4 | Self-supporting wall with solid-steel mullions spanning sixty feet vertically, view from the sculpture garden at the Museum of Modern Art, New York, N.Y.

fig. 5 | Absent columns in the Contemporary Galleries at the Museum of Modern Art, New York, N.Y., 2007

fig. 6 | Stair at the Gallerie dell'Accademia, Andrea Palladio, Venice, Italy

fig. 7 | Finite element analysis of stone treads for cantilever stair

figs. 8 + 9 | Cascade stair inspired by Andrea Palladio's stair at the Gallerie dell'Accademia and the tower stairs at the Ducal Palace in Urbino, Italy

The final project that I will discuss takes the classic principle of cantilever or cascade stairs and transforms it with glass. The concept goes back to Andrea Palladio's stair at the Gallerie dell'Accademia in Venice, Italy; before that, it can be traced to the tower stairs at the Ducal Palace in Urbino. These stairs were made of stone treads that interlock. | **fig. 6** By their interlock, they are able to cantilever out from a wall as the gravity load cascades from step to step, down to the base. We took that concept and reconceived it using glass. | **figs. 7–9** Four-by-six-inch steel tubes rest on fabricated steel "stirrups" in the glass wall. These are linked with aluminum plates to make a continuous cascade. The project illustrates not just a question of materiality and tectonics, but also an attempt to communicate a tradition, an idea, and a conceptual development historically over time.

In my mind there is a linkage between the invisibility of concepts, the thinness of the line, and the spatial qualities of light and line that result in this work. This directly relates to the opportunities that exist today with glass and that are being realized in work like that of SANAA and others who strive to embrace a heightened perception in glass.

Unclear Vision: Architectures of Surveillance

Beatriz Colomina

The relationship between glass and technologies of communication has been an ongoing inspiration in my research. The history of the modern window is a history of communication: Le Corbusier's horizontal window is unthinkable outside of cinema. The Eames House is unthinkable outside of the color slide. And the picture window at midcentury is unthinkable outside of television. | **figs. 1–3** In each case, the ambition of modern architecture to dissolve the line between inside and outside is realized by absorbing the latest realities of communication.

If communication is basically about bringing the outside in (as when reading a newspaper to bring world events into your life) and getting the inside out (as when sending a letter) then glass unambiguously represents the act of communication. It is as if glass literally takes over more and more of a building as the systems of communication became more and more fluid. Having dissolved the walls into glass, the question has become how to dissolve glass itself, the last delicate line between inside and outside. The relentless quest for greater fluidity between inside and outside is no longer simply a drive toward transparency. The glass box has become something else altogether.

SANAA's Glass Pavilion in the Toledo Museum of Art is symptomatic of this dissolution. At first, the building appears as the perfect example of transparency: an all-glass pavilion, for all-glass objects, in the glass city. In this sense, SANAA has inherited the Miesian tradition of radical transparency. In the standard publicity image of the project, the white-trimmed pavilion sits in the park, uncannily echoing some of Ludwig Mies van der Rohe's canonic projects, particularly the Farnsworth House and the Fifty by Fifty-Feet House. | **figs. 4 + 5** Mies famously deployed sheer glass walls to radically expose the interior. My interest in this phenomenon has been to explore the possibility that transparency in modern architecture was directly related to advances in medical imaging technologies for the human body. From that point of view, the logic of sheer glass walls is exactly like that of the X-ray; the inner structure is revealed by a new technology that allows you to look through the outer skin of the body. | **fig. 6** Mies himself even described his work as "skin-and-bones" architecture, referring to the structure of his Glass Skyscraper of 1922 as "the skeleton," rendering the project as if seen under X-rays. Mies was deeply interested in X-ray images and used them as illustrations in his article in the April 1926 issue of *G*.[1]

Mies was not alone. Books on modern architecture are filled with images of glowing glass skins, revealing inner bones and organs. Consider, for example,

fig. 1 | Strip window at Villa le Lac, built by Le Corbusier for his mother, 1924

fig. 2 | Details of the Eames House and studio, 1949–78

fig. 3 | Advertisement for picture windows published in the *Saturday Evening Post*, April 26, 1958

fig. 4 | Rendering of the Glass Pavilion, SANAA

fig. 5 | Farnsworth House, Mies van der Rohe, 1949

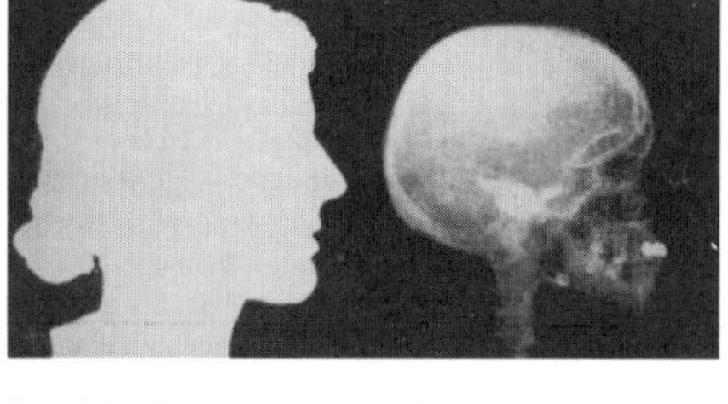

fig. 6 | Still from *Highlights and Shadows*, directed by James Sibley Watson Jr., 1937

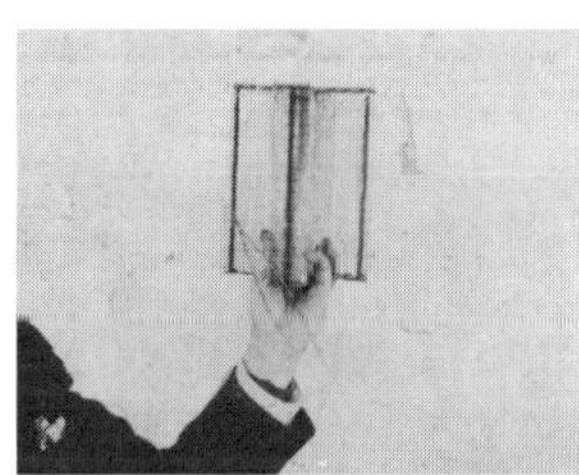

fig. 7 | The Cartesian Skyscraper, steel and glass model by Le Corbusier, film still from *Bâtir*, directed by Pierre Chenal, 1928

fig. 8 | Schunck Glass Palace, Frits Peutz, Heerlen, the Netherlands, 1935

fig. 9 | Crystal House by George Fred Keck (with a Dymaxion car by R. Buckminster Fuller parked in the garage), exhibition at the Chicago World's Fair, 1934

Le Corbusier's project for a glass skyscraper in 1925 | **fig. 7** ; Walter Gropius's Werkbund Exhibition in Cologne in 1914; Erich Mendelsohn's Schocken Department Store in Stuttgart, Germany, from 1926 to 1928; Frits Peutz's Schunck Glass Palace in Heerlen, the Netherlands in 1935 | **fig. 8** ; George Fred Keck's Crystal House for the Chicago World's Fair in 1934 | **fig. 9** ; and Paul Nelson's Suspended House in 1935.

These experimental designs from the early decades of the twentieth century formed the basis of everyday building by midcentury, when the see-through house had become a mass phenomenon just as the X-ray itself had. Screening the body for tuberculosis meant gazing into previously invisible areas of the body. X-ray technology had been available in sanatoriums since the beginning of the century. Only by midcentury did mass x-raying of citizens begin on a regular basis. With the spread of this technology, the newly visible interior of the body became not just a tool for diagnosis but the site of a new form of public surveillance. Policing the population by scrutinizing their insides, public institutions such as schools and the military began to manage the most private spaces of the body. Over a half-a-century period, an experimental medical tool transformed into a mechanism of surveillance for the entire population.

By midcentury, the association between X-rays and glass houses became commonplace in popular culture. For example, in *Highlights and Shadows*, a 1937 Kodak Research Laboratories film on the virtues of X-rays for disease prevention, a woman wearing a swimming suit is strapped to a laboratory table while her body is subjected to X-rays. As her photographic image gives way to that of her X-rayed body, the narrator declares: "This young lady, to whom henceforth a glass house should hold no terrors, will, after an examination of her radiographs, be reassured that she is indeed physically fit."[2] In this context, the glass house symbolized both the new form of surveillance and good health.

A similar set of associations can be found in the discourse surrounding canonic works of modern architecture. In an interview in *House Beautiful*, Edith Farnsworth, a successful doctor in Chicago, compared her famous weekend house, designed by Mies in 1949, to an X-ray:

> I don't keep a garbage can under my sink. Do you know why? Because you can see the whole "kitchen" from the road on the way in here and the can would spoil the appearance of the whole house. So I hide it in the closet further down from the sink. Mies talks about "free space": but his space is very fixed. I can't even put a clothes hanger in my house without considering how it affects everything from the outside. Any arrangement of furniture becomes a major problem, because the house is transparent, like an X-ray.[3] | **fig. 10**

The use of the metaphor of the X-ray was not accidental. Modern architecture cannot be understood outside of tuberculosis. It is not by chance that Farnsworth goes on to say of her house, "There is already the local rumor that it's a tuberculosis sanatorium."[4] The development of the X-ray and modern architecture coincide. Just as the X-ray exposes the inside of the body to the public eye, the modern building exposes its interior. That which was private became the subject of public scrutiny. A new clarity of vision—the penetrating gaze of medicine—liberated the new architecture, whose structure was meant to be as clear as the gaze looking into it; or so the story went.

What really fascinated architects, such as Mies and Philip Johnson, was not the way the gaze passed through the glass but the way it seemed to get caught in the layers of reflection. In canonic photographs, the Glass House becomes opaque, clad in what Philip Johnson described as wallpaper. | **fig. 11** In a television program, Johnson said the Glass House "works very well for the simple reason that the wallpaper is so handsome. It is perhaps a very expensive wallpaper, but you have wallpaper that changes every five minutes throughout the day and surrounds you with the beautiful nature that sometimes, not this year, Connecticut gives us."[5] For Mies and Johnson, reflections consolidate the wall's plane. Complex lines of trees become like the veins of marble in Mies's buildings. When explaining his house, Johnson cites Mies from twenty-five years earlier, when he said: "I discovered by working with actual glass models that the important thing is the play of reflections and not the effect of light and shadow, as in ordinary buildings." Mies may have been referring to the models of his Glass Skyscraper that he had repeatedly photographed in a garden, before arriving at the few canonic images released in 1922. | **fig. 12**

Charles and Ray Eames also went to considerable trouble to study the reflections in their house. For example, they placed a model of the original project, the Bridge House, on the site and photographed it from all angles. | **fig. 13** In doing so, they took Mies's experiment a step further. With the Eames house, the plane is broken. Reflections of eucalyptus trees endlessly multiply and relocate. As Ray Eames said after thirteen years of living in the house, "The structure long ago ceased to exist. I am not aware of it."[6]

In the Glass Pavilion, SANAA goes even further in producing a layering of reflection on the inside as well as the outside. The blurring no longer stops at the space's outside limit; the whole space is the limit. There is no clear-cut boundary between inside and outside. The space is neither in nor out; it seems to extend infinitely. In such a space, walls are not optical barriers, but optical intensifiers. They are exposed along with the people and the objects. The inner and outer edges

fig. 10 | View of bedroom in the Farnsworth House, Mies van der Rohe, 1949

fig. 11 | Reflections in the Glass House, Philip Johnson, New Canaan, Conn., 1949

fig. 12 | Model of glass skyscraper, Berlin, Germany, Mies van der Rohe,1922

fig. 13 | Model of first version of Case Study House #8, called the "Bridge House," Charles and Ray Eames

of the wall are revealed, but more importantly, the inaccessible gap between them takes over to become the real space of the project. The double line of the wall establishes and then undoes any sense of solidity. | fig. 14

SANAA's vision is far from crystal clear. In fact, the Glass Pavilion appears to be more interested in blurring the view and softening the focus than on sustaining the transparency of early avant-garde architecture. Within SANAA's architecture, structure is never revealed. Their buildings are not even meant to be looked into or out of. They are optical devices without any visible mechanisms. The real view is not from the outside looking in, or the inside looking out; it is from the inside looking even further inward. Its objective is not for the viewer to discover the inner secret of the building, but to be suspended in the view itself. In Toledo, the visitor is quite literally suspended between the curving walls of glass. What you see through the glass layer in front of you is another layer and then another and then another. Even the objects on display through all of these layers are themselves made of glass. Peering through the layers, vision softens and distorts as the curved glass accentuates the distortion. If Kazuyo Sejima is the inheritor of Miesian transparency, the latest in a long line of experiments, she is the ultimate Miesian, leaping beyond transparency into a whole new kind of mirage effect. After centuries of architecture organized by the straight lines of the viewing eye, we now have an architecture formed by the soft distortions of the gaze—a more tactile experience of vision. To enter a Sejima project is to be caressed by a subtle softening of the territory. Even the reflections of trees in the outer layer of glass have a delicacy that one does not find in Mies's work, whether in the renderings or the 1:1 scale models. With such a tactile sense of vision, models are crucial. In the studio, countless models are made of every possible solution that the effects can be felt before being fixed in a drawing. Indeed, SANAA seeks variations whose effects are unclear: "We try not to select options for which we can already imagine the outcome." Theirs is an architecture of deliberately unclear vision.

The modern discourse of X-rays—cutting through the outer layers to reveal secrets—gives way to inner layers, endlessly folded and overlapping fabrics that intensify the mystery rather than remove it. The X-ray logic, as it has been absorbed by modern architecture, culminates in a dense cloud of ghostly shapes. The clearest of glass is now used to undermine clarity.

Today, new forms of advanced surveillance technologies operate in the city, and these models of vision act as the new paradigms for the window. We cannot predict which of these technologies will be absorbed into architecture, but some are already having an impact on the built environment. Handheld scanning devices capable of seeing through clothing, walls, and buildings are already in use

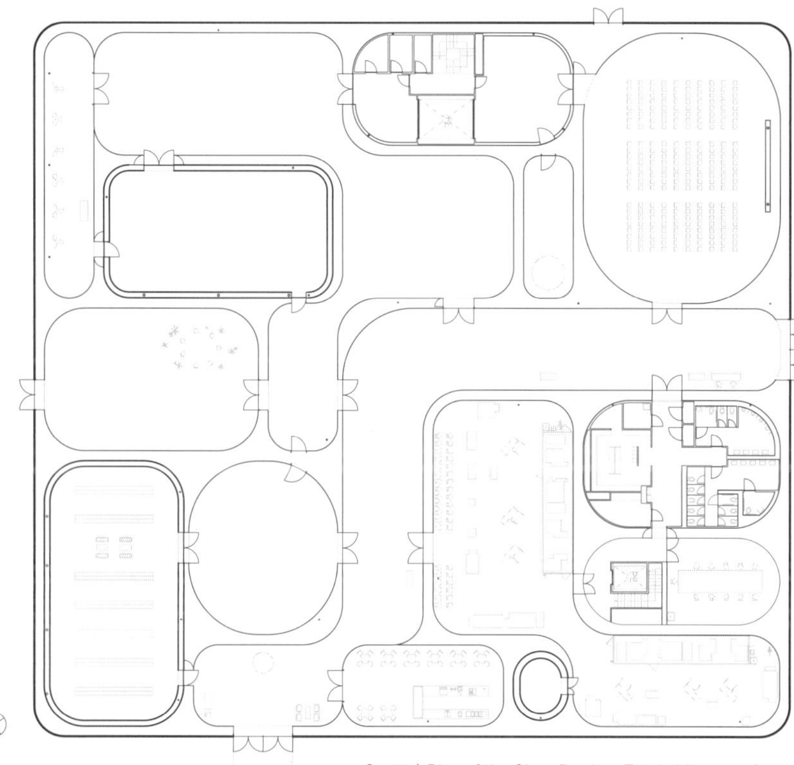

fig. 14 | Plan of the Glass Pavilion, Toledo Museum of Art, SANAA

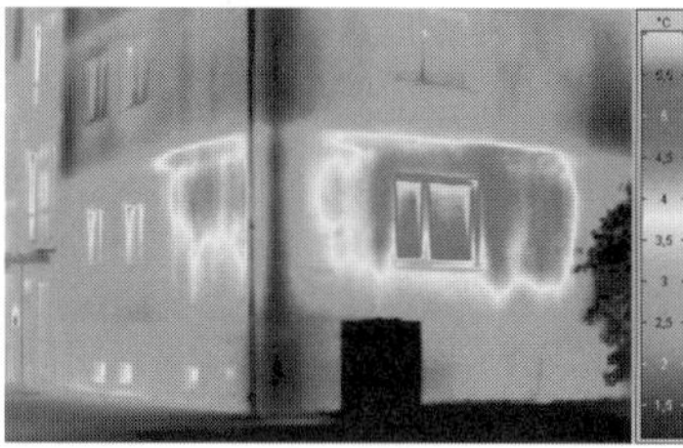

fig. 15 | Forward Looking Infrared Radar (FLIR) heat signatures radiating from organisms and structures

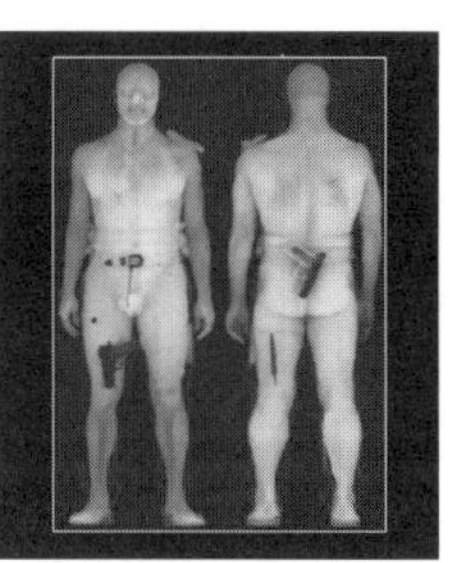

figs. 16 + 17 | Passive Millimeter Imaging (PMI), used to detect hidden weapons or contraband in clothing, bags, and vehicles

fig. 18 | Popemobile

fig. 19 | A High Mobility Multipurpose Wheeled Vehicle (HMMWV) modified with Popemobile glass

by the military and, increasingly, by the police. These devices effectively make solid walls behave like glass and they open up the possibility, even inevitability, for new kinds of architectural experiments.

Forward Looking Infrared Radar (FLIR), for example, detects the electromagnetic frequencies at which heat radiates from organisms and structures, exposing heat-emitting bodies inside. | **fig. 15** Seemingly solid walls no longer offer privacy. Indeed, FLIR scans can reveal activities that have already finished. You can be exposed even after you have left the building, because heat signatures remain for a while. This delay is incorporated into a new kind of vision. Again, bodies are treated the same as buildings. Passive Millimeter Imaging (PMI) is used by the United States Customs Department to detect hidden weapons or contraband in clothing, bags, or vehicles by stripping the outer layer away. | **figs. 16 + 17** With the KPF lens, anyone can use a regular camera, even a cell-phone camera, to see through clothing by concentrating on the infrared spectrum. These technologies are controversial. The use of PMI has been restricted due to privacy concerns, and the KPF lens is illegal in the United States and Europe.

The midcentury fear of loss of privacy in the glass house and with the X-ray has reappeared. It seems as if each new technology that exposes something private is perceived as threatening and then quickly absorbed into everyday life. The fear of the glass box or X-ray seems quaint today. Even the grainy images of video surveillance cameras seem already less invasive now, almost reassuring. Perhaps today's scanning technologies will also seem quaint in the future, as each new technology delves deeper and deeper into the private. With each new invasion, our definition of private changes.

Meanwhile, the original concept of the Glass House has reemerged in mobile form. Consider the protective bunker of the Popemobile, designed with four sides of bulletproof glass after the 1981 assassination attempt on Pope John Paul II. Mies and Johnson on wheels. | **fig. 18** More recently, soldiers in Iraq have appropriated this concept, with what they call "*Pope glass*," by welding old ballistic-proof windshields to the top of their Humvees for protection against snipers. | **fig. 19**

The point of these quick notes is simply to show that by changing our definitions of public and private, the new surveillance technologies that emerged in the early years of the last century have also changed our understanding of architecture. The question here is not how transparency has been dislocated into other fields, or how architecture affects other fields, but how architecture absorbs the latest communication systems. Architecture is never threatened by these technologies. On the contrary, it feeds on them. Our field is currently digesting new models of vision; new architectures will inevitably emerge.

1 | Mies van der Rohe, "The Pure Form is the Natural," *G*, no. 5–6, April 1926.

2 | James Sibley Watson Jr., *Highlights and Shadows* (Kodak, 1937), quoted in Lisa Cartwright, *Screening the Body: Tracing Medicine's Visual Culture* (Minneapolis: University of Minnesota Press, 1995), 155.

3 | Edith Farnsworth quoted in Joseph A. Barry, "Report on the American Battle between Good and Bad Modern," *House Beautiful*, May 1953, 270.

4 | Edith Farnsworth, "Memoirs" (unpublished manuscript), quoted in Alice T. Friedman, *Women and the Making of the Modern House: A Social and Architectural History* (New York: Abrams, 1998), 143.

5 | Philip Johnson in "The Architect (Philip Johnson and Louis Kahn)," *Accent*, CBS, May 14, 1961.

6 | Ray Eames quoted in Esther McCoy, *Modern California Houses* (1962), reprinted as *Case Study Houses 1945–1962* (Los Angeles: Hennessey & Ingalls, 1977), 54.

Is Glass Still Glass?

Kenneth Frampton

Glass has long been such an inseparable component of modern building that the intrinsic role it plays in contemporary architecture is more multiple than one might, at first, imagine. In fact, the physical attributes and phenomenological character of glass have led to a state of affairs in which the role of the designer is as varied as the material itself. This is made particularly evident in the quite distinct ways in which the architects and engineers in this book have approached the handling of this basic material. James Carpenter, by virtue of his initial formation as a fine artist, tends to emphasize the prismatic and refractory qualities of different kinds of glass and their effects under quite distinct lighting conditions. Of late, Guy Nordenson, a structural engineer, has become increasingly involved with the design of what he calls (after Marcel Duchamp) *infrathin* structures made entirely of glass. This expressive potential has been most brilliantly displayed in the Glass Pavilion at the Toledo Museum of Glass in Ohio, built to the designs of Kazuyo Sejima and Ryue Nishizawa, founders of SANAA.

In the Glass Pavilion, glass assumes the form of an exceptionally luminous, plastic, ultra-thin membrane, as opposed to Hans Schober's transformation of glass into faceted translucent elliptical forms made of specially designed glass lenses. I have in mind the glass monument designed by FAM Architects and built outside the new Atocha Station in Madrid, Spain, to commemorate the victims of the terrorist attacks of March 11, 2004. In this instance, borosilicate glass lozenges were glued to form a self-supporting elliptical shell of structural glass, thirty-six-feet tall and measuring twenty-six by thirty-six feet in plan. The space within the ellipse is protected by a thin translucent glass roof, held in place by trusses made of stainless-steel rods.

Lastly, the recent work of François Roche has consisted, in large measure, of recycled glass bottles, a proposition that recalls Martin Pawley's 1975 book, *Garbage Housing*.

In their demonstrations of the role of glass in contemporary building, Carpenter, Nordenson, Schober, and Roche have surpassed the rather limited use of plate glass that we find in the ubiquitous neo-Miesian curtain wall that, thanks to universal air-conditioning, has been realized virtually everywhere in the past half-century, regardless of prevailing climatic conditions. In the interim, our society has succeeded in producing glass of such different physical properties that it, as a substance, can no longer be regarded as a singular material having constant properties. Today, it may be employed as a self-sustaining structure through the use of invisible glues of exceptional strength; it may also be applied in multiple layers, having different properties, so as to act as an efficient sun filter or to provide levels of insulation and opacity that were formerly obtainable only with a solid material. Alternatively, glass may, as Carpenter has demonstrated, be polarized to achieve infinite aesthetic effects.

In fact there is perhaps only one area to date where the application of glass has not been as versatile as in the pioneering modern architecture of the 1930s: the use of colored glass or Vitrolite as an opaque, intrinsically chromatic, and self-cleaning cladding material.

Insulated Glazing Units: Fabrication and Memory of Weight and Stress

Michael Bell

Glass is flat. Its flatness is a key test of its quality. To that end, architects such as Philip Johnson have gone so far as to decline the use of safety features, such as tempering, to avoid the waves it causes in the glass's surface. The literal flatness of glass is rarely discussed in critical writing about architecture, because it is either assumed that imperfections are not present, or the lack of flatness is simply not noticed, even if it is flagrantly present. Examine, for example, the slight concavity of insulated glazing units (IGUs) within the curtain wall of a New York skyscraper or even the small-scale IGU of commercial-grade sliding or double-hung windows. Glass itself may be quite flat, but its assembly into insulated glazing units rarely is. The lack of flatness in an IGU offers a counter-critique to the ubiquitous reading of glass as planar or as a neutral and overtly transparent surface. Tolerances for glass in curtain walls have stated deflection limits, and the thickness of the lites or the IGUs' composition affect its planarity, as do tempering, heat strengthening, and laminating. Yet whatever means one uses to study the planarity of glass, there is arguably little reserve for imperfections or aspects of fabrication that are subpar. As a material, glass receives an inordinate amount of technological quality control. It also benefits from a high degree of projected or anticipated perfection that idealizes its ultimate qualities. In light of recent advancements in architectural construction and fabrication, these advantages are seen in a new context. Is glass still as perfect as it seems? Does it still carry the same iconic control and linguistic connotation, and does it remain a harbinger of private desecration?

In normative construction, there are limits to the sizes of continuous glass panels. Roller marks from tempering are less likely to show on smaller panels, as is defection in an IGU due the span of the cavity. Material thickness can compensate for some deflection. Thicker lites have more resistance, and lamination and field conditions (such as shadows, complex patterns from trees, or other environmental reflections) can also compensate for thickness, but an unbroken, strafing sun quickly reveals such flaws. Of course, the same can be said of a continuous drywall surface. Within the Museum of Modern Art's main atrium, for example, any unbroken aspects of construction reveal flaws when viewed from a distance. Yet, in the case of glass, it brings about thoughts of literal changes in manufacturing. If you seek to invest in the process, you will find yourself quickly assessing a very high-end form of fabrication; that is, you would find yourself addressing the degree to which glass, for all its apparent qualities of flatness, is the material that allows anything but flatness. Instead, it is the material of depth and complexity.

Glass forms a foundation for plastic space, and it is the securing device: the means for producing an inside that is anything but experientially flat.

In transcribing the works by Ludwig Mies van der Rohe and Le Corbusier, John Hejduk was said to have literally redrawn the plans and sections of both architects. Franz Liszt is heralded for his transcriptions of Beethoven's symphonies, and his transcriptions are considered to be among his most successful achievements. What is an architectural transcription? What is a transcription of a glass house or work of glass architecture, today? And how did Hejduk's transcription create new forms of space by conflating transcriptions?

Transcription

The essay "Out of Time and Into Space," by John Hejduk, was first published in 1969. I first read it in the context of his compendium of architecture, poems, writing, and interviews, *Mask of Medusa*. The essay ends with the incantation of what Hejduk saw as a new form of space that had emerged in his work just as his preoccupation with Cubism began to end. The essay focused on the work of Le Corbusier and in particular on the Carpenter Center in Cambridge, Massachusetts. Today, it is worth relooking at the analysis and, in particular, at a passage in which Hejduk tested what he saw as the limits of cubist composition in architecture. In regard to the Carpenter Center, he wrote: "The tension and compression, the push-pull may have therapeutic value to the docile...[but] the question remains, at what point do the harmonic fluctuations crack, causing dissolution and failure of the spatial organism?" Hejduk's analysis was testing the limits of the Center's cubist logic, its ultimate coherence, and its resolution as a plastic mechanism, despite the push and pull of tensions that were manifest in the composition. With a precise phrase, he described the Carpenter Center's spatial enterprise as being on the brink of dissolution, and with it would come the dissolution of the generative plasticity of buildings as organisms capable of defining themselves or their hosts or subjects.

figs. 1 + 2 | Renderings of the Gefter-Press House, Michael Bell Architecture, 2007

If the impetus to design new works of glass architecture—in particular, a glass house—is often and easily attributed to Mies van der Rohe, then the Gefter-Press House likely finds its impetus in the plastic qualities of Le Corbusier's work. A more precise source for this impetus would be the transcriptions and analyses of Le Corbusier by John Hejduk. The Gefter-Press House sought to move Hejduk's formulation of space a step further. It is also driven by a deep analysis of contemporary glazing technologies. | **figs. 1 + 2**

The glass itself and its formation into IGUs have demonstrative value, as does its installation within glazing frames by way of structural silicone. An IGU is at least twice as heavy as a single pane of glass, and its fabrication brings a

fig. 3| IGU installation maintains vertical integrity of assembled unit, as compared with horizontal production of float glass

particular spatial history of its own into the equation. While glass is formed in a horizontal cooling process, an IGU composed of two panes of glass is fabricated for vertical placement, and its structural logic requires that its orientation remain vertical for the duration of its lifespan. The combination of gravity, as an operational force during formation, allows glass to self-level as it cools; thus, it achieves an opaque flatness. Its transformation into a vertical element occurs during fabrication, transit, and installation. | **fig. 3** This instigates a web of contradictions: horizontal weight distribution, optical opacity, and extreme temperature transform the material into a highly brittle product capable of managing vertical surface tension and linear material compression with covalent qualities. Transparency may actually be glass's least interesting quality. If material formation and the processes of construction have deeper value in aesthetics, it would require us to remember processes that we have not witnessed. Glass is opaque in this way. It withholds much of its own history but dares us to look for it. Glass cools to a semiperfect planarity. In doing so, it creates a high degree of stress across the surface. Yet, we tend to remain oblivious to this strain. Instead, we look for the deeper vantage in space, and we discount the glass surface, which too often is far less perfect than we imagined.

In referring to the Carpenter Center, Hejduk attempted to describe a space that at its core was based on previous innovations; as a work, the center exceeded its own plastic limits. Hejduk depicted a work with its limits pushed past the breaking point. That marked the end of the formal or plastic cohesion of space, which would have been expected during a period of work that Robert Slutzky described as spatially viscous, even malleable. The Carpenter Center, however, extended past Le Corbusier's cubist era; as Hejduk noted, it marked a critical turning point. Hejduk's own experiments in design in the mid-to-late 1960s and, in particular, his work on the Wall Houses—and the antecedents of their spatial genesis in the Diamond House projects—were accomplished in tandem with painting by Slutzky. Hejduk's move from the Diamond House projects to the Wall Houses has been analyzed in texts by K. Michael Hays (as well as myself), but it is the ultimate limits of plastic space that Hejduk discussed in his own writings that offers a compelling link to the theme of flatness. In other words, you can trace Mies in Hejduk's most formally sculpted works, even when they appear to have been formally influenced by Le Corbusier. The Wall Houses are a case of Hejduk's work being attributed to a study of Le Corbusier, when they may have just as much to do with extending the work of Mies. It was the Wall Houses that exceeded plastic limits, ultimately erasing the bounding frame that secured Hejduk's previous works.[1] Instead, he substitutes an opaque, optically saturated pale gray wall as the new origin of plastic form. Instead of being seen as evidence or strata upon which the plastic form reveals itself, it could instead be seen as the imploding and densified frame of earlier works. Plastic space did not disappear, but it ceased to be understood as being produced by cubist forms of still life and its framing devices. Rather, it cast architecture and its subject into a continuously plastic field outside the newly dense wall. The wall had retreated; it became thin and self-supporting. To see this, examine the trees in Hejduk's drawing of the Bye House (also known as the second of his Wall Houses). They are drawn as surrealist forms, as biological shapes folded into the atmosphere surrounding them. | figs. 4 + 5 The house itself is depicted as essentially erased or removed from the otherwise continuously drawn field of organic life that surrounds the architecture. If the Wall Houses are still easily linked to cubist predecessors, it is by way of the still present picture plane and its ultimate flatness. But it is also critical to imagine this wall and its flatness not as a stable or formal given, but instead as a result of the extreme forms of tension and compression that have collapsed to form a dense and opaque surface. Hejduk described these qualities in his interviews as "the generators of the house's wall."

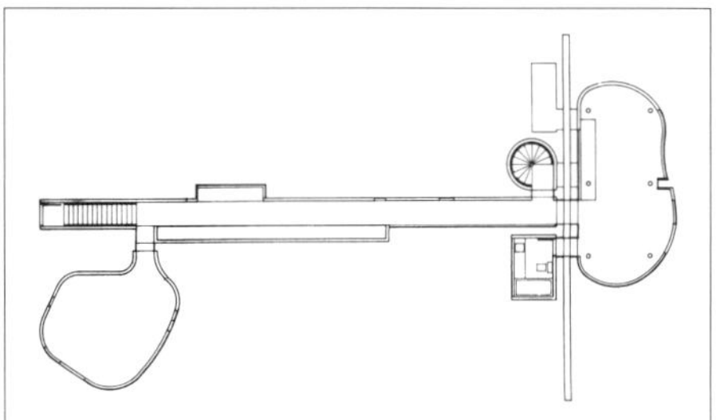

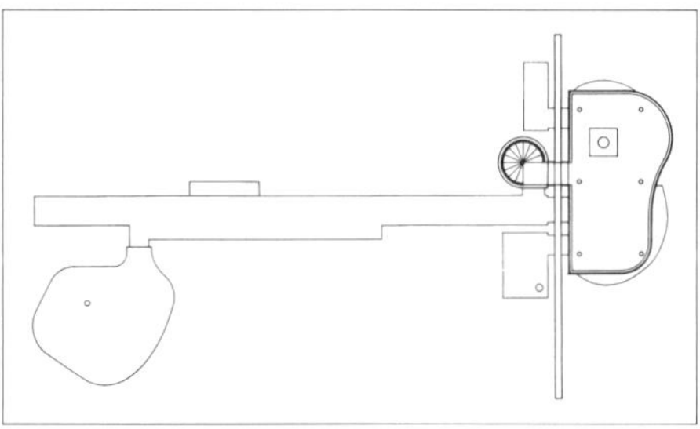

figs. 4 + 5 | Wall House 2 (A. E. Bye House), John Hejduk, plans, 1973

Like most of Hejduk's writing, "Out of Time and Into Space" reads as a partial unfolding of the spaces that had influenced him. The essay was seen as being an homage to Le Corbusier, but this limits its true significance. Seen as a moment or segment in a larger compendium of work, the essay was a single star in a constellation of insights, analyses, and formal transcriptions. It revealed the architectural potentials that he had intended to be witnessed in the form of a historical compendium, as a kind of memory of other inventions that he had set into place for his students. A single project gained its significance from its relation within the context of other works, as well as within the traces of an extended argument between his own work and that of others. The Gefter-Press House traces a similar trajectory; it arrives as a project in light of at least five glass houses I had designed prior to it and at least six other works designed before it that were invested in themes inspired not only by Le Corbusier but also by paintings created by Hans Hofmann and Robert Slutzky. A project of push and pull—or, to quote Hofmann, "push=pull"—and of "turning space inside," to quote Robert Slutzky. | fig. 6

fig. 6 | Layering of space against a deep flat background, model view, Double Dihedral House, La Cienega, N. Mex., Michael Bell Architecture, 1992

The Gefter-Press House embodies a set of attempts to measure flatness against a precipice of deep space by way of removing the middle ground. The layering manifests a tension between the foreground and the implications of a distant background; of depth pushed to troubled limits; and its visual compression layered against close and distant surfaces with no in-between. Also, the Gefter-Press House is literally Miesian in its origins. The client sought a house in dialogue with the Farnsworth House, but it was actually realized against a project analyzed from an earlier period of my own Corbusian work, a project based in Hejduk's writings but also having invocations of Slutzky's inside-out space. To arrive at Mies by way of Le Corbusier was to first note the flatness of glass as wall-surface and wall, rather than curtain, and to see this flatness as a refutation of the pleasure of depth and distance that was often available in Le Corbusier's work. This compelled a set of glass houses in my own work. It was not the transparency but the opacity or coplanar solidity that is viewable in the glass from a side view. But the IGU is also figured, in a large way, and it pushed the comprehension of visual space through Hofmann and Slutzky but also through Jackson Pollock; toward a recognition that the IGU has two postures and two relations to gravity. It seemed possible to accentuate the flatness of the glass in both its fabrication and implementation, in its horizontal origin and its vertical position, to see glass as an extremely dense wall, rather than a clear membrane. Here its transparency reveals a depth of field, but one also begins to tie its potential to readings of gravity drawn on a three-eighths-inch-deep pool of liquid glass. Glass is self-leveling and pools during formation. It forms while heat is slowly removed, before the material becomes stable but also causing it to become increasingly brittle. The lifting of glass from this state is crucial. Surface tensions, especially in tempered glass, allow it to shatter if hit on the edge while resisting damage from perpendicular force. It is the act of lifting it in place after fabrication and during installation that reveals the material's weight and limited stability. The weight formed in a three-eighths-inch pool is now staged through a nine-foot-high vertical pane, or two for an IGU.

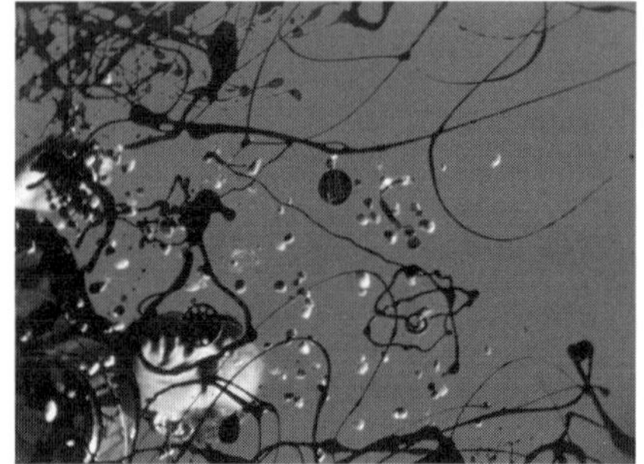

fig. 7 | Still from the Hans Namuth film, *Painting on Glass*, with Jackson Pollock, 1950

Horizontal to Vertical

For art historian Clement Greenberg, a Jackson Pollock painting—executed on the floor of his studio and choreographed by action, material weight and forces of velocity and viscosity—became a "painting" only when it was made vertical. | **fig. 7** If approached with a memory of its fabrication, glass is similar, and an IGU is even more complex. Deep visual transparency becomes apparent in the vertical panes but is simultaneously conflated with an opacity and sense of material weight, even density. If the glass is thicker—as it is in the Gefter-Press House at three-eighths-inch per pane and one-and-one-quarter-inch per IGU—the effect of the weight is palpable and structurally significant. The downward sense of weight is real; the pull into horizontal space is immense, and the architect's sense of surface tension is never far from one's awareness. These conditions were once set in construction: glass is set and it stays in place. They are easily understood as difficult, tenuous, and often characterized as ineffable, but as conditions they are also quite literal and carry didactic repercussions. Glass is a dangerous conflation of mitigating forces. Tension and compression race through its otherwise visually simple shape. | **fig. 8** It has distinct lives that demand different axes of sustenance. It then becomes glass, if we accept Greenberg's logic, only when it is placed in the vertical axis. These realizations about the nature of glass and an IGU are convened by way of Hejduk, by the nature of the material itself and by the production of an IGU. If read against the exceeded limits of the Carpenter Center's plastic apparatus—against the embodied tensions in glass, rather than transparency—and if the final evidence or literal transparency is mixed with the memory of the material weight when horizontal, a project for architectural space arises in which the curtain wall is based not in fabric, weaving, or surface texture but in a mix of depth and flatness, a visual field constructed by memories of a material field. The eye is being pulled into space, but so, too, it remains aware of the material's own weight. This is the nature of glass at its limits, as in the immense IGUs installed in the Gefter-Press House, which measure fourteen feet across and nine feet tall. Such proportions drive the Gefter-Press House's spatial tensions. This aspect of the glass is not Miesian; instead, it relates to the glass's own history and the literal aspects of its fabrication in completely contemporary terms and potentials.

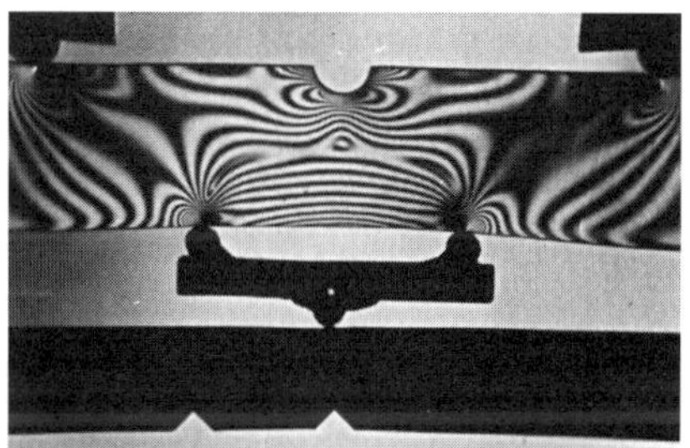

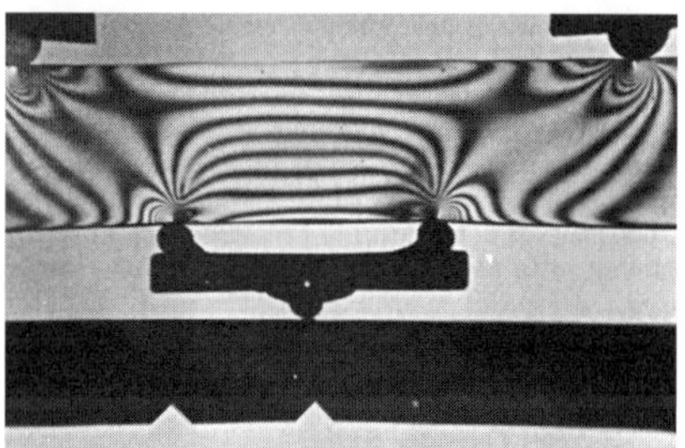

fig. 8 | Photo-elastic stress analyses, circa 1934

The Gefter-Press House was designed to form an extended edge: a 270-foot perimeter, compared to the 194-foot perimeter of the Johnson House. Composed of three-eighths-inch-thick glass set into IGUs, rather than the one-quarter-inch-thick, single panes of the Johnson house, the material produces a very different final effect. In terms of literal weight and optic density, this constitutes a far heavier perimeter than that of the Farnsworth House or the Johnson Glass House. Glass on its edge is in a different condition than glass on its surface. On it edge, glass is a myriad of planar stress; across its surface is a network of brittle stresses. The Gefter-Press House has a 24,000-pound surface; in comparison, the Johnson House weighs approximately 6,400 pounds.

A transcription is complex, and sometimes its derivations are driven by authorship or conflation of sources, such as with Mies and Corbu; or by analysis, as with Hejduk on Corbu; and sometimes by material, assembly, or the memory of all, including the labor of placing it in a frame.

1 | The Diamond House projects preceded the Wall House projects. The Diamond projects gave rise to a fully viscous and robust exercise in the push and pull of plastic space. Completed in the mid-to-late 1960s, the projects were defined by bounding frames, which gave plastic reply to varying forms of centrifugal and centripetal space in the project plans. If spatial tension and compression were tested, it was allowed to remain ultimately stable. Here, space was viscous, and it was manifest in a later version of the *brise soleil*.

Projects

Nelson-Atkins Museum of Art, Kansas City, Mo.

Steven Holl Architects

Steven Holl

An addition, not an object but a new paradigm of fusing landscape and architecture

Near the end of his life Edgar Allan Poe wrote "The Poetic Principle," an essay that published posthumously in 1849. He argued that there are three kinds of writing: transparent reporting, translucent prose, and opaque poetry. John Hejduk spoke about the opacities of architecture, and I also remember reading similar statements made by Le Corbusier and Louis Kahn. Thinking about it in my own personal history, I was never really interested in just transparency. In fact, I was always suspicious of it. The zone I feel very comfortable in is the distance between the translucent and the opaque. For me, light is for space what sound is for music. The experience of architecture and its overlapping perspectives is the equivalent of spatial acoustics in light. If you have a piece of music, you have the score, you have the rhythm, you have some kind of polyphony, you have some kind of a structure, and then there is sound that executes and brings it all to life. Otherwise, it is just an abstraction. The same applies to architecture; you have the spatial conception, the conceptual strategy, the integration of lenses in the landscape, the fusion of architecture and landscape and urbanism, but none of that is anything really alive until you infuse it with the light.

The idea of trapping light or building out of blocks of light is something I've long been obsessed with. It was already reflected in the project for the Bronx Gymnasium Bridge in 1977; over the years, it is coming back in different ways. In 2004, Jene Highstein and I were invited to participate in the Snow Show in Rovaniemi, Finland. Conceived as an experience of space and light trapped in ice, the interior of the nine-meter-tall cube was modeled on the absence of a huge monolithic shape, which is characteristic of Jene Highstein's sculptures. For this piece, it was very important that the ice be harvested from pure water, as seawater turns slightly bluish when it freezes. We cut it out of freshwater ice to prevent green light from getting trapped in the ice.

In April of 1999, we began our sketches for the Nelson-Atkins Museum of Art. The original competition brief asked for the new addition to be against the existing building to the north. When I first visited the site, the feeling of the landscape and the integrity of the original 1933 building impressed me. I felt the new addition could fuse with the landscape, offer new views out to the gardens, and connect to the existing building without blocking the north facade.

The idea of "complimentary contrast" drove our design for the addition. The original building would be the opaque, the new building the translucent. In contrast

For me, light is to space as sound is to music. It is the equivalent of spatial acoustics in light.

to the stone building, a new lightweight architecture of glass lenses is now scattered about the landscape, framing the sculpture gardens. The movement of the body as it crosses through overlapping perspectives—through the landscape and between the light-gathering lenses of the new addition—creates elemental connections between ourselves and the architecture.

The external austerity of the new building, which has been described as being "like shards of glass emerging from landscape," is fully intentional. I believe a building should always be much more about the interior experience than the exterior. The visitor experiences an external austerity followed by an inner immensity. It is the same strategy Matisse used for his astonishing chapel in Venice, France, completed in 1952; a similar philosophy informs our Chapel of St. Ignatius in Seattle, Washington, completed in 1997. I believe it is the correct strategy for the original stone building to stand free, with integrity in the overall composition; while the new lenses, or shards of glass, stand minimally, forming garden courts for outdoor sculpture. The blank background of the glass planks is perfect for a foreground with a piece of sculpture.

Today, we can finally see and experience this architecture the way it was imagined, in a view from the inside out. The fluttering *T*'s subtly mix the cool north light with the warm yellow light of the south. Structural glass lenses, luminously bracketing the landscape of the sculpture garden, begin to glow from within at dusk. The dream of constructing in light reaches a comprehensive passion in this building. The interiors of overlapping perspectives, bathed in the subtle changes of natural light, are constructed from an exterior architecture of translucent prisms that emerge from the ground . . . an architecture of sculpted bars of light and time. One can really see that intensity in the billowing cloudlike spatial energy above the gallery floor. This light changes by the hour, by the day, and by the season. It is as ephemeral as time. The spatial parallax experienced in moving through these galleries is also loosely related to time, whose passage is never in a straight line. Time is more mysterious; without a beginning, without an end, and without a final event. Likewise, these spaces turn and overlap with cadence or rhythm, but, like time, without an absolutely defined direction.

External austerity followed by inner immensity

Nelson-Atkins Museum of Art, Kansas City, Mo.

Steven Holl Architects

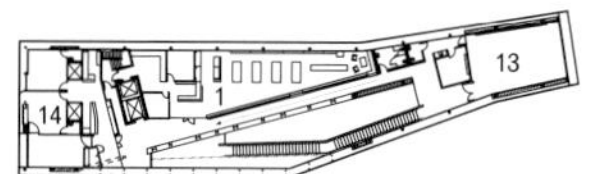

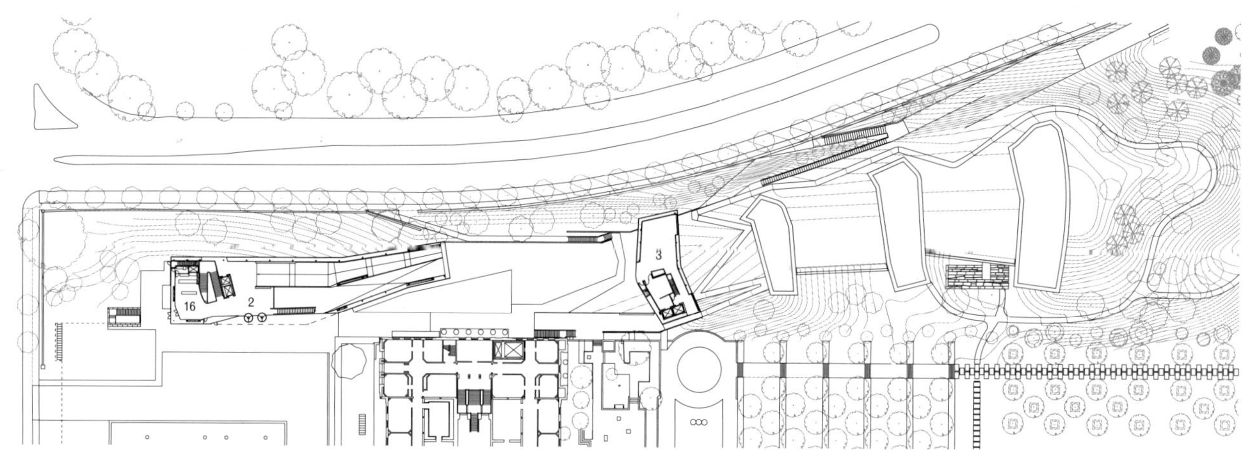

First and second floor plans

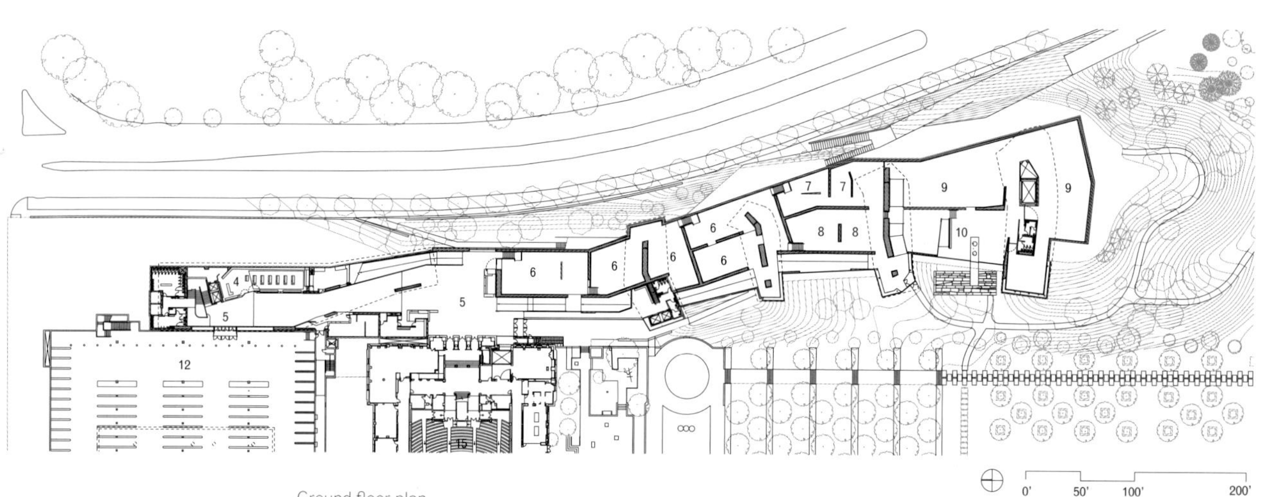

Ground floor plan

library 1
upper lobby 2
garden dining room 3
museum store 4
lower lobby 5
Contemporary Art Gallery 6
Photography Gallery 7
African Art Gallery 8
featured exhibition space 9
10 Noguchi Court
11 art service level
12 parking
13 multipurpose room
14 executive offices
15 auditorium
16 cafe

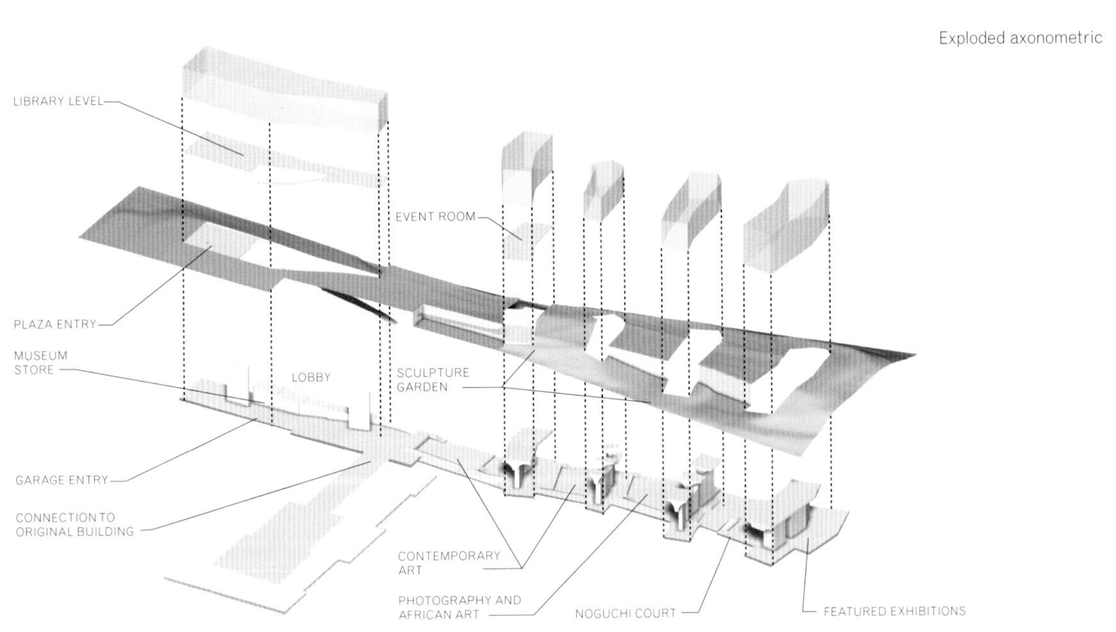

Exploded axonometric

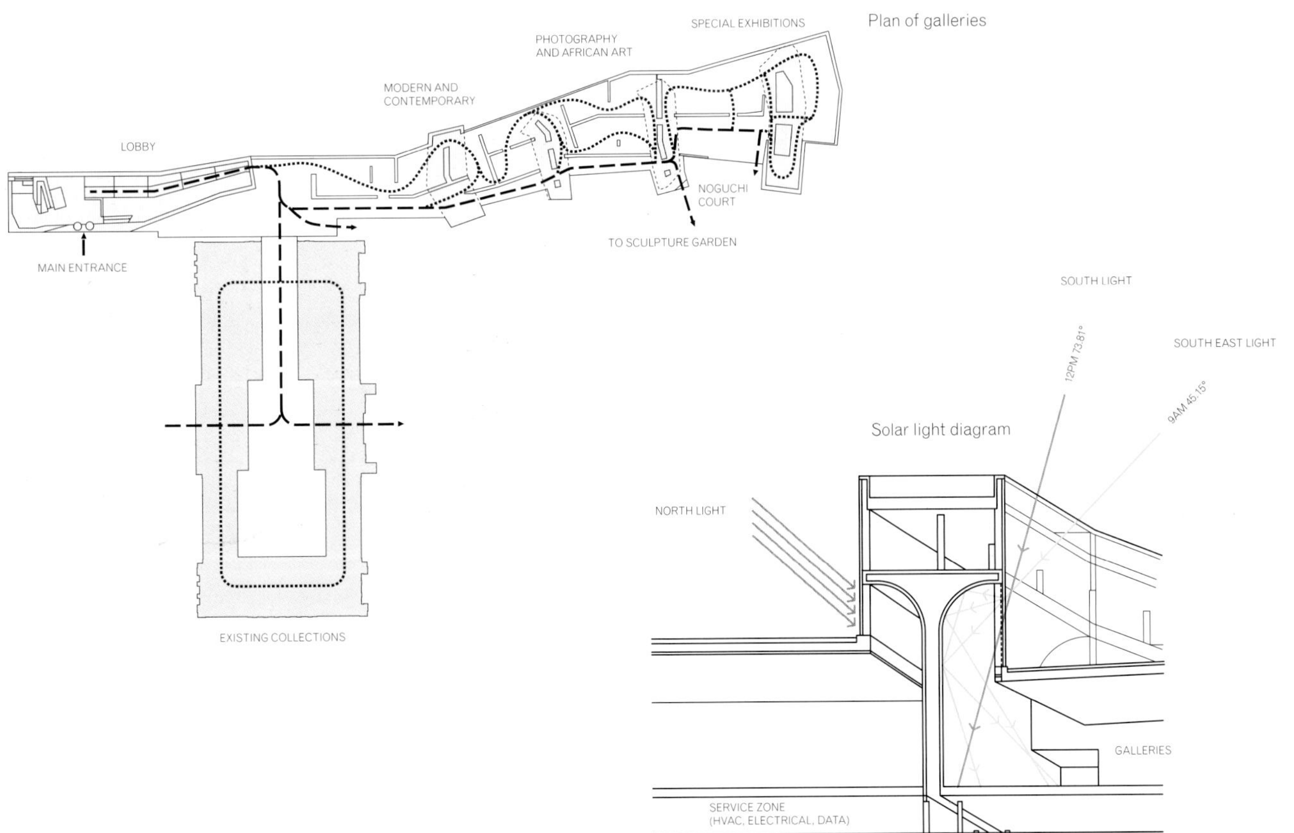

Plan of galleries

Solar light diagram

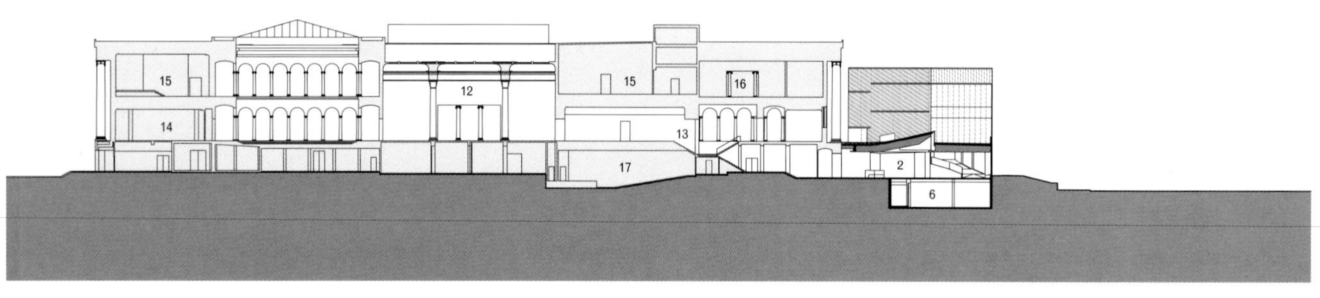

Cross section: lower lobby and original building

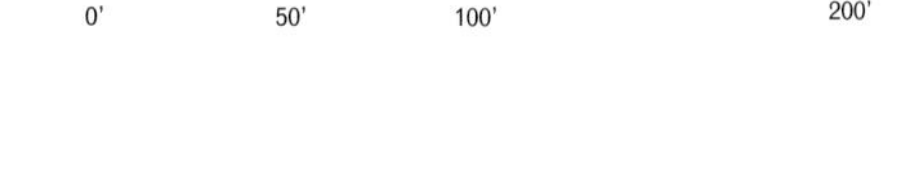

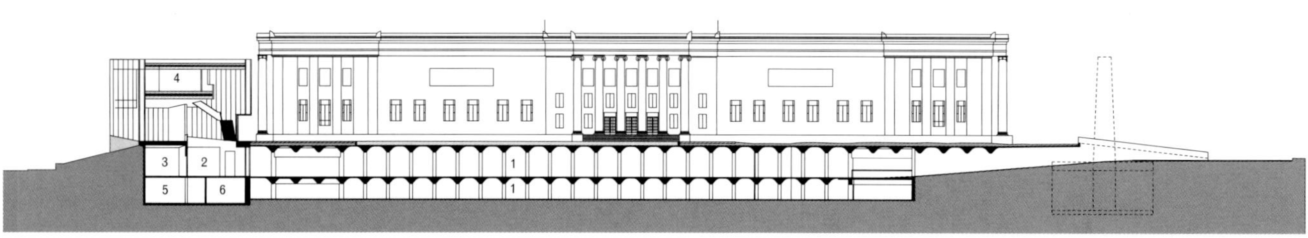

Cross section: lower lobby and garage

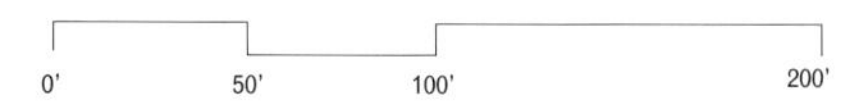

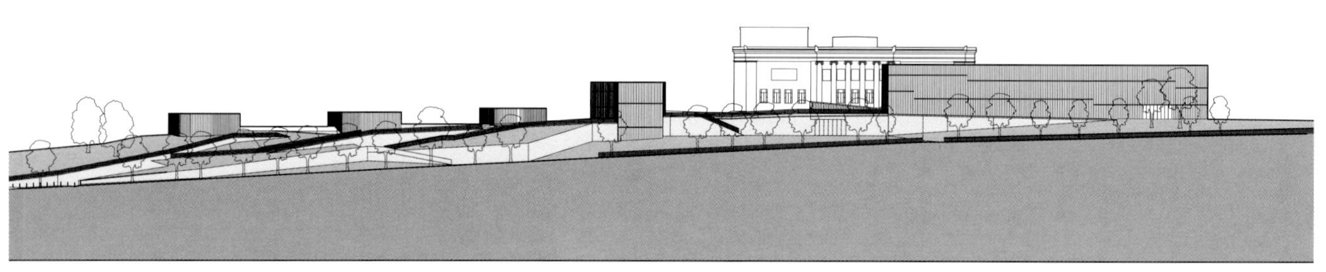

East elevation

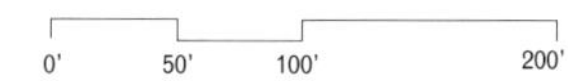

parking garage 1
lobby 2
museum store 3
library 4
stacks 5
mechanical 6
Contemporary Art Gallery 7
collection storage 8
Noguchi Court 9

10 featured exhibition space
11 art receiving
12 original building
13 new opening and stair
14 European Art Gallery
15 Asian Art Gallery
16 American Art Gallery
17 auditorium

Gefter-Press House, Ghent, N.Y.

Michael Bell Architecture

Michael Bell

Exterior view

The Gefter-Press House is sited on a twelve-acre property accessed by crossing a quarter-mile expanse of farming fields before reaching the forested site. The slow approach is the initial phase instigating the organization of movement and time in the house. A series of planar groupings—along with the pictorial depth of the approach and the view through the house—runs counter to the interior movements and shallow spaces, where the buildings is as narrow as ten feet. The programming of the building is coordinated with visual depth; social relations are reflected in the floor and grade heights (above, at, or below) and diagonal vistas though the house and across the courtyard. The building's structural glazing system, consisting of insulated glazing units measuring nine by fourteen feet, allows one's gaze to pass through private as well as public spaces. The glazing has two details: it is either flush with the building volume and projected inboard of the structural framing (on the east/west elevations) or it is six inches outboard of the structural framing (on the north/south elevations). Sills are recessed two inches below floor level. The effect is to project the interior margins of the volume outward and to asymptotically flatten the exterior view against the interior surfaces. The background is pulled elastically to the foreground, diminishing the sense of middle ground. The interior is precisely defined but also dissolves into the extended spaces and clearings in the forest. Vision is immediate and close but also distant. This simultaneity brings the space of the forest into the immediate circumstances of private life. The house can be opened to form a single volume. The two bedrooms open with interior sliding doors that match the glazing systems and form two oculus openings. When approaching the house, they form a binocular effect that bifurcates the house's singular vantage point.

Gefter-Press House, Ghent, N.Y.

Michael Bell Architecture

Gefter-Press House, Ghent, N.Y.

Michael Bell Architecture

Gefter-Press House, Ghent, N.Y.
Michael Bell Architecture

Gefter-Press House, Ghent, N.Y.
Michael Bell Architecture

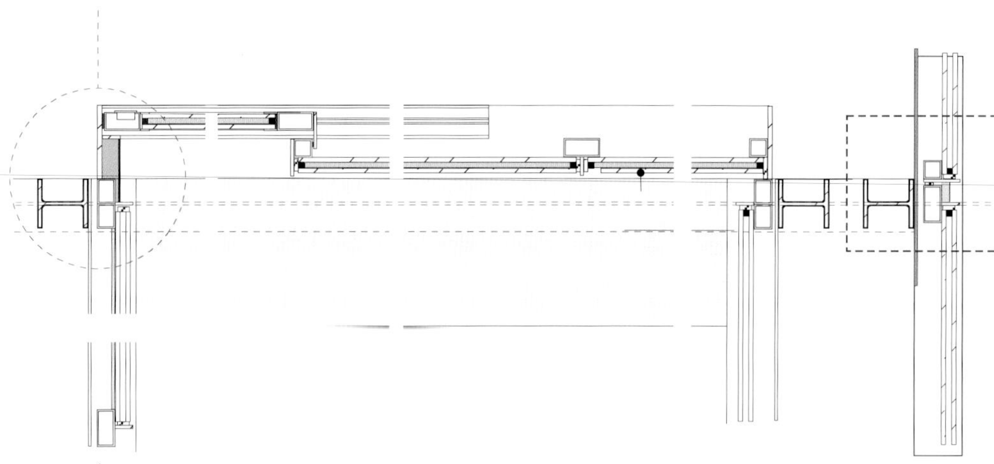

Plan detail at curtain wall

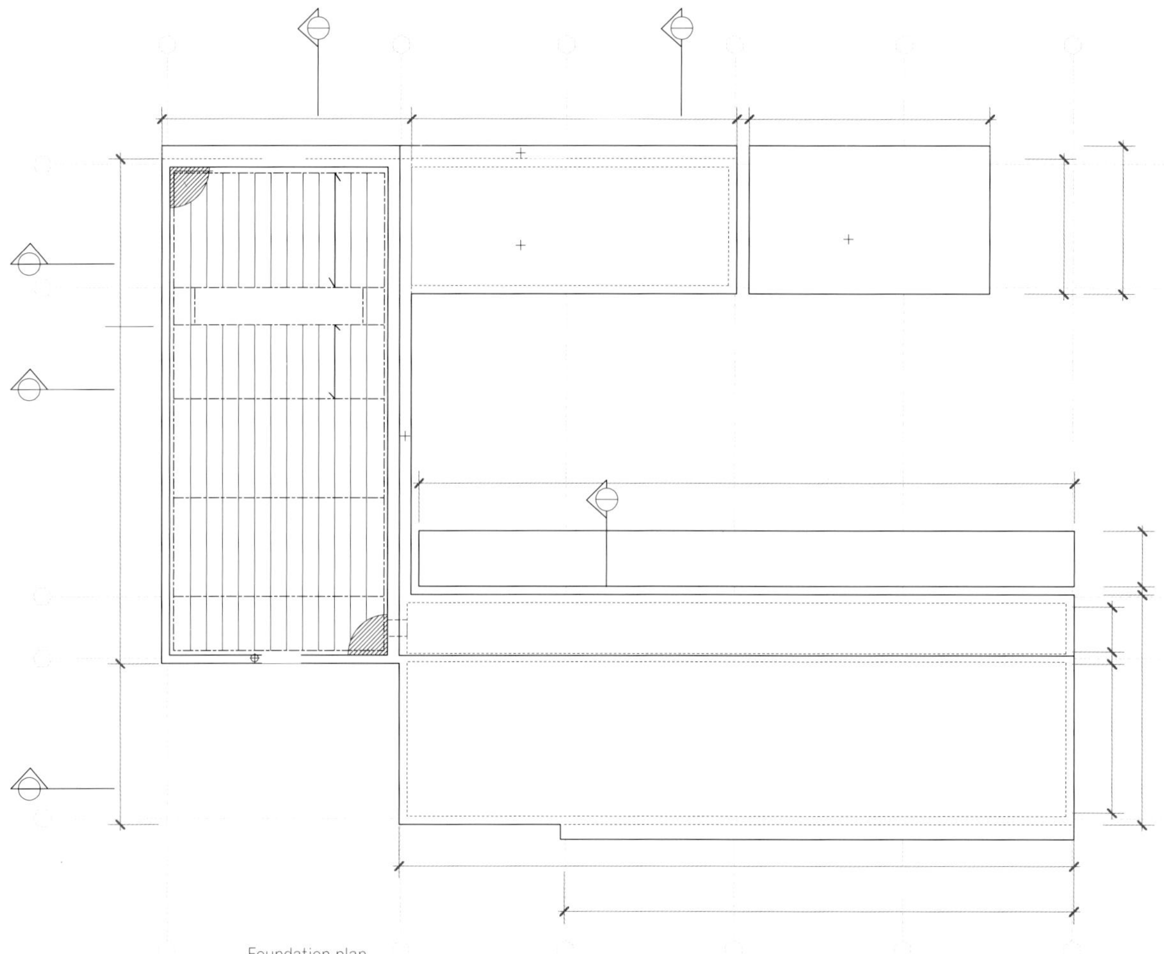

Foundation plan

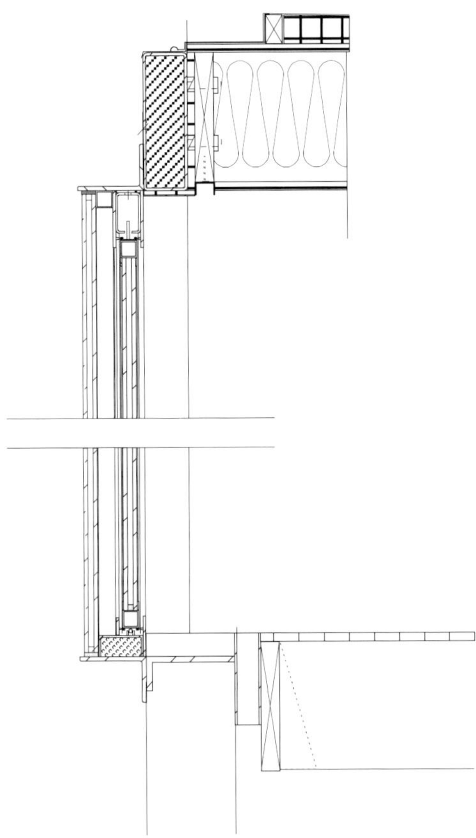

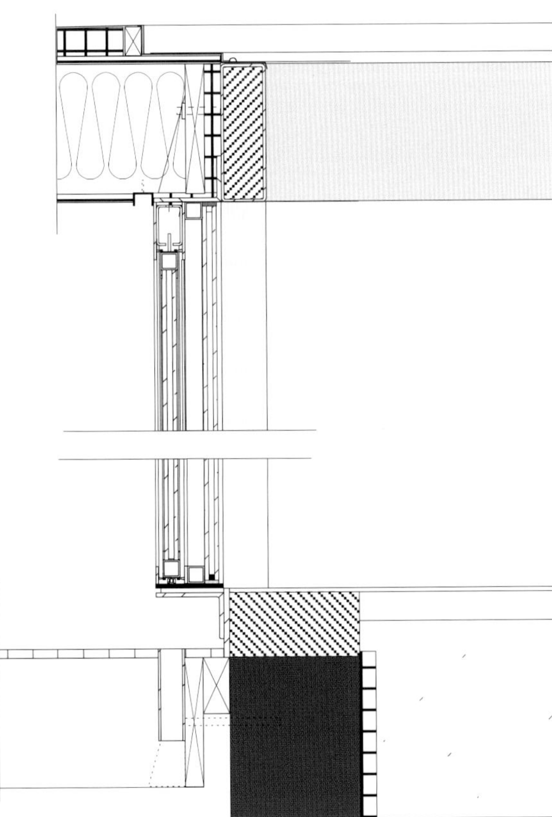

Sections through sliding doors

Gefter-Press House, Ghent, N.Y.
Michael Bell Architecture

The Glass Pavilion, Toledo Museum of Art, Toledo, Ohio
SANAA

Toshihiro Oki

Bare roof structure during construction

Located in a grove of 150-year-old trees, the 76,000 square-foot, single-story Glass Pavilion contains the Toledo Museum of Art's extensive glass art collection, temporary exhibition galleries, and glassmaking hot shop. The building's low profile preserves the view outside, while its glass walls interact with the colors and characteristics of the surrounding environment.

The programmatic requirements were to combine the seemingly opposite functions of rough glass-making studios with refined galleries, highlighting both functions equally and concurrently. Glass walls are used both as physical separators and visual connectors, bringing far to near, outside to inside, and molten glass to exhibited art, and they allowed for further layering of the complexities of light. Spanning uninterrupted from floor to ceiling, the walls are composed of two layers of glass separated by a dynamic buffer or cavity zone. This buffer emphasizes separation (as spaces slide past each other) and connectedness, revealling adjacent sights, programs, and activities such as the motions of a glassblower.

The design depended on a viable envelope. In this case, the cavity was the catalyst. It functions like an insulated glazing unit (IGU). Radiant heating and cooling in the floor and ceiling combine with a low-velocity air system to create a thermal buffer. This mitigates temperature extremes between exterior and interior spaces and between the hot shop and galleries. Other systems were also employed to maximize efficiency, such as mapping sun angles to manage heat gain; recycling heat from the glassblowing ovens; balancing mechanical, electrical, and plumbing (MEP) systems with structural systems; and using heat-gain reflecting curtains to reduce energy loads. With such large amounts of glass being used in the building, balancing and controlling daylight became a major issue. Mapping was used to quantify direct and indirect daylight levels. In the galleries, model analyses were used to gauge optimal accumulated light levels for artwork.

Structural engineering was critical to keep the roof thin and the structural columns minimal. Intense calculations and coordination were undertaken to minimize deflections and dimensional tolerances of the roof structure while maximizing spans. This data was mapped over the glass to identify conflicts and inefficiencies. Engineering was crucial to understanding the complexities of the building in terms of budgetary, environmental, and programming needs. By doing so, it allowed further exploration of glass as an experiential medium.

View of gallery and glass envelope

Foyer 1 and main corridor

View of hotshop, from main corridor

Interior view showing reflections on glass

Roof structure under construction

Laminated glass panels being fabricated in China

Installation of glass panel

Interior under construction

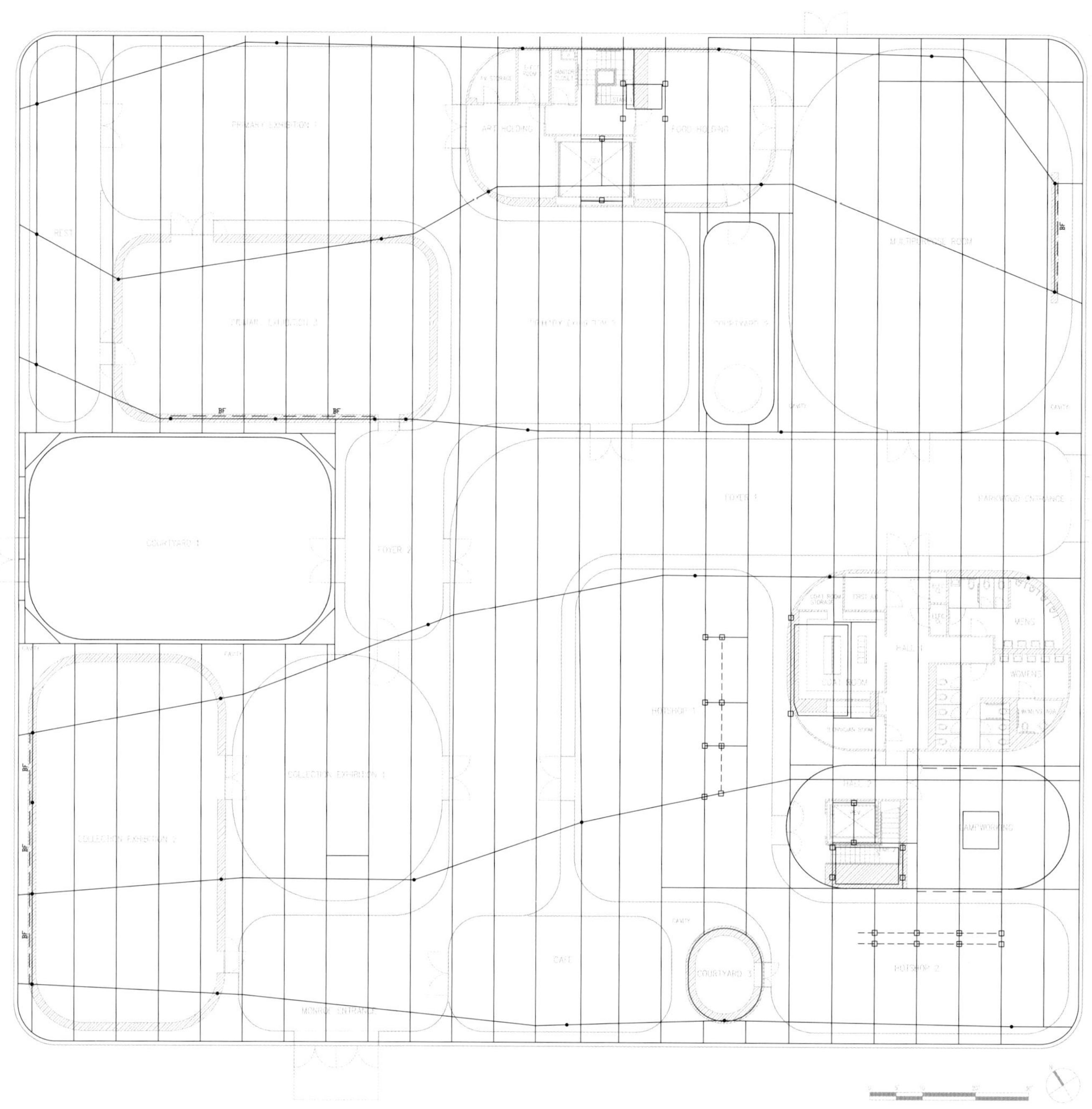

Steel roof structure overlaid on ground floor plan

Section diagram of curtain wall

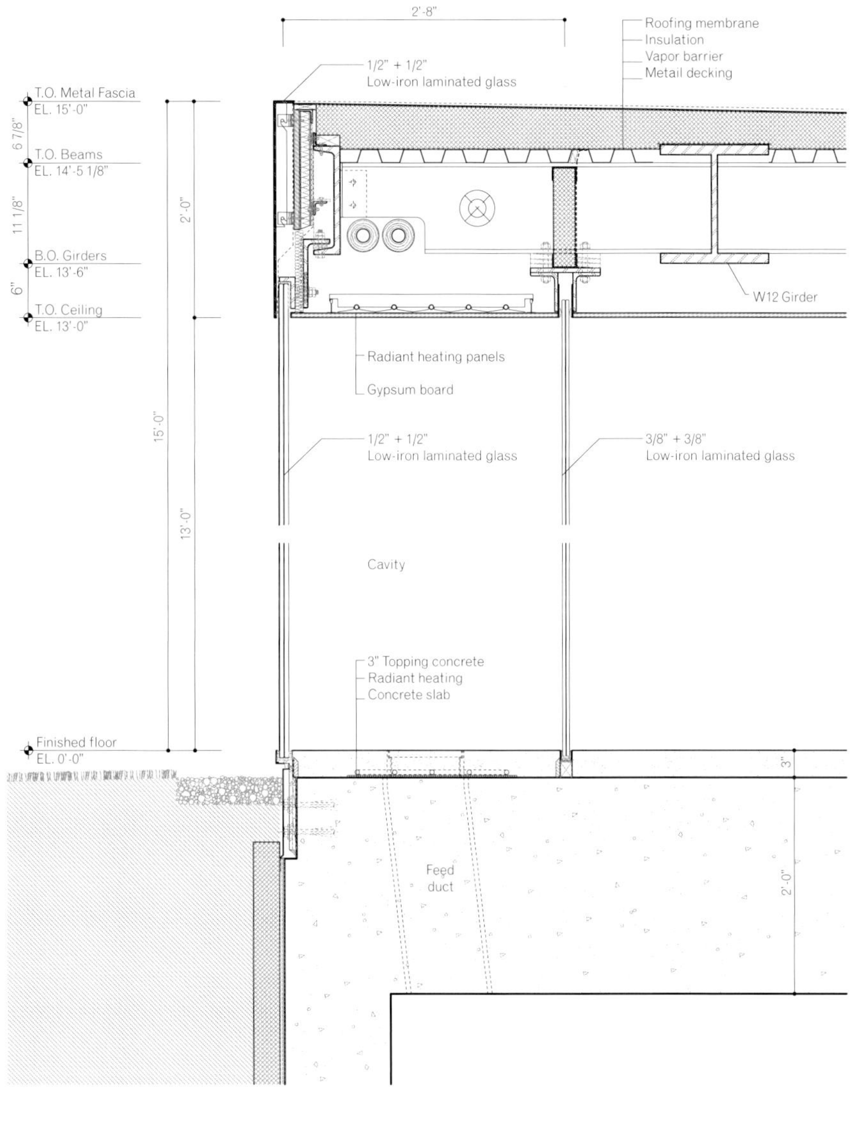

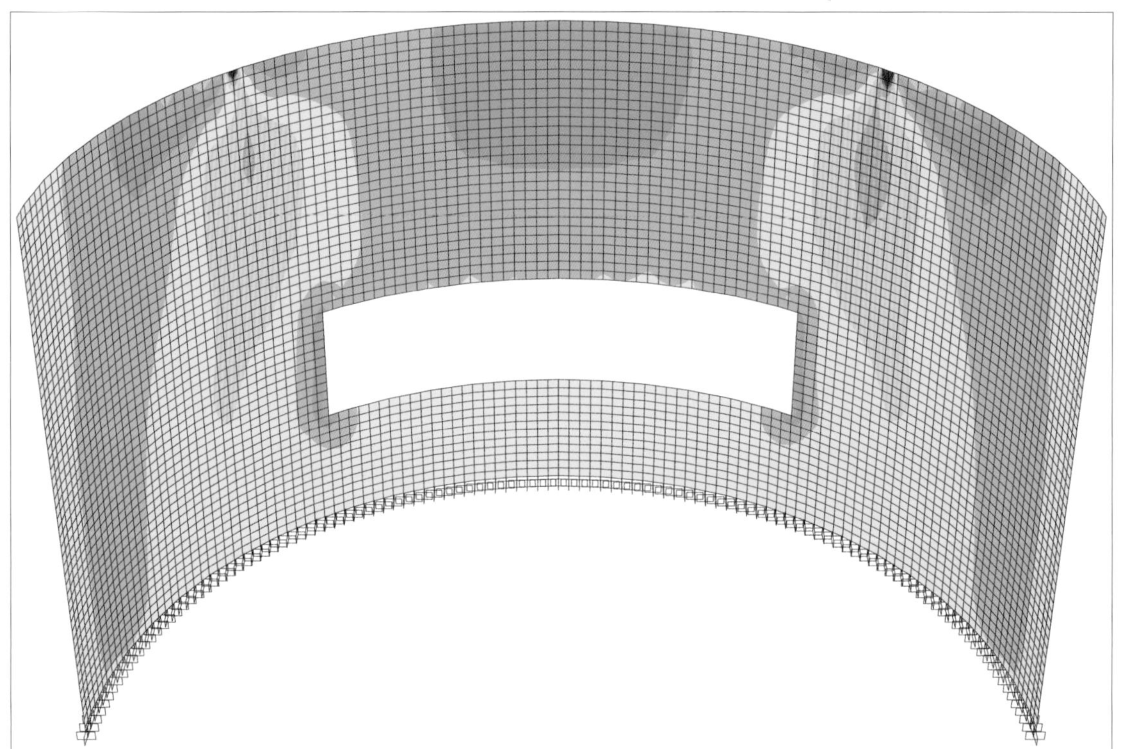

Stress distribution in steel plate shear wall from structural finite-analysis model

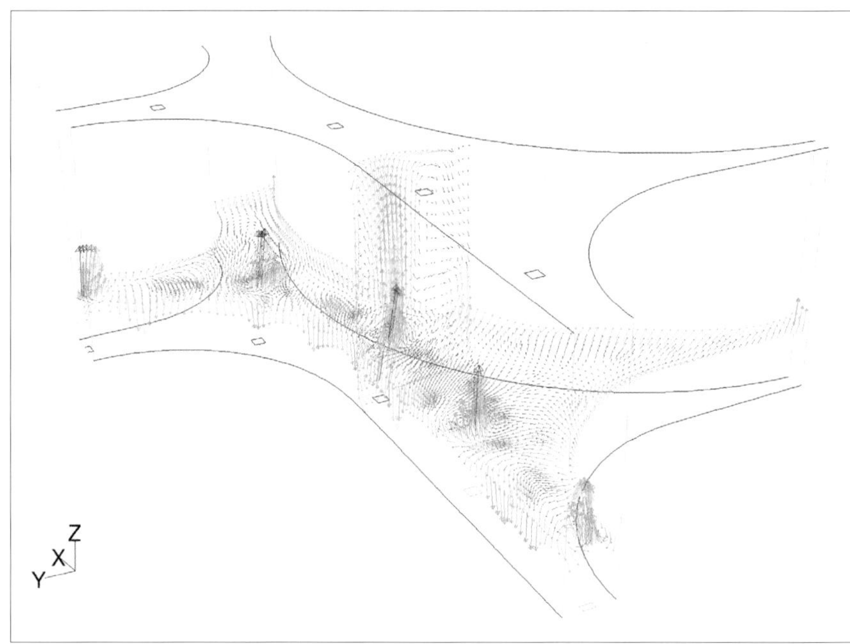

Airflow optimization model at cavity space

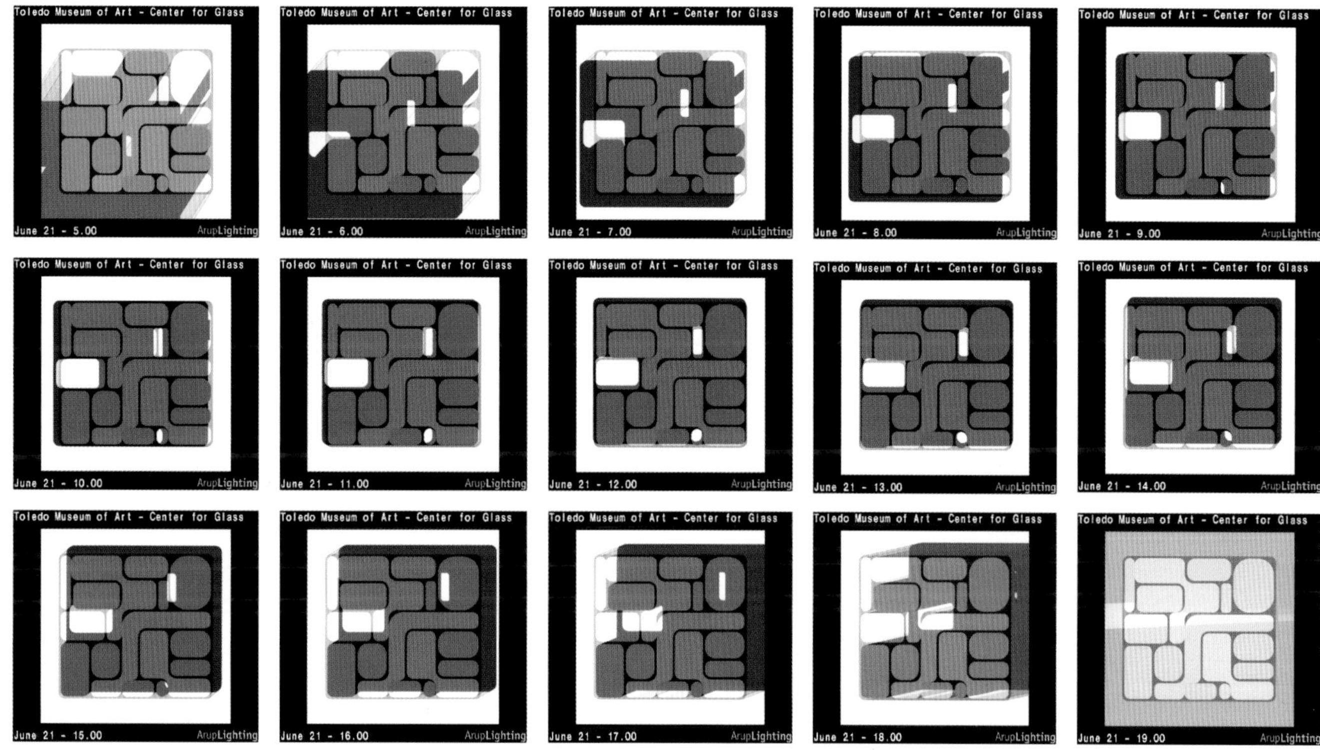

Direct daylight exposure analyses

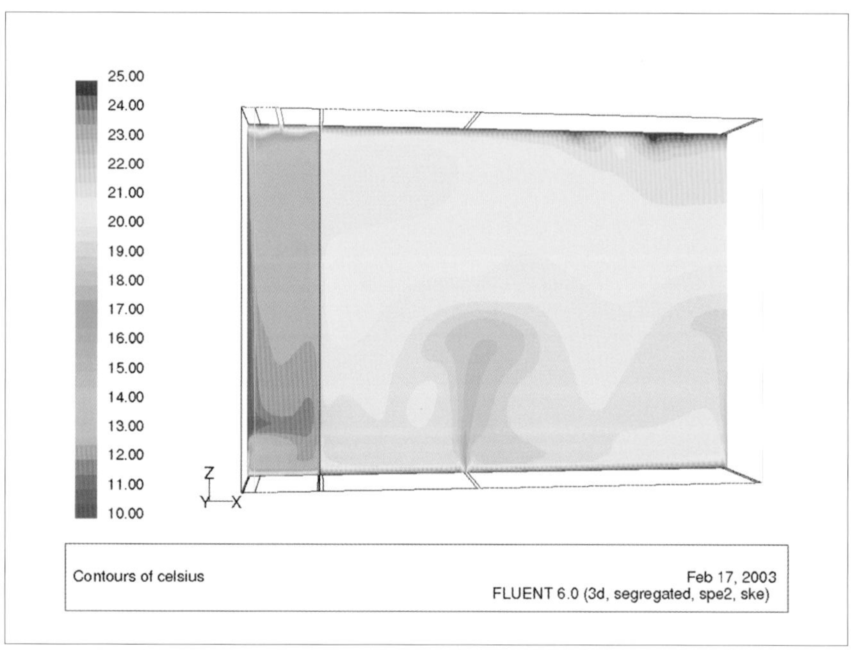

Computational fluid dynamics (CFD) temperature analysis of cavity and interior

:: PORTAL COMPOSITION LIST ::

Portal #	03		04		06		10		12		14		15	
Type	TYPE A	TYPE A OPP.	TYPE C	TYPEC OPP.	TYPE J	TYPE J	TYPE E	TYPE G	TYPE D	TYPE D	TYPE A	TYPE A OPP.	TYPE A	TYPE A OPP.
Top Details	02	02	02	02	36	40	04	20	10	14	02	02	02	02
	04	04	08	08	38		16	22	12	04	04	04	04	04
Bottom Details	01	01	01	01	35	39	03	19	09	13	01	01	01	01
	03	03	07	07	37		15	21	11	03	03	03	03	03

Portal #	16		17		19		23		25		26		27	
Type	TYPE A	TYPE A OPP.	TYPE I	TYPE I	TYPE B	TYPE B OPP.	TYPE E	TYPE F OPP.	TYPE E OPP.	TYPE F	TYPE B	TYPE B OPP.	TYPE F	TYPE F OPP.
Top Details	02	02	28	30	06	06	04	14	04	14	06	06	14	14
	04	04	32	34			16	18	16	18			18	18
Bottom Details	01	01	27	29	05	05	03	13	03	13	05	05	13	13
	03	03	31	33			15	17	15	17			17	17

Portal #	50		51		65		68		69	
Type	TYPE E SIM.	TYPE E SIM.	TYPE H	TYPE E SIM.	TYPE E	TYPE E OPP.	TYPE E	TYPE E OPP.	TYPE E	TYPE E OPP.
Top Details	04	04	24	04	04	04	04	04	04	04
	16	16	26	16	16	16	16	16	16	16
Bottom Details	03	03	23	03	03	03	03	03	03	03
	15	15	25	15	15	15	15	15	15	15

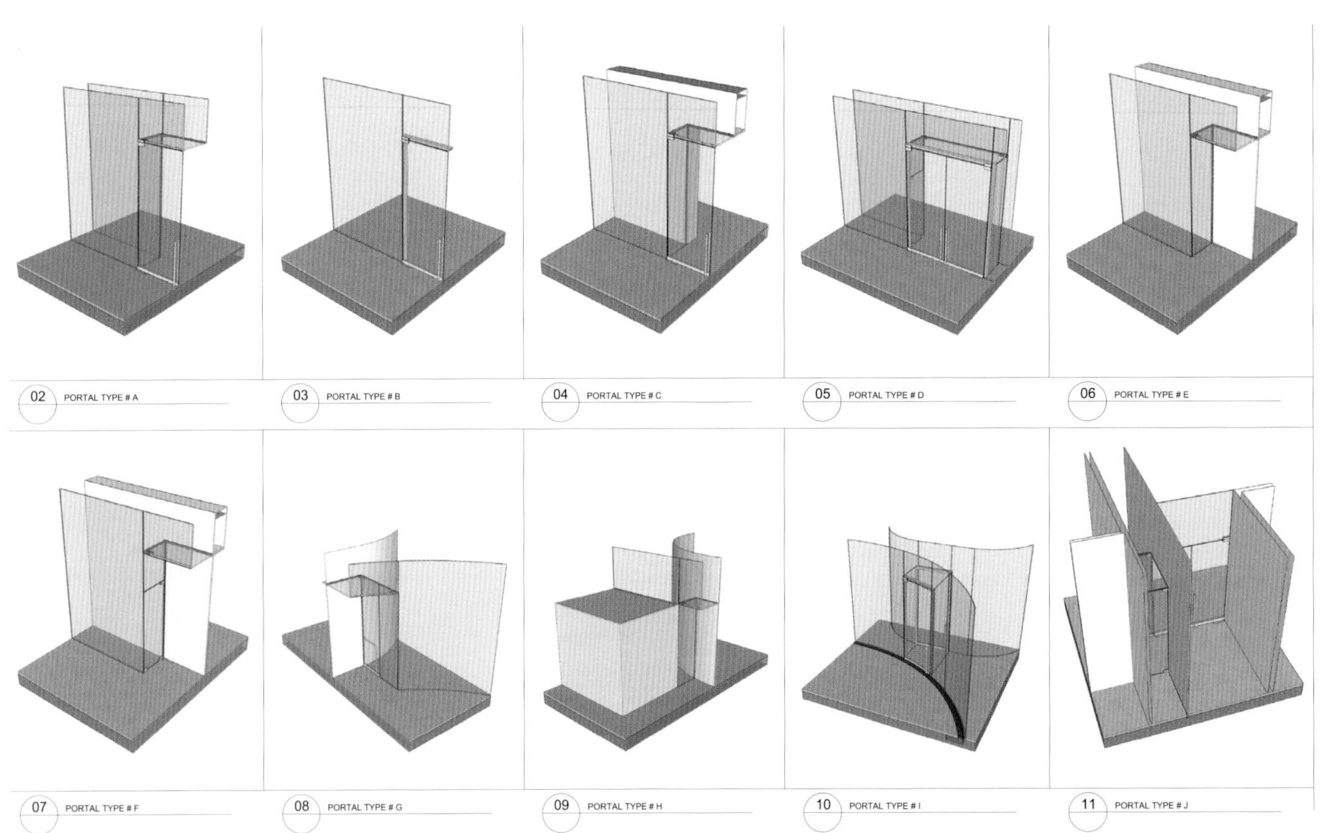

Portal types

IAC/InterActiveCorp, New York, N.Y.

Gehry Partners

Michael Bell

Exterior view of IAC/InterActiveCorp, Gehry Partners, New York, N.Y., 2006

The IAC/InterActiveCorp in New York City was designed by Gehry Partners, with significant input from Permasteelisa and, in particular, by engineer Roberto Bicchiarelli, who oversaw the implementation of parameters and control factors for cold bending the building's curtain wall. Unlike the heat processes used in Gehry's previous curved-glass architecture, or in the works of SANAA and others, the cold-bending process required that the IGUs be formed on site. The curtain wall is composed of 1,330 unique units; each is situated within a matrix of possible rotational axes established by the allowable limits of bending. There are three folds on the building's top tier and five on ground level. Together, they form a modulated and repeated torqued structure that diminishes as it meets the ground. The flow of the folds and the incisions that these edges portend are not based on a regular curve but a continuously changing spline that plies its elegance against the force of the city grid. Glass fritting diminishes the edges between opaque and transparent, without negating the visual effect of floors as segregate zones, resulting in the horizontal stripe of a quasi–ribbon window and the occupation of the building as a set of stacked floor plates. If the IAC project was a virtual partnership between architects and engineers, it is difficult to imagine how one could have worked without the other. For all of Gehry's incantations of technology—and he is the leader in this arena—his work is never far from that of the artists that he so often claims as partners or inspirations.

IAC is a structural-silicone installation. As such, it is a curtain wall sustained by the bite and adhesion of silicone. DOW Chemical and others have perfected this product for thirty years, but its essential make-up is long-standing. Silicone grips glass from behind, yet curtain walls are often understood as being woven and based in metaphors of fabric. A structural silicone wall is therefore an unwoven curtain, one that is exceedingly flat and in which glass is set in place from the exterior and then pulled into a sustained position. Given the building's conflated image of rotational torque (in its massing) and its perpetual inward pull (through the use of structural silicone), one senses the building as a form of still life with immanent motion. Its stasis and potential energy situates this building with the art of Robert Morris, Robert Smithson, and Eva Hesse; works that critic Rosalind Krauss refers to as "immobile cyclones" in the way they propagate sensations of motion.

Gehry Partners' software, Digital Project (developed from CATIA), is central to the design, as well as to Permasteelisa's engineering. The first step in both CATIA and Digital Project is to scan a physical model of the proposed work. Scanning translates curved surfaces to the digital model. While easily understood as a form of translation, it is critical to note the complexity of this process as a form of exterior analysis. It is therefore the elastic space between the flatness of the scanning mechanism and the curved surfaces of the model that represent the true innovation and breakthrough of Gehry's work; a transaction that threatens to overshadow the plain feat of cold-bent IGUs. Gehry and Permasteelisa have found a latent ductility in glass, creating a taut-surfaced structure that denies the ease of perception it so fully embraces.

IAC/InterActiveCorp, New York, N.Y.
Gehry Partners

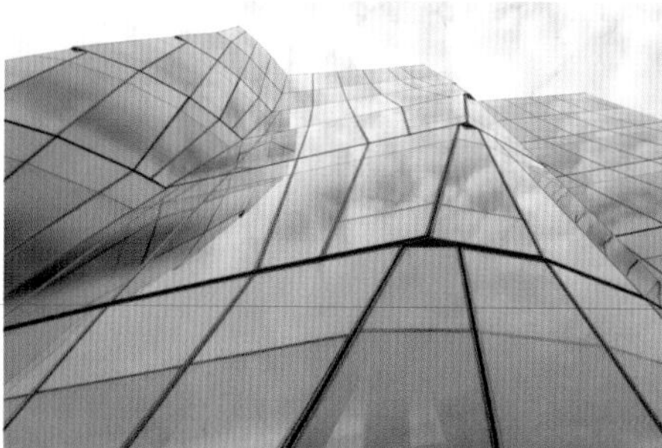

Elevation

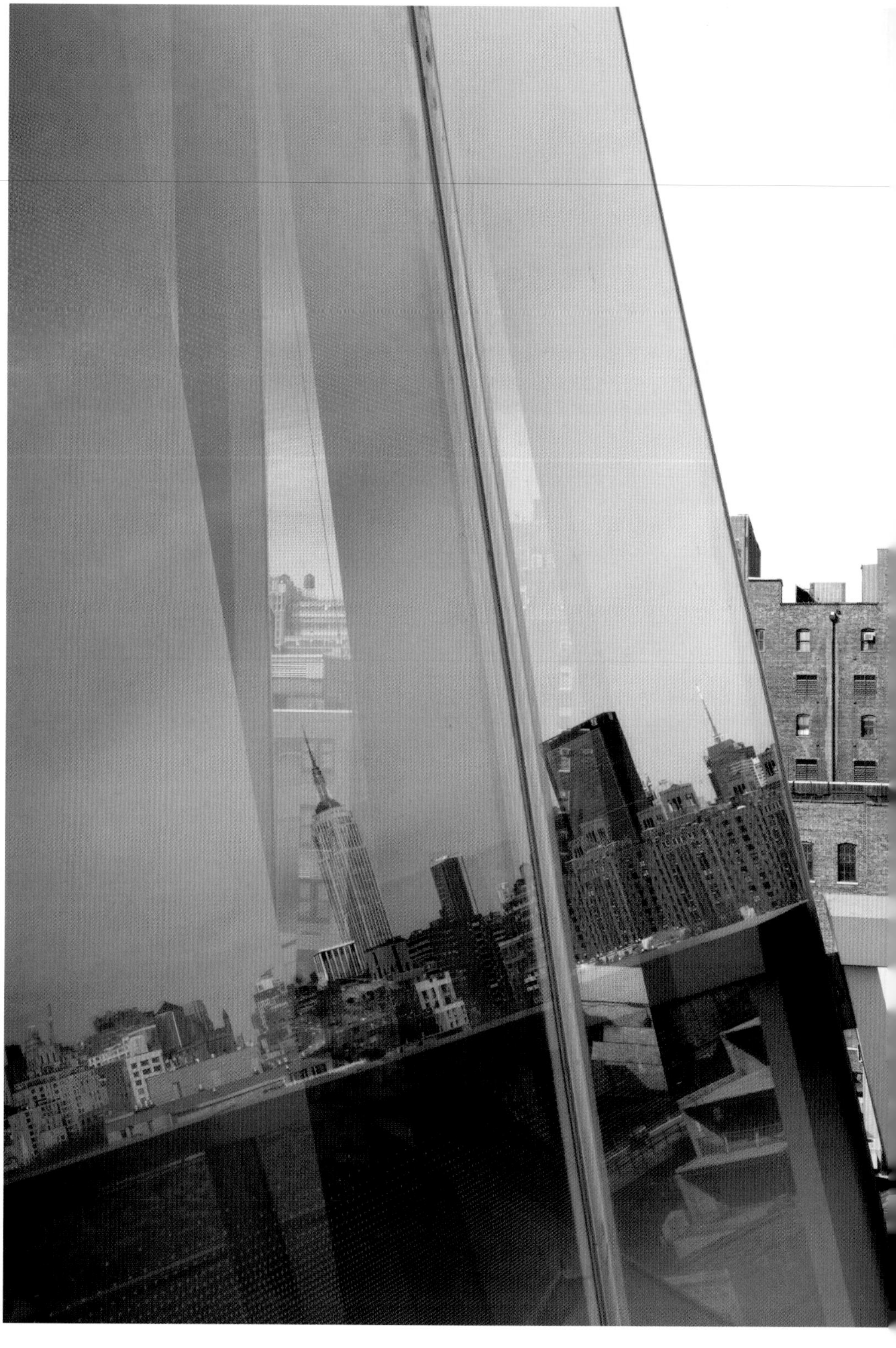

Detail of glass installation

7 World Trade Center, New York, N.Y.

James Carpenter Design Associates

James Carpenter

Tower merging with sky

Seven World Trade Center was the third building to collapse on September 11, 2001, and it is the first to be rebuilt. Designed by David Childs of Skidmore, Owings & Merrill (SOM), the new building is composed of forty-two floors of office space set above eight floors of Con Edison transformers (located in large concrete vaults at street level). James Carpenter Design Associates (JCDA) was invited to join the design team in late 2002, after the building's prismatic form—derived from significant site planning—was already established. We were asked to collaborate on the curtain wall, the base of the building containing the transformers, and the lobby.

The site's new master plan radically altered the building's context. Before its destruction, the original 7 World Trade Center was accessible only from the complex's podium, four stories above street level, where the blank granite box was dominated by Con Edison's industrial louvers. With the loss of the World Trade Center's raised podium, by necessity, the new design had to accommodate the transformers and also respond to a new public and urban presence at street level. The concept for the new design was to create a parallelogram in plan, extruded into a sixty-story-high crystal prism. The base volume grounds the single extruded parallelogram and supports the tower visually. SOM proposed locking the base and tower with a third interior volume of light, the shape of which becomes most apparent at night. We sought to embed light in all of the building's levels. From the podium to the special linear-lap curtain wall, light appears to emanate from the building itself. Our contribution to the design included glass panels that overlap the building's floor plates and a spandrel system that reflects light from behind the panels, creating a luminous tower that extends light into the public realm.

The curtain wall combines low-iron glass with a reflective coating, allowing light to enter the tower and reflecting it into the public realm.

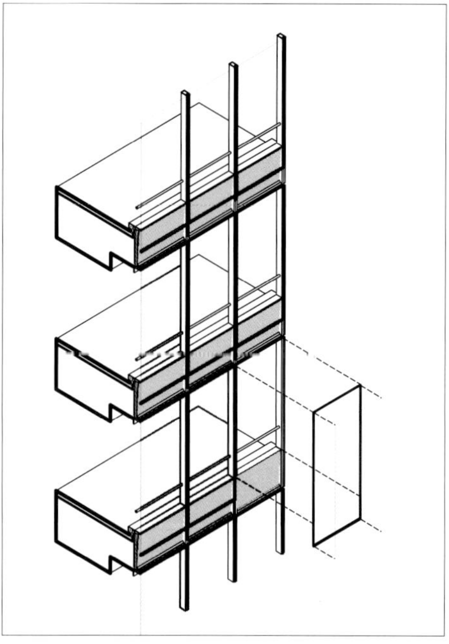

Exploded axonometric diagram of the curtain-wall system

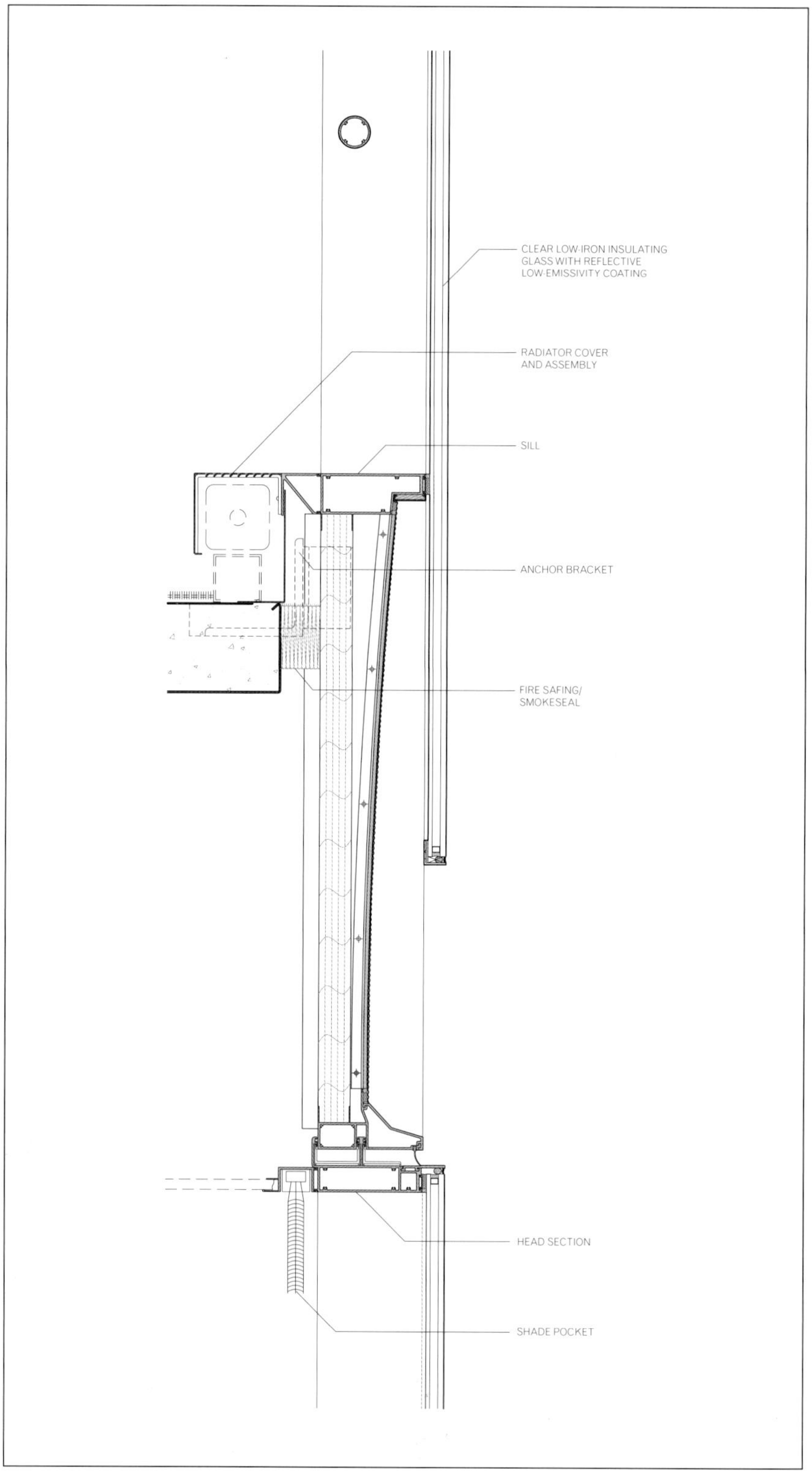

Detail section of curtain wall

CLEAR LOW-IRON INSULATING GLASS WITH REFLECTIVE LOW-EMISSIVITY COATING

RADIATOR COVER AND ASSEMBLY

SILL

ANCHOR BRACKET

FIRE SAFING/ SMOKESEAL

HEAD SECTION

SHADE POCKET

View of the curtain wall during installation

Mock-up of the curtain-wall spandrel featuring the linear-lap detail

Sequence of photographs showing the installation process of the curtain-wall panels

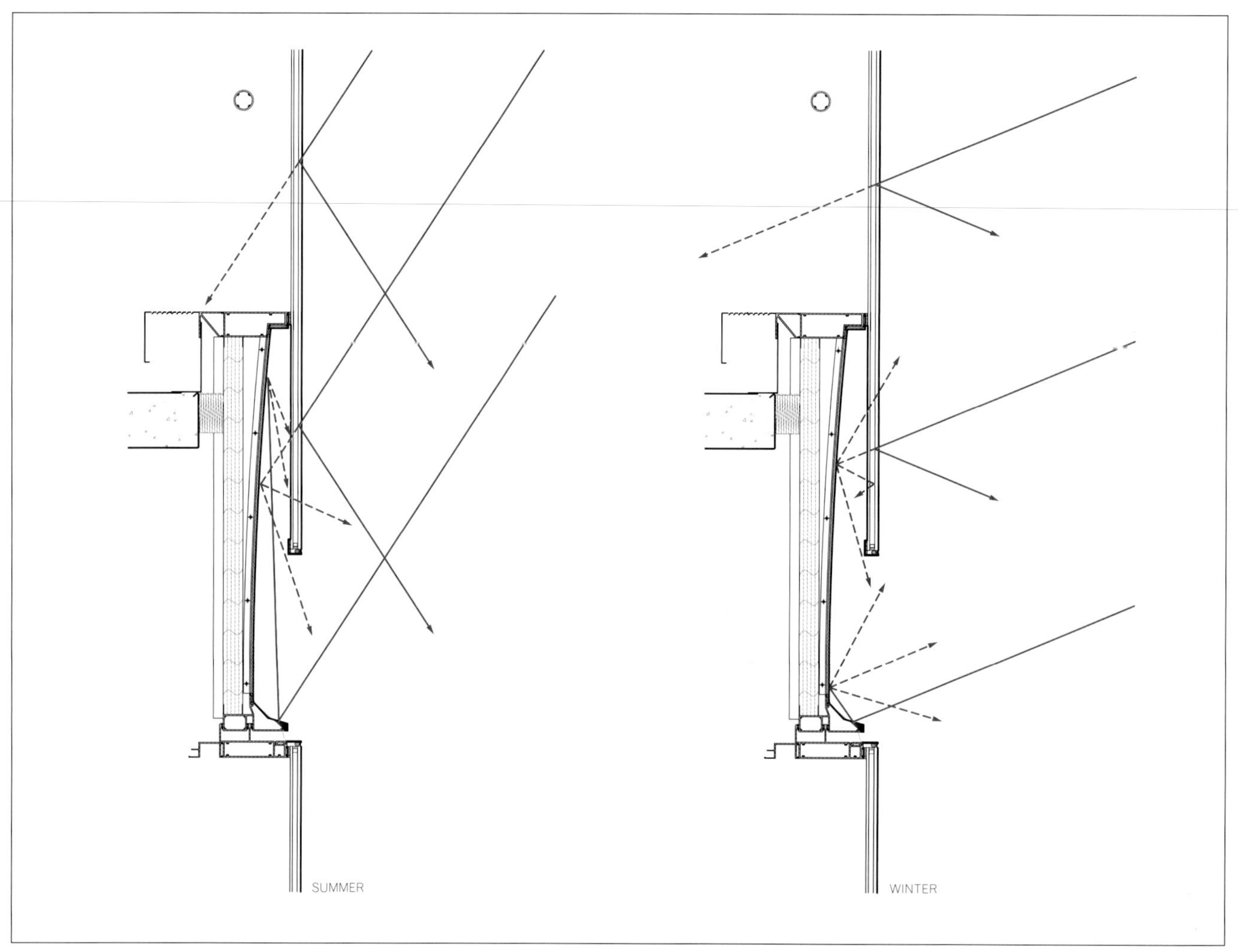

Section showing the interaction of daylight within the spandrel

11 March Memorial, Atocha Train Station, Madrid, Spain

FAM Arquitectura y Urbanismo S.L.

Miguel Jaenicke Fontao

Eleven March Memorial was inaugurated at the Atocha Train Station on March 11, 2007, the third anniversary of the Madrid train bombings. The oval-shaped glass cylinder weighs 140 tons and is eleven meters tall, with exterior and interior diameters measuring eight and ten-and-a-half meters respectively.

A luminous monument, it is built out of 15,000 curved glass blocks glued with a liquid-acrylic material and hardened by ultraviolet light. Inside the tower, an ethylene tetrafluoroethylene (ETFE) membrane is printed with messages left at the station by mourners in the days after the bombings. Thousands of marks of condolence are inscribed on the inside of the tower. Sunshine hitting the bricks focuses light into an empty blue chamber, which the public can access via Atocha Station. From below, visitors can peer skyward to read hundreds of messages wrapping internally around the cylinder. After dark, the volume radiates softly from lights at the base. During the day, sunlight produces an ethereal glow as it filters through the tower and reflects against the deep blue surfaces in the underground chamber.

Mourners' messages printed on ETFE membrane

In addition to commemorating the tragedy, the monument's structure is something of a novelty. For the first time in engineering history, massive glass blocks connect, forming a structure through the use of transparent adhesive and without the need for additional mechanical elements. The blocks were rigidly bonded on site with a UV-hardening acrylic adhesive. Normally, acrylates are applied in very thin layers—roughly three tenths of a millimeter—but due to unavoidable tolerances between the blocks, the intermediate material needed a thickness of 2.5 millimeters. Small and large samples were tested and verified with regard to resistance to aging, including long- and short-term resistance for temperatures between 20°C and 80°C. Also, due to the fact that acrylates tend to creep under permanent loads, creep performance was tested under a constant temperature of 60°C for different stress levels. Shear and compression levels, below which no creep could be observed, were considered sufficient for the structure.

The outer layer of the eleven-meter-tall monument consists of approximately 15,100 massive glass blocks. Made of extremely clear borosilicate glass, the bricks were manufactured to be convex on one side and concave on the other. The eleven-meter-high external wall is nearly elliptical in plan, and the curvature lends greatly to its rigidity, creating a shell of structural glass without steel elements, which would otherwise have disturbed the visual impression of the memorial.

Construction view from above

View of monument from underground blue chamber

Madrid

Blocks being joined with transparent adhesive

View of assembly

Transverse section showing underground chamber beneath the highway

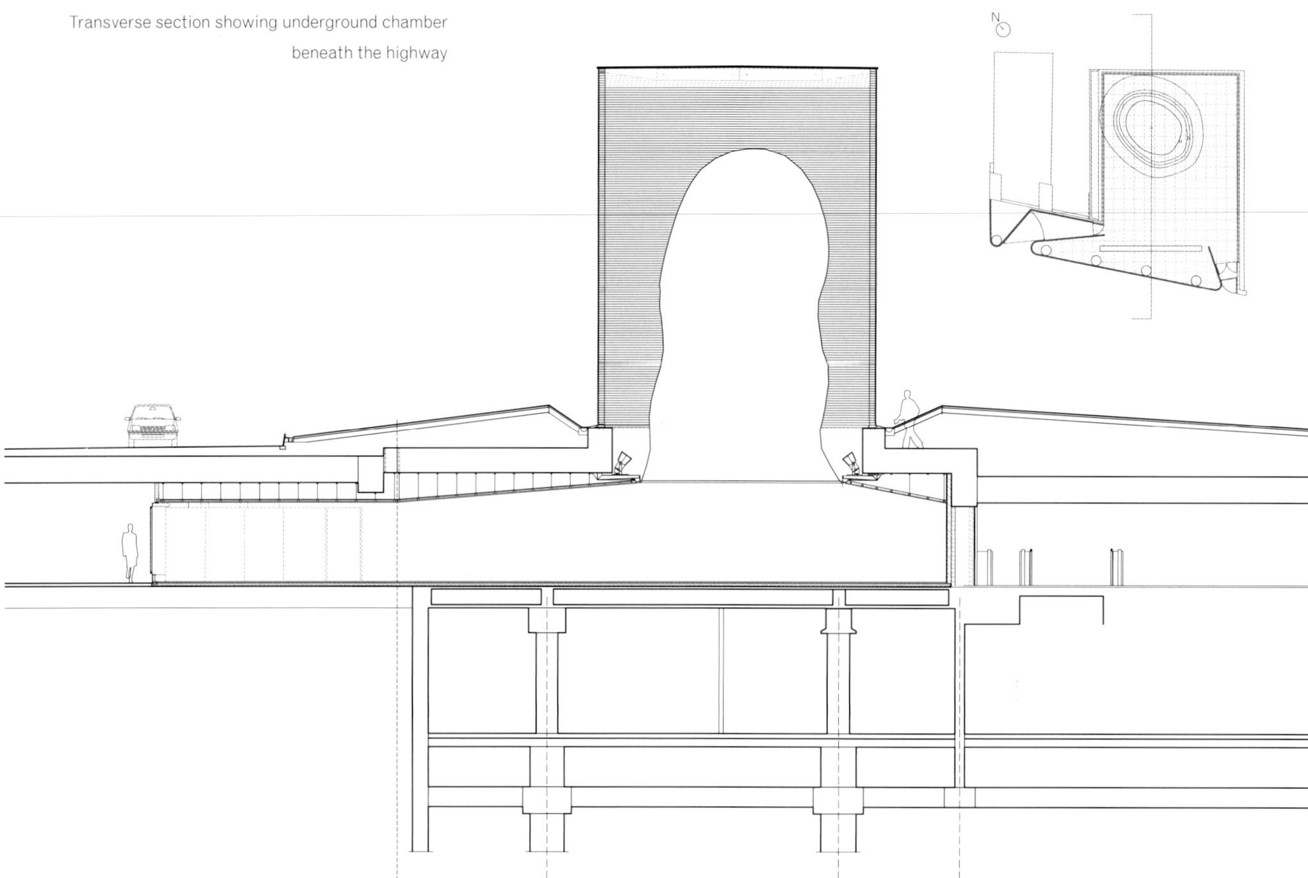

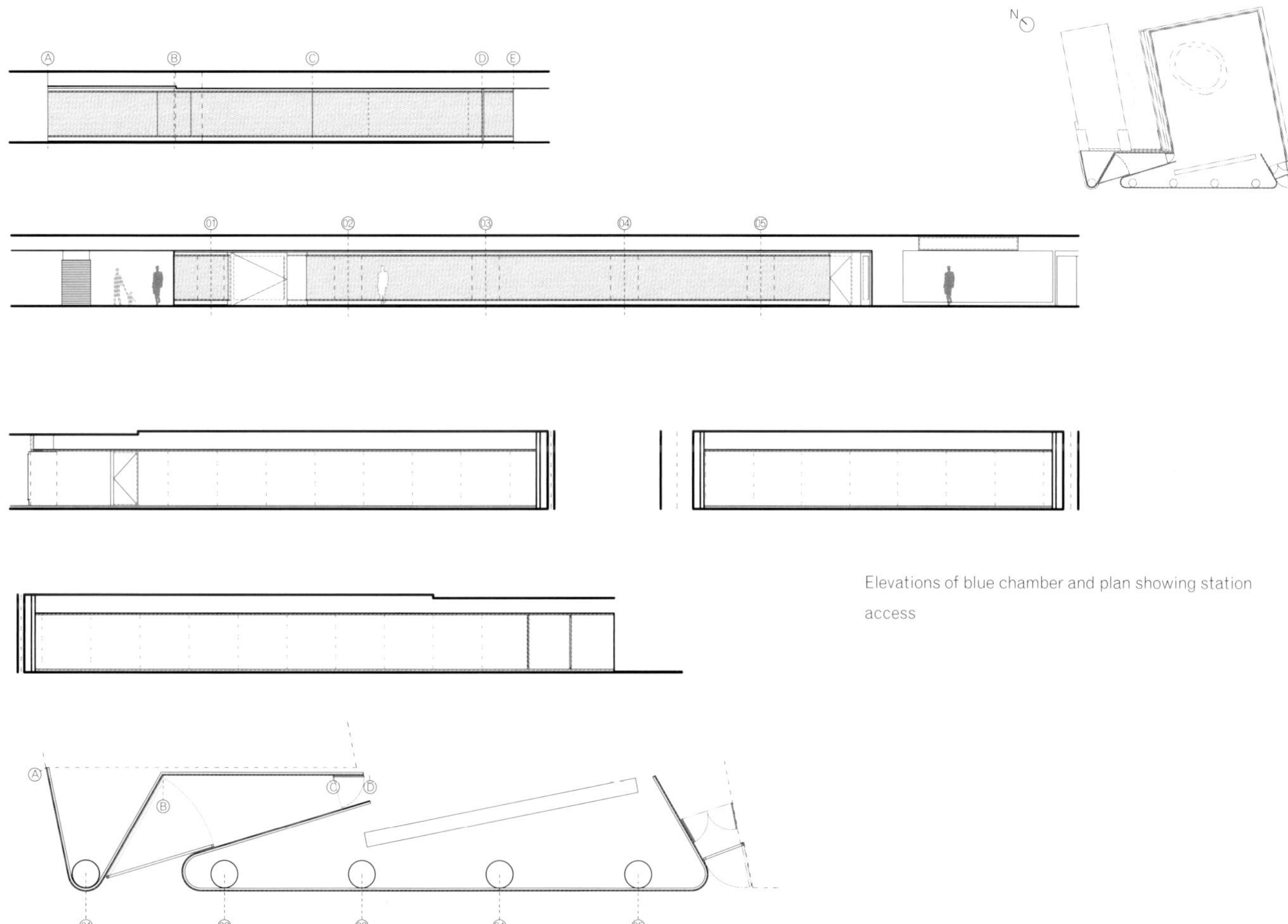

Elevations of blue chamber and plan showing station access

Technical Innovations: Material and Light

Electrochromic Windows

Thomas J. Richardson

Significant progress has been made in three decades of research and development of dynamic solar control glazing; however, products now on the market are expensive and offer limited ability to control and direct solar radiation. For example, Sage Electrochromics produces skylights and windows that range in visible light transmittance from 75 to 5 percent and offer good visual quality and superb thermal stability. These devices use tungsten oxide, which can either absorb or transmit light depending on their chemical state, which alters with applied voltage. There is little difference, however, in reflected visible light between the clear and dark blue states, and there is little change in the transmission of infrared light, which accounts for almost half the solar energy reaching the earth's surface.

Electrochromic technology that blocks light by reflection, rather than by absorption, offers a number of advantages over light-absorbing windows. These include the ability to admit or reject all wavelengths of visible and infrared light; to provide sufficient opacity for privacy; and to substantially reduce glare. In addition, light-absorbing electrochromic windows can become quite hot when exposed to direct sunlight, making it necessary to place an expensive low-E coating on the interior pane to keep radiant heat out of the building. The exterior surface of a light-reflective electrochromic window can be up to 20°C (36°F) cooler, which also contributes to its durability.

The reflective metal-hydride system currently being developed at Lawrence Berkeley National Laboratory[1] utilizes a thin-film magnesium alloy that becomes transparent when absorbing hydrogen. These films exhibit very large changes in both transmission and reflection, across the visible and near-infrared spectral regions. They can be switched by simply exposing the coated glass to a stream of diluted hydrogen gas. Exposure to oxygen or dry air causes the window to convert back to a mirror state. | **fig. 1**

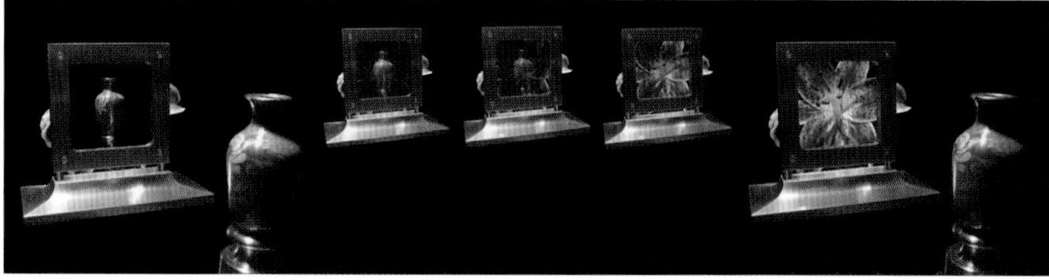

fig. 1 | Time sequence showing the conversion of a reflective electrochromic window at Lawrence Berkeley National Laboratory (LBNL)

This can also be done electrochemically, giving the user greater control of intermediate states of partial reflection. Although this sounds more complex, the design has fewer components compared to light-absorbing electrochromic windows. Because the layers are thinner, the entire stack sequentially deposited films may also be less expensive to manufacture.

Computer simulations show that in climates with wide ranges in temperature between seasons, as well as in regions that undergo rapid temperature changes, light-reflective electrochromic windows can substantially reduce energy consumption for cooling and lighting, and the reductions are greater compared to light-absorbing electrochromic windows. Tests indicate a potential 50 percent reduction relative to static low-E windows, with low visible transmittance. | **figs. 2 + 3** Commercial electrochromic windows are currently undergoing testing in a simulated environment at Lawrence Berkeley National Laboratory, where heat and light conditions are being monitored daily and throughout the seasons.[2] | **figs. 4 + 5**

1 | Thomas J. Richardson, "Chromogenic Materials," Windows and Daylighting Group, Lawrence Berkeley National Laboratory, http://windows.lbl.gov/materials/chromogenics/.

2 | "Advancement of Electrochromic Windows," Environmental Energy Technologies Division, Lawrence Berkeley National Laboratory, http://windows.lbl.gov/comm_perf/Electrochromic/electroSys-cec.htm. This work was supported by the Assistant Secretary for Energy Efficiency and Renewable Energy, Office of Building Technology, State and Community Programs, Office of Building Research and Standards of the U.S. Department of Energy under Contract no. DE-AC03-76SF00098.

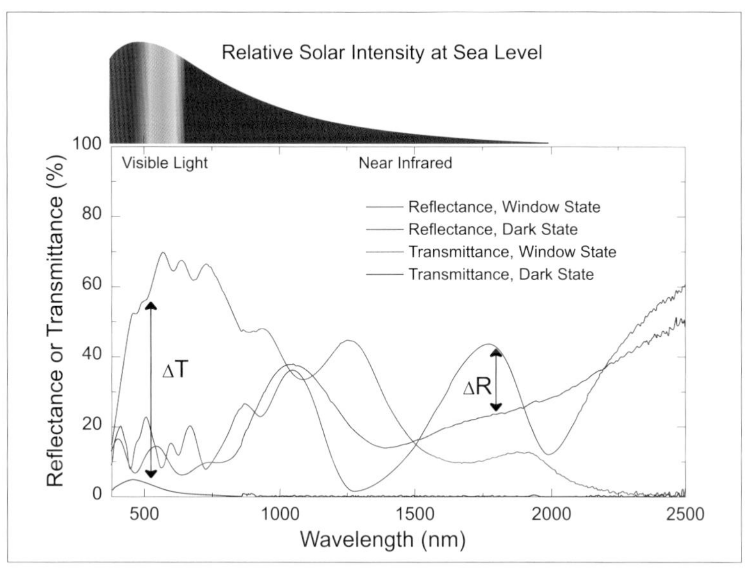

fig. 2 | Relative solar intensity at sea level of a static low-E window with low visible transmittance

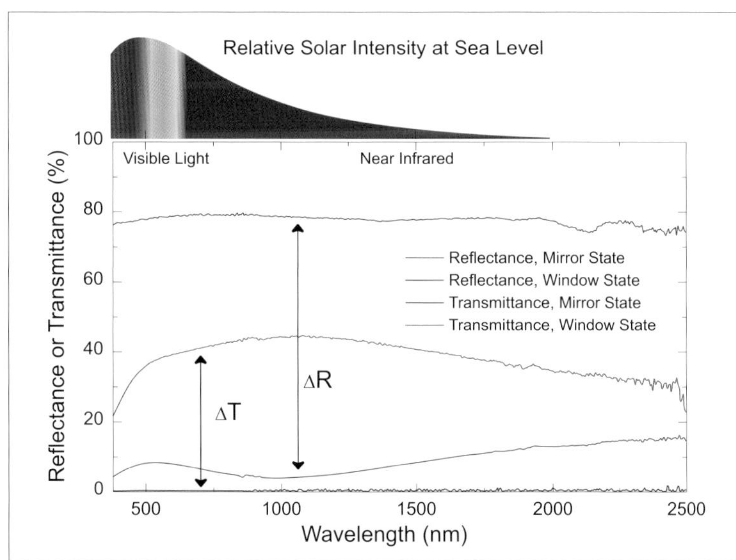

fig. 3 | Relative solar intensity at sea level of a light-reflective electrochromic window

fig. 4 | Office environment test facility at LBNL

fig. 5 | Interior of office test environment at LBNL

Double Performances

Scott Marble

Within the title *Engineered Transparency* lies one of the more important issues confronting architects and engineers today: how to utilize the expansive body of new and developing technologies for socially and culturally significant effects; how to use quantitative techniques to create qualitative results;[1] or, to cite an example specific to the topic of this book, how to "engineer" transparency. Ironically, the renewed interest in glass as a building material coincides with growing environmental concerns and the significant impact that buildings have on energy consumption. The demand to increase the environmental performance of glass while maintaining its property of transparency has led to the development of thin surfaces of films and applied coatings that can reflect, absorb, fracture, or convert the energy of light and heat.

fig. 1 | Ceiling view of Student Hub, Toni Stabile Student Center, School of Journalism, Columbia University

Arguably, this emphasis on technical performance is what drives the development of most new materials today, and while this is an obvious concern for engineers, the extent to which it influences architects' thought processes and design methodologies raises broader questions about meaning in architecture. There is a tendency to simultaneously embrace and be ambivalent toward the instantly verifiable results of advanced technology, which may unknowingly overshadow potential consequences. The degree to which materials and their effects are engineered, and equally important, the degree to which their properties and behaviors can be analyzed and predicted under virtually any condition through digital simulation, runs the risk of becoming the endgame of design. More alarming is the thought that the development of new materials and design techniques, driven by an emphasis on technical performance, become void of cultural signification. Regardless of the level of technological precision, buildings are always subject to interpretation and to the subsequent development of social and cultural meaning over time that extends well beyond their original production. It is worth considering whether the cultural intrigue of a building, such as SANAA's Glass Pavilion for the Toledo Museum of Art—already celebrated by architects, engineers, and critics alike—might be due to the extreme technical and performance-based requirements that so significantly influenced its design and construction.

With the power of new digital design and production technologies also comes the temptation to either slip passively into a new type of technical determinism or to reject the opportunities that technology affords as a form of oppressive control that diminishes individual imagination. Between these two extremes is an option to engage in the logic of technical knowledge and to critically evaluate its cultural implications, feeding this critique back into the further development of technology. The technologies that increasingly organize and structure our design and engineering methodologies, seemingly expanding our knowledge base and productive skills, simultaneously establish the logic of how we make decisions without revealing the underlying biases of that logic. The relationship between programmers, who write, and designers, who use software, serves as just one example. While this could be said about many historical moments—particularly since the first industrial revolution—it is worth noting that what makes our current condition distinct is our relationship to technical and social production methodologies.

The tendency to define new materials and their performances in purely technical terms can be expanded by acknowledging the double meaning inherent in the term *performance*, which can be understood as having both technical (quantitative) and phenomenal (qualitative) characteristics. | **figs. 1 + 2** This dual definition is demonstrated, throughout this book, by images of highly refined details, charts, and graphs that explain properties and behaviors through verified results (quantitative proof), as well as by images of light and transparency that transcend our limited understanding of glass as merely the result of technical criteria (qualitative effects). This double meaning of performance also provides the framework for renewed modes of collaboration between engineers and architects. The old model of the architect making technically uninformed and nearly impossible requests to the engineer is being replaced by reciprocal inputs and an increasingly integrated design process driven by new forms of digital communication. This stretching and overlapping of boundaries between architecture and engineering involves challenging the assumptions of our respective disciplines with respect to quantitative concerns, qualitative desires, and how the two relate.

fig. 2 | Student Hub, view of digital perforation pattern on west wall

1 | The distinction between quantitative and qualitative criteria, while admittedly arbitrary on some levels, is intended to acknowledge and probe differences between technical and social production for the purpose of expanding both. For a contemporary definition, one can say that quantitative criteria can be numerically defined and written in computer code, while qualitative criteria are open-ended and rely on social interpretation to be useful.

Conversions of Light

Graham Dodd

New materials made by new processes or new combinations of processes are increasingly used to reduce the environmental impact of buildings and change the ways in which they are occupied. These new materials rely on a variety of strategies, including systems, composites, and structures.

The systems strategy utilizes a number of components, each serving a different function. For example, consider the color red. Under a system strategy, it is created by passing sunlight through a prism, then selecting the red portion with a slotted plate and projecting red light onto a surface. | **fig. 1** The composite strategy combines materials with complimentary properties. A composite strategy for achieving the color red involves mixing red pigment into a clear resilient binder to make paint. | **fig. 2** The structured strategy is lean on materials but rich in information. A single material is arranged in numerous different forms, sometimes on a microscopic scale, to change its properties. For example, butterflies create the colors of their wing scales through the use of diffraction gratings. | **fig. 3**

Glass performs several functions within a building: transmission of light and heat, reflection of light and heat out of and into a room, changing the quality of light through transparency, translucency, reflectivity, and texture; and conversion of light to other forms of energy. Sunlight can be converted into heat, chemical energy, or electrical energy. For example: body-tinted, solar-control glass absorbs light and gets hot; electrochromic glass adjusts to convert more sunlight to heat; and solar collectors convert light to heat in water. Photocatalytic self-cleaning glass converts a tiny amount of solar energy to chemical energy as it breaks down organic chemicals, and photosynthetic glass uses solar energy to assemble chemicals into more useful ones. Currently, research is underway to produce hydrogen directly from rain and sunlight. Photovoltaic cells have been developed to harness the high concentration of energy in the visible band of light, but if photovoltaic devices were cheap enough and capable of covering a wider range of wavelengths, it would convert unwanted heat to electricity with greater efficiency. | **fig. 4**

New design objectives should revolve around sustainability. If glass is recovered from buildings, contaminants prevent its reuse in float glass. One challenge for the glassmaking industry is to close the technical cycle by using and refining glass waste, or overhauling the process altogether so that glass can be returned to the soil or the sea as a nutrient, without loss of valuable metals and possibly even powered by solar energy. Future coatings might consist of nanostructures of glass constituents, such as in the structured color of a butterfly wing. | **figs. 5–7**

fig. 1 | A systems strategy selects portions of the solar spectrum.

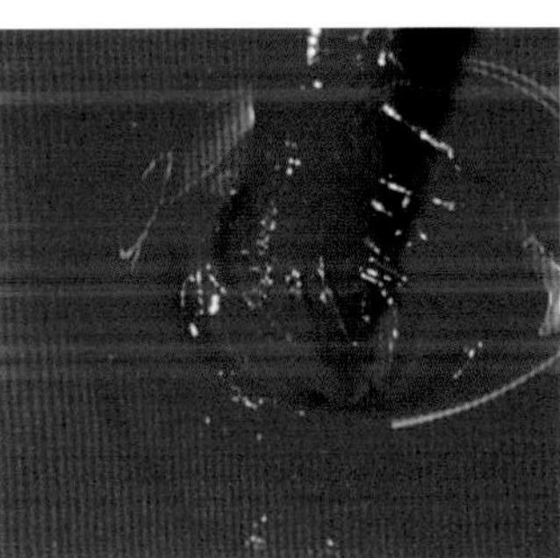

fig. 2 | Two or more materials are mixed or joined to achieve combined properties.

fig. 3 | A structured composite material akin to the keratin wing structure and diffraction grating of a butterfly wing produces unexpected color.

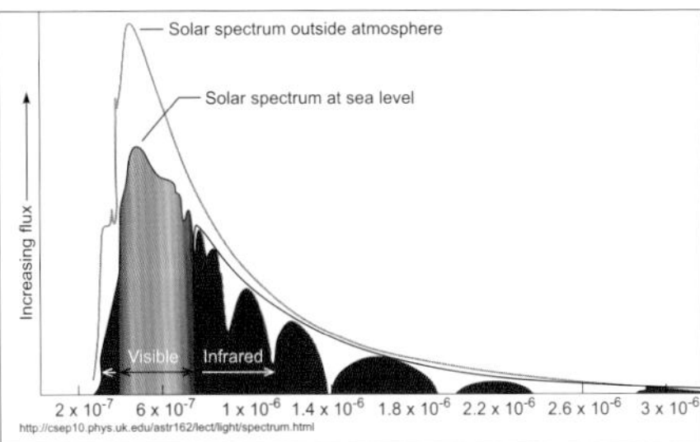

fig. 4 | Wide range of wavelengths available for use in photovoltaics

figs. 5–7 | Transparency at different scales

Solar Vision

Bernhard Weller, Susanne Rexroth, and Stefan Unnewehr

The introduction of photovoltaics has brought solar cells and photovoltaic modules into the architectural marketplace. Solar cells convert the sun's rays into electricity. A sufficient amount of useable sunlight is available in central Europe and at similar latitudes throughout the world. The more directly the solar surface is exposed to the sun, the greater the amount of energy it yields. Since the amount of electricity generated by individual solar cells is small, a large number of them are typically connected to photovoltaic modules. These modules are often embedded in the lamination between glass sheets. | fig. 1

fig. 1 | Contact image sensor (CIS) modules offer flexibility and antiglare protection

A single module is usually incapable of producing enough electricity to meet consumer demand. Therefore, a series of modules are connected to one another to form a solar generator, which is then able to support, if not cover, the entire electrical load. In central Europe, solar generators with a rated output of one kilowatt are capable of delivering an annual output of seven to eight hundred kilowatt-hours. This translates to one kilowatt-hour per square meter, assuming a system efficiency of 10 percent and optimal orientation of the generator.

Photovoltaic modules can be easily integrated into common types of facade and roof constructions. Modules can either replace an entire building envelope or be combined with typical facade elements. Crystalline silicon cells are generally spaced two to five millimeters apart to create expressive light as well as cast diamond-shaped shade patterns within interior spaces. A standard module composed of silicon cells and measuring 150 square millimeters, when spaced two to three millimeters apart, offers approximately 10 percent light transmittance. This is enough to provide natural daylight to rooms that do not have specific requirements, such as staircases and lobbies. | figs. 2–5

Thin film solar cells are more flexible in terms of geometric dimensions. The cells consist of four- to twenty-millimeter-wide strips at intervals of 0.2 to 0.3 millimeters. The barely visible cell spacing is particularly suitable for glare protection. From a distance of about two meters, the planes merge visually. Small areas of electrically active coatings are removed, based on the required level of transparency. The resulting patterns are very fine, with hole sizes of one millimeter; or they have narrow transparent stripes that result in homogeneous illumination for interiors. Since modules can be adapted to a building's textures, structures, and colors, these recent developments in thin film technology promise great potential for architectural design.

fig. 2 | Integrated CIS thin-film modules curve from the top of the roof to a water harvesting pool, OpTIC Centre, St. Asaph, North Wales, United Kingdom

fig. 3 | A colorful facade composed of back-painted glass elements

fig. 4 | The interior of double-glazed windows containing thin-layer modules of colored amorphous silicon

fig. 5 | A combination of semitransparent photovoltaic modules and screen-printed double-glazed windows

Optics, Waves, and Particles

Michelle Addington

As a transparent artifact, glass appears to eliminate much of the messiness involved in tracking the movement of light. The complex three-dimensional behavior of light is collapsed onto a picture plane, from which figural tracings can project onto another plane. This behavior neatly fits into the most common descriptive model of light, geometric optics. The model of geometric optics is convenient for architecture, as its representation follows the rules of orthographic projection. Vectors are stripped of their temporal component; volumes are reconfigured as closed surfaces; and dimensions assume a dimensionless form. Geometric similitude—in which dimensions are scaled in proportion to size—governs both orthographic representation and geometric optics. The light path is represented by lines that follow the same relational rules, regardless of length. Principles—such as the angle of incidence being equal to the angle of reflection or the angle of refraction being proportional to a ratio of material indices—hold true if the path of light is one-millimeter long or one-million miles long.

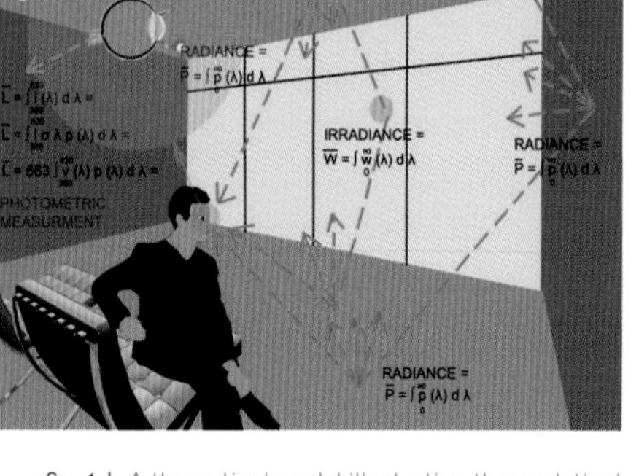

fig. 1 | A theoretical model illustrating the analytical behaviors of light as it interacts with different surfaces, by Adriana Lira

Geometric optics is so pervasive that we often overlook the fact that it only provides a descriptive model, not a behavioral one. The two behavioral models for light—particle physics and classical wave theory—offer no aspects in which geometry plays a role. Many of the advanced materials entering the discipline of architecture have features that demand the application of behavioral models. | **fig. 1** From diffraction-grating films to light-emitting capacitors, physical materials process light rather than simply redirect it. The interaction of light with conventional materials such as glass is also governed by behavioral models. By resetting the frame of reference to behavior rather than form, unprecedented opportunities for activating a static material emerge. The three doctoral projects presented here investigate the interactions of light and materials.

Reflectivity

A particular wavelength of blue light, when delivered diffusely to the retina, regulates the body's circadian rhythm. Although abundant in daylight, this wavelength is almost nonexistent in most interiors. A variety of devices have been developed for framing the face with blue light-emitting diodes (LEDs), but Adriana Lira developed a method for extracting the critical wavelength from surfaces and glazings and then imperceptibly concentrating it at eye level through microscale modifications of a material's spectral and directional reflectivity.

Emissivity

Urban heat islands are presumed to result from built geometries. The pro forma geometry for preventing heat islands is to space buildings at a distance of two times their height. This generous spacing opens up the sky view, enabling buildings to radiate heat to the upper atmosphere instead of toward adjacent buildings. What matters, however, is not the view from the building surfaces but the features of the surface materials. By manipulating emissivity in relation to reflectivity, Naree Phinyawatan experimented with undetectable changes in surface coatings or glazings on upper floors, producing a virtual sky view in dense urban areas that appears equivalent to sky views produced from optimally spaced buildings. | **fig. 2**

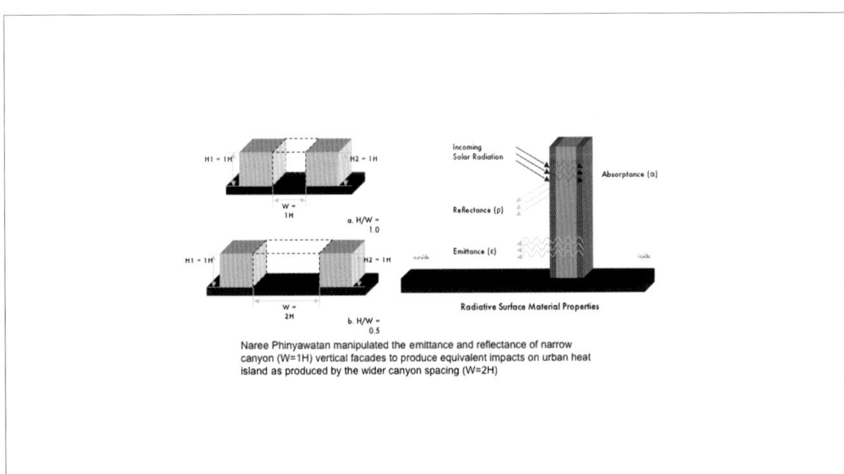

fig. 2 | The relationship between material properties and urban geometries: narrow canyon vertical facades produce heat islands equivalent to those produced by wide canyon spacing, by Naree Phinyawatan

Frequency

The desire for daylighting has led to larger and larger surface areas of exposed glazing. This, in turn, has increased our dependence on both electric lighting (for managing contrast) and environmental systems (for managing envelope loads). Nasser Abulhasan worked with a visual psychologist to develop a method for dramatically reducing the surface area of glazing by establishing sequential contrast zones within the field of view, thereby improving daylighting. By manipulating the frequency with which these zones appear on the retina of an ambulatory occupant, Nasser was able to demonstrate that much lower light levels in the interior could be perceived as having improved daylighting. | **figs. 3 + 4**

fig. 3 | Test facility to demonstrate the relationship between glazing area, contrast ratio, and perception of brightness, by Nasser Abulhasan

fig. 4 | In situ experiments in which Abulhasan varied the frequency and alignment of contrast zones within the field of view

Technical Innovations: Structure and Glass

Engineered Glass

Werner Sobek

Of all the building materials used today, textiles and glass hold the greatest potential. Textiles are fascinating because of their breathability, their capacity to integrate different types of phase-change materials (PCMs), and their high tensile strength, which allows them to span large distances. Glass, on the other hand, provides high compression strength and perfect transparency, as well as integration of switchable light transmissivity for altering transparency. Today's coating technologies—and the possibility of reinforcing glass with different stiffening materials—offer a nearly endless range of new techniques. While there is room for further research and development in regard to glass, its structural properties only became a matter of serious research in the late 1980s. Since then, the load-bearing behavior of glass, its failure characteristics, and the possibility of influencing its transmissivity for radiation have been widely researched; however, a series of interesting questions remain unresolved.

Structural Behavior

The mechanical properties of glass as a structural material have been widely researched and discussed in recent years. Simply put, glass has perfect elastic behavior: it shows no ability to plastify or yield in local regions of overstressing. The problems resulting from this fact have also been widely researched, but not solved. While compression strength is unaffected by microscratches on the surface, tensile strength is dramatically affected by the unavoidable existence of scratches. Tempering and heat and chemical strengthening help reduce this problem but only to a very limited extent; the allowable tensile stress levels are shifted to 30 to 50 newtons per square millimetre, a number that remains disappointingly low. Also, the lack of any plastic properties limits the range of thinkable designs and necessitates the introduction of failure scenarios, even for simple structures. Unless a composite or treatment is found that allows the material to plastify in regions of local overstressing, limited tensile strength and spontaneous breaking are the two characteristics that will continue to govern the design of load-bearing glass elements.

One method of ensuring postbreakage, load-bearing capacity is to laminate glass panes with polyvinyl butyral (PVB), a method widely used over the last four decades. Broken pieces will stick to the unbroken pane via the PVB film. If both panes break, the viscous behavior of PVB does not provide sufficient load-bearing capacity, especially under high temperatures and over longer periods of time.

A remarkable improvement of the postbreakage behavior of laminated glass can be achieved by introducing a fibrous or thin-sheet reinforcement between the two panes. This idea goes back to research performed in 1996 that quickly revealed how interlayers can dramatically improve postbreakage behavior. The interlayers tested were stainless steel fibers and strands of glass and carbon in parallel arrangements. Fine fabrics made of the same materials were also considered. In a second step, perforated metal sheets were introduced. In all cases, the reinforcement was embedded between two layers of PVB embedded between two glass panes.

The load-bearing capacity of a fully broken PVB-laminated glass pane depends on two factors: the compression strength of the "glass crumbs" and their ability to transfer compression forces via contact pressure, respectively; and the PVB's ability to take-up tension forces. This capability is relatively small, and it is further weakened by high temperatures, humidity, and creeping. If a fiber or thin-metal sheet reinforcement can absorb the tension forces, the PVB only has to withstand shear transfer. Fiber or metal-sheet reinforcement is much stiffer than PVB; it thus acts in the same way as steel reinforcement in cracked concrete, leading to excellent postbreakage behavior. Of course, additional local reinforcements can be used to strengthen broken glass laminates around point fixings or other areas where concentrated forces are introduced into the pane. [1 2 3 4]

Manipulation of Transmissivity

There are situations where nonpermanent modification of glass's high transparency can be useful. The search for temporary privacy or the reduction of thermal-energy flow through a glazed facade are two examples.

The possibility of modifying glass's transmissivity for light—or, in more general terms, for radiation—allows for a wide range of new applications. Adaptive facades or building skins with an optimized light-and-energy flow suddenly become possible. In our research on adaptive building skins made out of textiles, we widened our scope to include the field of adaptive glass. In contrast to other systems currently being developed—such as thermochromic, gasochromic, or electrochromic systems—ours uses a technology that allows for more than just a switch from transparent to translucent or opaque. Our system makes the transmissivity of glass infinitely variable. This can be achieved by using nematic liquid crystals embedded between two glass panes. [5 6]

Systems that exploit the smart properties of nematic liquid crystals allow for active, high-speed control of radiation and light transmission. These systems are derived from well-known liquid-crystal cells used in displays. Previously, they were not deemed suitable for similar applications on the exteriors of buildings because of the sensitivity of some of the system's components to external factors, such as temperature stresses and ultraviolet radiation, as well as their prohibitively high cost of production. Recent developments now make it possible to apply liquid-crystal technology to window systems without the aforementioned problems of cost and durability.

The advantages associated with liquid-crystal windows over other elements based on thermochromic, electrochromic, or gasochromic principles are considerable. The essential advantages include fast switching; low energy consumption; infinitely variable radiation transmission within given limits; small color error; and low installation and maintenance costs. Various prototypes have been developed, produced, and tested under long-term weather exposure, as well as under accelerated conditions. The results demonstrate that these new systems are very stable and maintain their switching properties over a long period of time. This research is currently underway in cooperation with partners from the glass industry.

Joining Glass

Joining glass elements so that loads can be transferred from one element to the other is typically done through point fixings, which create stress concentrations in the glass and reduce its structural efficiency. Clamping builds up geometrically, thus destroying the smooth surface. Welding and soldering—a technology widely applied in the chemical industry—is not applicable for glass used in the architecture and construction industry. Therefore, the only way to achieve a structurally efficient and smooth load-transfer from one glass element to another is through the application of glue.

Glueing glass is widely used in industrial applications, especially in the automotive industry. Windshields on buses and other vehicles are used as a stiffening element by activating the glued joint, located between the glass, and by using the metallic body as a load-transferring element. With few exceptions, structural gluing is not allowed by the building industries of most countries. The most important reasons for this regulation include the lack of fully tested long-term weather resistance and the loss of strength in glued joints at around 158 to 248 degrees Fahrenheit; however, these obstacles only apply to glued joints of small thicknesses. Those with thicknesses ranging from 0.39 to 0.47 inches—the width needed for typical tolerance effects—are considered impossible with existing gluing technologies.

In the context of our research on metal-free glass shells, it was necessary to find a solution to this problem. After intensive discussion with leading producers of glue systems, modified compositions were produced and then tested at different temperature and humidity levels under short-term and creep loading. After evaluation, the glues were modified and tested again. The results obtained were encouraging enough to warrant continued development. The current status of our research has already allowed for the creation of a spherical glass shell with a diameter of 28 feet with laminated glass having a total thickness of 0.11 inches. Joints between the curved glass panes forming the shell have a width of 0.39 to 0.79 inches. The glass shell has sustained all temperature, wind, and snow loads since April 2004 on a site located near the Institute for Lightweight Structures and Conceptual Design at the University of Stuttgart in Germany.

Glass as a Cladding Element for Very Flexible Cable Substructures

Cables and cable-net structures were one of the earliest directions of research in the pursuit of transparency and lightness. They were widely researched by Frei Otto and others.[7] The technologies to design, produce, and install such structures are highly developed.

Cable nets form very effective structural systems, especially for midsized and largespan bridges. The efficiency of the typical double-curved and square-meshed nets due to only having tensioned members. This means that no material is necessary to prevent buckling, however, the cladding necessary to enclose the interior space of a building can be difficult if transparency is desired. The roof structures built for the Olympics held in Munich, Germany, in 1972 were the first to demonstrate transparent cladding, which at the time was a requirement for color-television broadcasting. Due to the double curvature of the roof and unresolved safety issues associated with the use of glass in this context, it was clad with polymethyl methacrylate (PMMA), which is known to have a relatively high coefficient of temperature elongation in addition to being hydrophilic. Both properties necessitate the use of large neoprene joints between the panes, which has a considerably adverse influence on architectural appearance.

When our office was asked to build a 43,000-square-foot cable net in Bad Neustadt, Germany, we decided to use glass as a cladding material. The cable net has, in total, 24,000 meshes with 15.75 inches between nodal points. Since the geometry more or less differs for each mesh, it was necessary to use either 24,000 different pieces of glass or to develop a new method of fixing glass to the net. For the sake of simplicity, the latter was chosen. After a research and development process, a method of installing glass shingles was created using square-sized glass panes measuring 20 by 20 inches clasped together using a 0.5-inch-diameter stainless-steel wire. The wire frame was fixed to two of the mesh's opposite nodal points. The patented system allows for quick and easy installation. The whole system was very cost-competitive compared to other roofing techniques. The distance between overlapping shingles can be up to 0.79 inches from surface to surface; therefore, sufficient overlapping of the shingles had to be ensured. Moreover, the shingles had to be arranged in such a way that rainwater flowing down the roof would not leak inside. This was achieved by arranging the cable net along the roof's surface to guarantee a perfect flow of water. The computer program needed to rotate a formerly plain and square-meshed cable net onto a double-curved shape. Though based on very simple principles, the process was actually quite complicated.

The glass-shingle solution was undoubtedly successful, but we decided to use another technique for the double-curved, cable-net-supported glass walls of the Audi exhibition in Tokyo, Japan. Here, the indoor application did not require waterproofing, but the glass surface needed to be as smooth as possible. To achieve this, 13,500 triangular glass pieces grouped in 350 different geometries were installed so that the corners of each glass piece slipped into a rubber sleeve within the net's nodal points, avoiding any bolting. The speed of erection was so fast that all 13,500 pieces were installed within ninety-six hours.

Parallel Cable Systems

Cable nets lose an important part of their stiffness if they are planar rather than double-curved. A glazed-plane cable net was first designed by Jörg Schlaich for the atrium walls of the Kempinski Hotel in Munich, Germany. Cables run horizontally and vertically in the net. Typically, forces in horizontal cables are difficult to anchor—they require abutment walls or equivalent solutions—and the design of a glazed corner is more or less impossible. We therefore developed a system using only vertical cables.[8] The first building to utilize this solution was the Central Foyer of Bremen University in Germany. The glazed hall measures 72 by 143 feet in plan. The building and its glass wall are 49 feet high. The cables, forming the load-bearing structure, span from the roof to the ground and are anchored by springs to guarantee a more or less constant state of prestress, independent of temperature variations and foundation settlement. The cables have a spacing of 71 inches. The glass panes are fixed onto the cables using a clamping system to avoid drilling in the glass.

The horizontal deformation of the cable net in Bremen is 14 inches under severe wind loads. To avoid secondary stresses within the glazing, the clamping system for the glass panes has to allow each pane to rotate within certain limits. This is ensured by rubber pads mounted between the glass and the fixture. Since deflections of the wall might cause geometrical conflicts, the corners are uncoupled, self-standing structures. All relative movements occur in the joint between the corners and the flexible-cable facade.

Another system was developed for the corners of the glazed entrance hall of the Bayer World Headquarters in Leverkusen, Germany. A steel column was placed inside the corner area. The column carries thin steel profiles, which cantilever horizontally to a length of 10 feet on each side. The two vertical cables to the left and right of the column are horizontally stiffened. The relative softness of the profiles—which act as leaf springs—allows for a smooth transition of deformations from the central area of the facade to the corners. In the central area, deformations can amount to 14 inches; in the corner area, they are at zero.

This easy and elegant solution was also implemented in the cable facade of the Chicago O'Hare International Airport extension, which is currently under construction. Insulated glazing units (IGUs) are used for the facade. The IGUs, which are very sensitive to twisting and warping, had to be designed for bomb-blast loading. Calculations and deformation and blasting tests demonstrated that the facade works perfectly well, even under critical load conditions.

At the moment, the largest, parallel cable system under construction is for the Lufthansa World Headquarters in Frankfurt, Germany. Here a total of ten cable walls are to be built, each 62 feet wide and 66 feet high.

Structures Made Out of Glass

Of course, one goal for the structural engineering of glass could be to create structures of perfect transparency—structures made totally out of glass. The bus shelter we designed in 1995 for one of the leading firms in urban furniture systems was an innovative glass building at the time. The glass panes formed part of the structural system and were joined with minimized point fixings. As expected, the point fixings required drilling and caused stress concentrations around the edges of the drilled holes. Our research showed that these stress concentrations—calculated for a perfectly homogeneous and isotropic material—are overlaied by additional stresses caused by small grooves and microcracks from drilling. Therefore, other types of connections had to be found to allow for the use of load-bearing glass at a larger scale.

The high compression strength and rather limited tension strength of glass led to the idea of using glass only for those structural elements that undergo compression. Building an arch out of glass panes would mean that contact pressure is transferred in the joints only. Buckling stability and stiffness—required for non-symmetric loading—could be ensured by a lightly underslung and diagonalized tension rod. Glass Arch I was designed and built according to these principles with a clear span of 33 feet. The thickness of the laminated glass is 0.26 inches. The outstanding structural lightness, high load-bearing capacity, and high stiffness of the structure encouraged us to design and build Glass Arch II with a clear span of 66 feet. Glass thickness here was 0.27 inches and the width of the arch was 13 feet. Total weight of the glass panes was approximately 5 tons.[9] Glass Arch II was shown at Glasstec, the international fair for glass technology in Düsseldorf, Germany. After the fair, the structure underwent controlled destruction in order to study the breaking behavior of highly loaded, lamintated safety glass (LSG) structures. The experiment demonstrated outstanding postbreakage qualities.

Given the fact that a shell loaded with deadweight stays under a biaxial state of compression above the failure joint, and taking into account the excellent load-bearing behavior of the two glass arches, we decided to research the constructability of a spherical glass shell of excessive slenderness. Glass Shell I, with a diameter of 8 feet, was built as a small-scale prototype to test the joining technique and to ensure that spherical elements could be produced within a limited range of tolerances. The glue used for Shell I was a modified polyurethane glue. The glass thickness was 0.11 inches and the widths of the joints were between 0.24 and 0.39 inches. Following the success of Glass Shell I, the second shell was built in April of 2004 near the Institute for Lightweight Structures and Conceptual Design. With a clear span of 28 feet, a thickness of 0.39 inches, and a slenderness factor of 1/850. Glass Shell II is a long-term experiment for studying the behavior of a glued shell under natural weathering conditions. [10]

While both Glass Shell I and II use LSG; a combination of PMMA and chemically strengthened glass will be used for a 66-foot-diameter shell currently being researched that will be built as an enclosure for a fully self-contained house called R129. In this house, PMMA is intended for use as a load-bearing matrix containing PCMs to regulate light transmission. Our research is specifically focused on the possibility of using microsphere-enclosed PCMs with thermotropic qualities. The thin upper-protection layer of the shell (made out of chemically strengthened glass) is for scratch resistance, weathering resistance, and antistatic qualities.

Design for Postbreakage Stability

All glass qualities used in the building industry show spontaneous breakage behavior. Using glass as a load-bearing element in a primary structure therefore requires a different design approach. Typical design methods are based on the fundamental assumption that single load-bearing elements will not fail as long as their loading level does not exceed the maximum stress level. Glass can show spontaneous breakage below the maximum stress level because of vandalism or local damage. The establishment of a "guaranteed safe-life" quality for a glass element is therefore impossible. Any design scenario for glass structures—or for structures using glass as a load-bearing element—has to take into account either the failure of a single structural glass element or a group of them. The design method must show that even a partially damaged structure will remain safe. Such a technique is called fail-safe design.

Of course, determining which element failed and how many of those elements were damaged can be difficult. Vandalism and terrorism complicate such assumptions even more. In general, different scenarios have to be assumed.

While single glass panes lose their load-bearing capacity immediately after breaking, laminated glass can continue to carry loads. The remaining force-transfer capability depends on whether one or all of the LSG panes are broken. In the case of total breakage of an LSG unit, residual load-bearing capacity is governed by the PVB film that bonds the broken pieces together and through its behavior under changes in temperature, time, and humidity. It is widely known that the remaining load-bearing capacity of a fully broken LSG unit is rather limited. In contrast, reinforced LSG shows excellent postbreakage behavior with a remarkably high, residual load-bearing capacity with relatively small deformations. A design method for a force-transfer with fully broken LSG is currently under development at the Institute for Lightweight Structures and Conceptual Design. Once this method is fully developed, the design of partially broken, load-bearing glass structures will be possible.

1 | Werner Sobek, Frank Maier and Matthias Kutterer, "Versuche an Verbundsicherheitsgläsern zur Beurteilung der Resttragfähigkeit und des Verbundverhaltens," Institut für Leichte Flächentragwerke, University of Stuttgart, *Forschungsbericht* 1|98, November 1998.

2 | Werner Sobek, Frank Maier and Matthias Kutterer, "Bewehrtes Verbundsicherheitsglas," Institut für Leichte Flächentragwerke, University of Stuttgart, *Forschungsbericht* 1|99, June 1999.

3 | Werner Sobek, Frank Maier and Matthias Kutterer, "Tragverhalten von bewehrtem Verbundsicherheitsglas," Institut für Leichte Flächentragwerke, University of Stuttgart, *Forschungsbericht* 2|99, October 1999.

4 | "Untersuchung der Resttragfähigkeit von Verbundglaselementen mit Bewehrungsschichten," Otto-Graf-Institute (OGI/FMPA), University of Stuttgart, *Forschungsbericht* Nr. 25-27686, May 1999.

5 | Walter Haase, "Adaptive Strahlungstransmission von Verglasungen mit Flüssigkristallen" (Ph.D. diss., University of Stuttgart, 2004).

6 | Werner Sobek and Walter Haase, "Adaptive Systeme und Materialien," *Deutsches Architektenblatt* (January 2005): 14–17.

7 | Frei Otto, ed., *Netze in Natur und Technik* (Stuttgart: IL Mitteilungen 8, 1985).

8 | Werner Sobek and Norbert Rehle, "Beispiele für verglaste Vertikalseilfassaden," *Stahlbau* (April 2004): 224–29.

9 | Werner Sobek and Matthias Kutterer, "Experimenteller Glasbogen auf der glasstec 98," *Glas: Architektur und Technik* (March 1999): 34–38.

10 | Werner Sobek and Lucio Blandini, "Structural Gluing: A Prototype Glass Shell," in *Translucent Materials. Glass – Plastic – Metals*, ed. Frank Kaltenbach (Munich: Institut für internationale Architektur-Dokumentation, 2004): 30–31.

fig. 1 | R128 House, east elevation at dusk, Stuttgart, Germany: The basic idea of the house is to live in a soap bubble, surrounded by trees, fresh air, and with rain dripping down the walls. The building is completely recyclable and runs on solar energy. There are no chimneys or exhausts.

fig. 2 | House H16, Tieringen, Germany: This residential house for a family of four was envisioned as a completely transparent glass box.

fig. 3 | SWM office building, Heilbronn, Germany: At the headquarters of the German steel industry, transparency is achieved through a facade composed of woven stainless steel struts.

fig. 4 | ICE train station at the Cologne-Bonn Airport, Germany: Through extremely refined structural analyses, an enormous roof is supported by a minimal amount of metal.

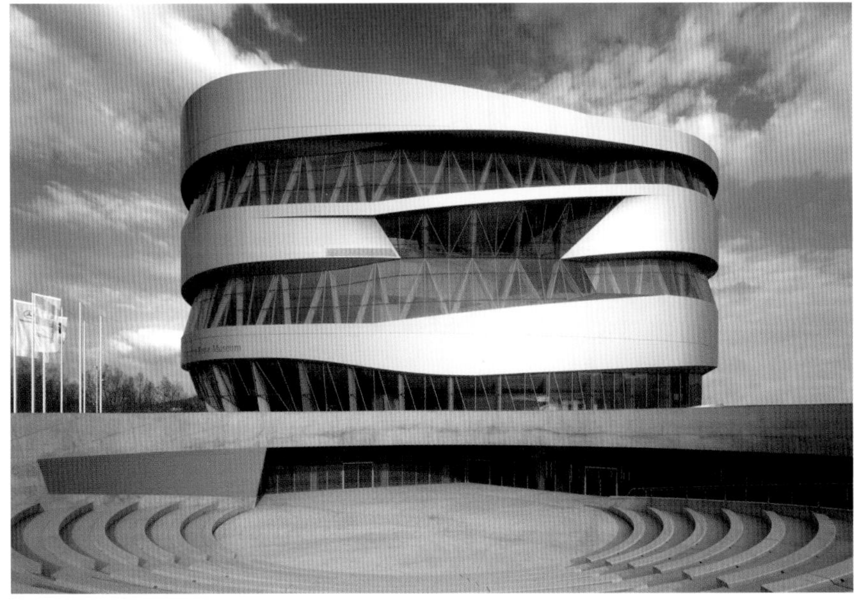

fig. 5 | Mercedes-Benz Museum, Stuttgart, Germany: The double-curved surface of the facade designed by Ben van Berkel is composed of 1,500 pieces of insulated glass, each unique.

fig. 6 | Audi exhibition stand, Tokyo Motor Show: This project was a collaboration with architect Christoph Ingenhoven. The geometry of the pavilion was realized using 13,500 pieces of triangular glass.

fig. 7 | Cité du Design, St. Etienne, France: Designed by Finn Geipel, the skin is a combination facade and roof composed of 14,000 triangular elements grouped according to function. Some provide heat insulation, others transmit light or produce energy.

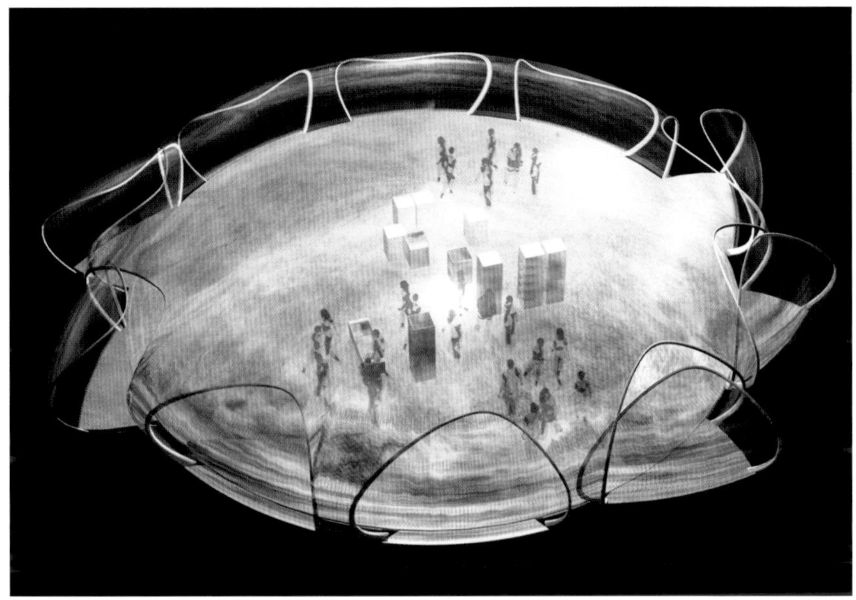

fig. 8 | R129 House (unbuilt): What would it mean to live in a zero-emission building? This monospace environment is planned to be totally recyclable and independent from the public utility grid.

fig. 9 | Glued glass cupola, Stuttgart, Germany: Almost like building with paper, this laminated glass cupola has a clear span of 8.5 meters and a total thickness of 10 millimetres (1/10 the thickness of an eggshell).

fig. 10 | Station Z, roof structure over the remains of the concentration camp in Sachsenhausen, Germany. With architect H.G. Merz, the decision was made to produce an architecture so modest that it virtually disappears. The building is stabilized by a vacuum, resulting in a long-span steel structure covering approximately 2,000 square meters of column-free space. Fabric is vacuum-sealed around a spatial truss using a tiny pump and a few square meters of photovoltaics. Vacuumatics are potential alternatives to pressurized air-inflated structures because they allow for reduced heat transfer while producing a homogenous surface that is free of details and can easily decompose or be recycled.

Making Visions Reality

Jens Schneider

The following is a short introduction to the application of annealed, tempered, and laminated glass from the point of view of structural engineering. Three examples of recently realized projects demonstrate innovative approaches and the potential for glass to be used as a real structural element in modern architecture.

fig. 1 | Fracture mechanics for describing the effects of surface scratches and flaws

Annealed Glass

Glass is an inorganic product of fusion that has been cooled to a rigid condition without crystallization. Glass is also a linear elastic material: the Young's modulus of the most common soda-lime silica is approximately E= 70.000 megapascals with a Poisson's ratio of m=0.22. The strength of annealed flat glass (the dominant architectural glass) is not constant but depends on the surface condition and the duration of the applied load. The fracture mechanics developed by Alan Arnold Griffith in the 1920s and George R. Irwin in the 1950s can be used to describe the effect of surface scratches or flaws in strength by using a stress-concentration factor that depends on crack depth and geometry. | fig. 1 The critical-stress intensity factor K_{Ic} at breakage is only about 0.76 MPaxm$^{3/2}$ for glass. This factor demonstrates the brittleness of glass. Moreover, glass strength is also affected by load duration from air vapors that seep into cracks, increasing the flaw depth. | fig. 2 Drawn on a logarithmic scale for critical failure stress, this dependence is almost linear. A commonly accepted value in standards for glass bending strength is 45 MPa (6.525 psi) for annealed glass. This corresponds to a load duration of 22 seconds and a flaw depth of 0.1 mm (0.004 inches). Compression strength is much higher but can never be reached in practice, due to local tensile stresses from load introduction or lateral tension stress.

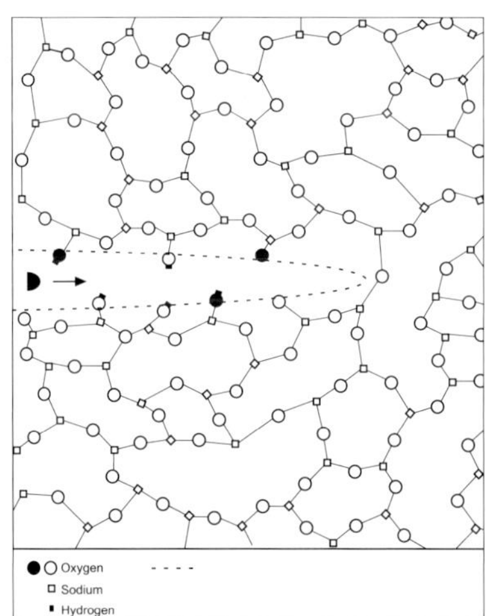

fig. 2 | Air vapors that seep into cracks affect glass strength

Heat-Strengthened and Tempered Glass

Strength can be increased by a factor of 1.5 for heat-strengthened glass and 3 for tempered glass. The thermal process—heating the glass to 620°C (1148 °F) and rapid-cooling (quenching) the surface—creates a favorable residual stress field, with compression stresses on and near the surface and tensile stresses in the core. Because the core does not contain flaws, it is unaffected by tensile stress. Surface flaws remain "closed" by compression stress and can only grow if tensile stress from external loads, such as bending, exceeds compression stress. | fig. 3 In practice, applied stress always remains below compression stress, and no crack growth or dependence on load duration will occur.

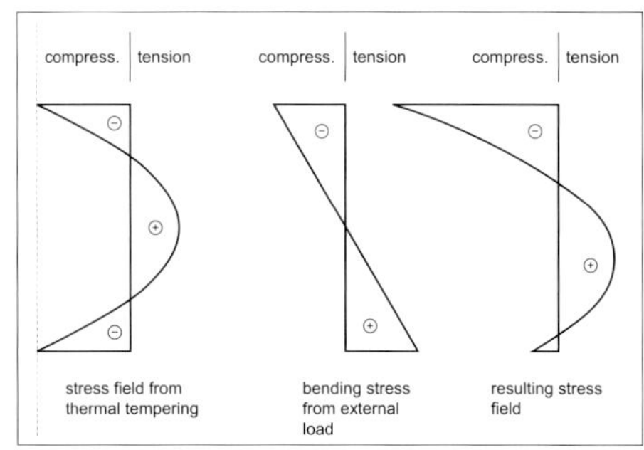

fig. 3 | Stress fields caused by various compression-tension scenarios

figs. 4 + 5 | Fragmentation patterns within laminated glass layers

Laminated Glass

Two or more annealed, heat strengthened, or tempered flat-glass panes of equal or unequal thickness can be bonded together with a transparent plastic interlayer, commonly PVB (Polyvinyl butyral). Here the lamination process is achieved through autoclaving at about 140°C (284°F) with a pressure of about 14 bar (1.4 MPa or 203 psi). Heat and pressure ensure that no air inclusions form between the glass and the interlayer. Lamination of a transparent plastic film between two or more flat-glass panes enables significant improvements in postbreakage behavior. After breakage, the fragments adhere to the film so that a certain residual structural capacity is obtained as the glass arches or locks in place. This capacity depends on the level of fragmentation within the glass and it increases with larger fragment sizes. | **figs. 4 + 5** Therefore, laminated glass elements retain a particularly high structural capacity when made from annealed or heat-strengthened glass that is capable of breaking into large fragments.

Insulating Glass Units

An insulated glazing unit (IGU) is a multiglass combination consisting of two or more panes enclosing a hermetically sealed air space. The most important function of an IGU is to reduce thermal loss. Panes are connected by a spacer, using sealants to reduce water-vapor penetration. The hermetically sealed space is filled with dehydrated air or gas. In combination with special coatings, modern IGUs achieve overall heat-transfer coefficients (U-values) of 1.1 W/m^{2}K for double-glazed units and 0.7 W/m^{2}K for triple-glazed units. All types of annealed, heat strengthened, tempered monolithic, or laminated glasses can be used as part of an IGU.

Lehrter Bahnhof, Berlin, Germany

Experimental testing and detailed finite-element analysis in combination with different fail-safe scenarios were required to ensure the safe use of these structural glass beams. The central hall of the new station Lehrter Bahnohf in Berlin has two entrances, from the north and south side respectively. The hall is circumscribed by two exceptional glass facades. The structure of these facades consists of only steel cables and glass. Similar to the roof of the main hall, the facades have many special details and were a challenge to design. The special glass connectors are described here in detail.

The original idea of architects van Gerkan Marg und Partner and engineer Schlaich Bergermann und Partner was to design a new type of cable-structure facade using glass connectors between two layers of prestressed steel cables. The glass connectors create an innovative pattern when seen from the inside, as the light refracts within them. The connectors demonstrate the use of structural glass in a new dimension, since they can carry up to 70 kips. Their load-bearing capacity was proven based on experiments and finite-element calculations. Principally, the glass connectors take the differential shear forces caused by wind loading between the front layer of cable and glass and the back layer. As this differential force increases toward the top and bottom of the facade, the center connectors are smaller (200 millimetres in height) than the edge connectors (400 millimetres in height). A special fail-safe concept was developed to ensure that the structure would not collapse, even if one or several glass connectors were to collapse completely. | **figs. 6–9**

fig. 6 | Experimental set-up for testing the strength of a maximum height connector

fig. 7 | Failure at approximately 300kN

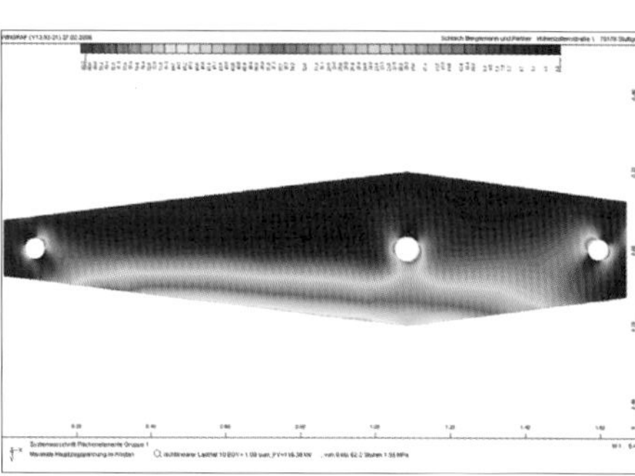

fig. 8 | Finite element analysis showing maximum principle tension and stress distribution

fig. 9 | Lehrter Bahnhof facade, Berlin, Germany

Leonardo Glass Cube, Bad Driburg, Germany

This project shows the potential of large IGUs (6.5 x 20 feet) in combination with an invisible connection to a prestressed steel bar in vertical glass joints. Anchoring of the steel bars was done using disc-spring packages, taking into consideration any creeping of the adjacent concrete plate.

Architects 3deluxe created this distinctive corporate architecture for the brand Leonardo, a German manufacturer of glass accessories. The integrative design concept combines architecture, interior design, and landscape design into a complex aesthetic entity. One of the design features is the multilayerd composition of the building. The silhouettelike genetics overlay with the graphic design of the glass facade and the elements on the inside. The connection between the soft organic structures and a clear linear-glass cover convey the company's core brand values: inspiration, emotion, and quality. This project shows the potential for using large IGUs (measuring 6 x 36 feet) in combination with an invisible connection to a prestressed steel bar within vertical glass joints. Anchoring of the steel bars was achieved using disc-spring packages, taking into consideration creeping of the adjacent concrete plate. This technology was used for the first time and allowed for expansive glazing without the need for disturbing posts or columns. | **figs. 10 + 11**

fig. 10 | Facade composed of 16 IGUs measuring 6 x 36 feet per side

fig. 11 | Night view

Glaspool Cyberhelvetia at EXPO.02, Biel, Siwtzerland

This small project shows the potential of glass in a virtual context. The idea was to create a pool made of glass for one of the Arteplages of Expo.02. Cyberhelvetia was opening up rooms for encounters in two worlds. The glass pool replaces the real swimming pool. Different internet-based games projected onto its surface allowed visitors to play with or contact others. The pool was filled with "virtual water" that could be enriched with fantasy avatars created by the visitors. The avatars could be produced before visiting and were projected onto its surface and manipulated. The glass surface changed over time, also taking into account weather conditions outside. The atmospheric pictures on the glass surface and its changes let visitors assume that the glass pool was a living organism, and many asked if real water was in the pool. Viewed form different angles, the glass could appear clear, semitransparent, or opaque. Numerous cushions made of transparent gauze inside the pool helped create the illusion that it was filled with water. Artificially projected "waves" on the surface changed according to external weather conditions.

The structural innovation in this project was the use of laminated tempered glass as a shear element. The glass pool structure consists of twenty-four horizontal and sixteen vertical panes. A structural shear panel was created using a grid of prestressed steel cables within the glass joints; these cables were then anchored at the edge panes. An epoxy mortar was used between the glass and steel to prevent local glass failure as the result of direct contact with the steel.

| figs. 12–14

figs. 12 + 13 | Glaspool Cyberhelvetia, Biel, Switzerland

fig. 14 | Inserting the epoxy mortar

Maximum Glass

Richard L. Tomasetti

The structural capabilities of glass have evolved from minimizing stress through the use of rigid and heavy support structures to minimizing support and maximizing transparency. Throughout the ages, the relationship between glass and structure has always affected a building's architecture and engineering. Romanesque-period design was heavy, with small windows that resulted in dark oppressive spaces. Advances in window and structural know-how permitted the development of Gothic designs with lighter columns and larger windows that reached upward, enhancing the building's natural light.

Nevertheless, buildings from both periods had extremely rigid structures that imparted negligible deflections to the glass openings, and the glass transferred only a small amount of wind load to the structure. In 1851 Joseph Paxton's famous Crystal Palace in London made a major contribution to architecture and engineering by introducing a monumental building with an essentially all glass facade. | **fig. 1** We can see a distinction between the primary structure and a secondary glass support system, which permitted both curvature and transparency.

fig. 1 | Joseph Paxton's Crystal Palace, 1851

I would like to demonstrate the evolution of maximizing transparency by citing several projects that our office had the pleasure of being involved with that use double curvature and lightweight support framing to maximize transparency. They represent a more integrated approach for combining the primary structure with the support framing. In this approach, however, the structural role of glass is still minimal, as it floats in its supporting frame. | **figs. 2 + 3**

fig. 2 | Entry atrium, Lucent Technologies, Kevin Roche John Dinkeloo and Associates, Lisle, Ill.

With advances in glass technology, we are now using more of the structural properties of glass to maximize transparency. Discrete corner supports can eliminate the frame and more directly transfer forces to the primary structure. This results in much greater transparency. High-strength prestressed tension-support systems are also becoming popular when transparency is desired. As in the previous example, these discrete supports are also very flexible. and provide the added advantage of decreasing forces from dynamic blast loads. More rigid tension-support structures have also become prevalent, and maximum transparency has been achieved through the use of glass mullion systems. In this case, the support system is also composed of glass. | **figs. 4–10**

The engineering of transparency has been around for a while on iconic projects and special structures. What I find exciting is its ever-increasing use on more commercial and residential projects. Current advances in glass technology promise to increase the ways that glass contributes to the built environment.

fig. 3 | Interior, University of Chicago Graduate School of Business, Rafael Viñoly Architects, Chicago, Ill.

fig. 4 | Detail of glass connection, West Midtown Ferry Terminal, William Nicholas Bodouva + Associates, New York, N.Y.

fig. 5 | Detail of glass connection at curve, West Midtown Ferry Terminal, William Nicholas Bodouva + Associates, New York, N.Y.

fig. 6 | Exterior, West Midtown Ferry Terminal, William Nicholas Bodouva + Associates, New York, N.Y.

fig. 7 | Net wall, UBS Tower, Lohan Caprile Goettsch Architects, Chicago, Ill.

fig. 8 | Connection detail, UBS Tower, Lohan Caprile Goettsch Architects, Chicago, Ill.

fig. 9 | Exterior construction view, Winter Garden, Pelli Clarke Pelli Architects, New York, N.Y.

fig. 10 | Detail, Winter Garden, Pelli Clarke Pelli Architects, New York, N.Y.

Fifteen Proposals

Ulrich Knaack

These proposals represent the work of the Facade Research Group. As a collection of future facade principles, they are an invitation to imagine building facades and systems through the innovative use of familiar materials. The Facade Research Group exists as an expansive network of faculties and industry partners within the Industrial Building Lab at Delft University of Technology.

fig. 1 | Modular air-filled boxes

CubeX

Creating modular air-filled boxes with a plug system makes it possible to build different types of walls or display stands. The system can also be used as a temporary partition to keep dirt out of an area while working. The plug system relies on air-filled tubes with valves resembling those of a bicycle tire. Foam plugs can also be used to connect the elements. | **figs. 1 + 2**

fig. 2 | Connecting the modules using foam plugs

Deflated Cardboard Facades

Air pressure can be used as an integrated element in the structure of facades. The goal is to design structural elements that allow for free-form constructions that can be stiffened by a vacuum. The elements are formed, then they are interlocked through pressure, fixing the shape of the construction. The benefits of the cardboard-facade system include: quick and simple assembly, easy transportation, transparency, and excellent insulation values. Cardboard is lightweight, cheap, and can be easily processed. The deflated foil works with the cardboard to provide watertightness and stiffness in all directions. The dimension of the cardboard components can be designed for specific structural needs.

Bookshelf Facade

The construction of the bookshelf facade is based on a cardboard grid structure. Two-dimensional elements are precut, preshaped, and assembled on site to produce a three-dimensional facade structure resembling a bookshelf. It can also be combined with sun-shading devices, such as Balloon Sun-Shading.

Deflated Envelopes

The inherent force of air pressure can be used as an integrated element in the structure of facade systems. This system also takes advantage of the enhanced insulation properties of the deflated construction.

Air-B-Wall

Using an air-filled balloon as a flexible airtight bag, an adjustable wall can be created that produces several possibilities: fill all of the balloons to create a rectangular wall after deflation; fill lines of balloons to create a moving wall; fill each balloon separately to form an organic shape; attach the pipes to a computer-controlled valve system to produce a wall that moves under different conditions. | figs. 3–5

Ball-Envelope

A filler material and foil supply a pretensioning force for the system. The filler's ability to maintain its shape under pressure of deflation is important for strength as well as for precision of form and prevention of creeping. Hollow plastic balls, for example, are strong, lightweight, and translucent. Packing is essential for the construction's formal flexibility. Ball-shaped elements in a single size tend to interlock into an ideal position with minimal volume, limiting the form's freedom. A filler with multi-sized elements is more difficult to control; likewise, a filling made of oddly-shaped elements can only be as strong as the balls, at the expense of a higher weight-to-strength ratio. Packing can be controlled either by shaping the upper and lower foil into a quiltlike volume or by packing the filling material into premanufactured units. For the Ball-Envelope, a strong transparent foil was desired. Stretching the foil and using a soft filler allowed for greater flexibility in construction. Too much flexibility causes a lower elasticity-modulus and has a negative influence on stiffness. The strength is, of course, also limited by air pressure.

Balloon Sun-Shading

The combination of a deflated facade and inflated-balloon construction can be used to create sun-shading devices with different transparencies. Generally, there are two possibilities for adjustment. In an open system, the balloons are connected to an independent pressure system. The relationship depends on the pressure differential between interior and exterior. In a closed system, the balloons are not connected to exterior pressure. The pressure differential is created simply by changing the vacuum within the facade. The balloons must be filled with a certain amount of air before being enclosed; this allows the device to grow and shrink. The first option has greater structural complexity but allows for better regulation of size without altering the vacuum in the facade or its insulating properties. Tests have shown that both principles work. Homogeneous pressure distribution is the critical factor. | fig. 6

fig. 3 | An adjustable wall is made of air-filled balloons.

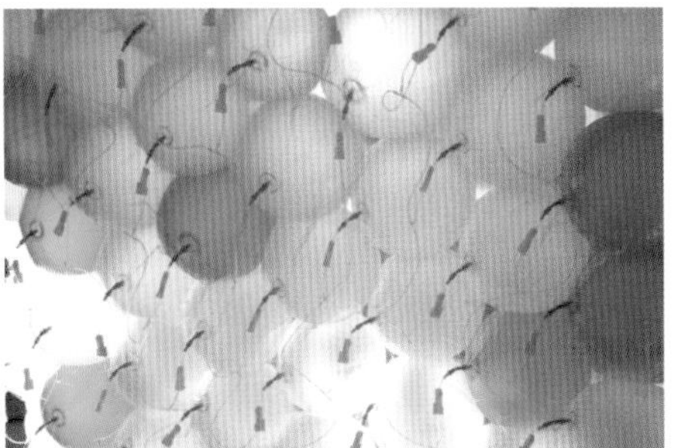

fig. 4 | A computer-controlled valve system allows for movement under different conditions.

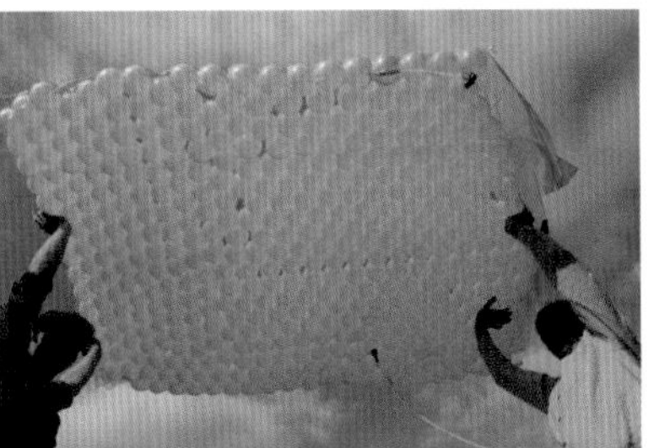

fig. 5 | The inherent force of air-pressure can be an integrated element in structural facade systems.

fig. 6 | Proposed sun-shading devices for facade constructions

Vacuum-Kinetic Structures

Inserting a structure that is capable of rolling into an airtight bag increases the potential of a kinetic structure. The cardboard rolls in under vacuum pressure and out when inflated. As a result, vacuum pressure ensures the smallest dimension and shape. This technique is possible for packaging, covering, and structural use due to the high stiffness of the evacuated core.

Self-Erecting Construction

Inserting precut elements into an airtight bag creates a self-erecting construction. By exploiting this phenomenon, biform construction is possible and the elements require less space. Every construction has two shapes and also employs the kinetic principle of growing until the final shape is formed.

fig. 7 | Unglazed units for heating and cooling surfaces

fig. 8 | Fiber-reinforced concrete for heat conduction and stability

Liquid Facade 2

The idea is to create a climate-adaptive facade in which liquid materials are used as a medium to vary the building's physical properties of thermal insulation, daylight access, and solar shading. The solution focuses on the symbiosis of different properties in a single materialization. One could, for instance, think of a system of multilayered cushions (or Lexan panels) with different compartments that can be filled and refilled with water, air, or other liquids. On the one hand, dynamic climate-controlled facades adapt their physical properties to changes throughout the day or seasons; on the other hand, they make optimal use of the collection of solar energy, which can play an important role in improving energy performance.

Facade Heating Cooling Panel

To avoid the use of traditional heating units in front of the glass, these unglazed units can be used as heating and cooling surfaces. The facade panels are formed from fiber-reinforced concrete embedded within a textile. They are used as load-bearing constructions and can be inserted into the framework of the facade. Oriented toward the room, the surface is inlaid with meadows of capillary tubes that heat in summer and cool in winter. The use of fiber-reinforced concrete provides good heat conduction and stability. | **figs. 7 + 8**

Integrated Sandwich Construction: Jackbox

Jackbox refers to a sensible combination of technical possibilities and intelligent materials capable of producing multifunctional system components. The sandwich panels are made through a vacuum procedure and have the following construction components: external glass-reinforced plastic skin (as weather-protective coating);

sandwich core of polyurethane foam, which also provides heat insulation; inner layer of fiber-reinforced concrete with integrated heating and cooling; capillary pipe mats that also provide efficient radiation heating

Parts of the building conceived as single modules were produced as a GRP sandwich with a fiberglass-reinforced plastic skin and hard foam cores. The modules are designed to be folded based on incisions in the roof area and possibly wall elements. After the elements are fixed in their desired form, they become the inner layer of textile-reinforced concrete with inlaid capillary pipes. | **figs. 9–11**

fig. 9 | A panel of GRP skin, PU foam, and fiber-reinforced concrete for the production of multifunctional system components

fig. 10 | Installation of an inside layer of textile-reinforced concrete (inlaid with capillary pipes) to seal the shape

fig. 11 | A jackbox, a sensible combination of technical possibilities and intelligent materials for producing multifunctional system components

Fiber Concrete Facade

Within the course of glass construction this research presents a facade of fiber-reinforced concrete and an integrated building services element. Until now, only traditional materials like aluminum, steel, wood, and glass have been used for extensive curtain walls. The development of fiber-reinforced concrete makes it possible to produce slim profiles and frames that have nearly the same dimensions as those manufactured in aluminum or steel. The approach of a modular facade in fiber-reinforced concrete demonstrates potential future applications of this material, as well as the possibility of extending the existing limits of design. While the use of fiber-reinforced concrete within a facade is common for the panels of curtain walls, its application within the facade's supporting elements is relatively new. A face dimension of 2.5 inches—as well as rigid foam-filled supporting elements with an average thickness of 0.4 inches—allows for significant design flexibility. This project was supported by Metallbau ErhardHolz of Leopoldshöhe, Germany, for the facade and glass; Durapact, of Haan, Germany, for fiber-reinforced concrete; and Krülland, of Kaarst, Germany, for the shading devices. | **figs. 12 + 13**

Edged Glass

Future glass may be shaped like steel or other metals. Creating a tool that heats a line within a glass plane could make edged-glass construction possible. These folded glass elements also make transparent construction possible. | **figs. 14 + 15**

Welded Glass

Welding glass would allow for free-form, highly transparent load-bearing structures without the use of steel. Pieces of molded curved glass that have been precut into exact shapes could then be welded together on site. Scaffolding would only be needed to support the panes and hold them in position during welding. After the glass is welded, diamond-tipped grinding tools could smooth the seams, producing a highly transparent, monolithic glass envelope. | **figs. 16–19**

fig. 12 | A modular facade in fiber-reinforced concrete, a future field of application for this material

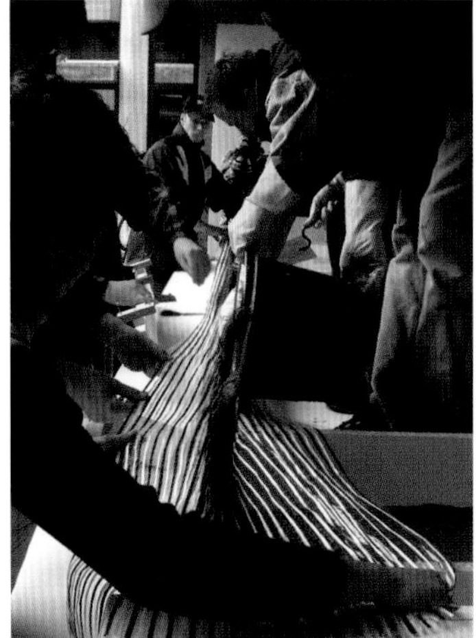

fig. 13 | Fiber-reinforced concrete process

fig. 14 | Glass molded into shapes like that of steel or other materials

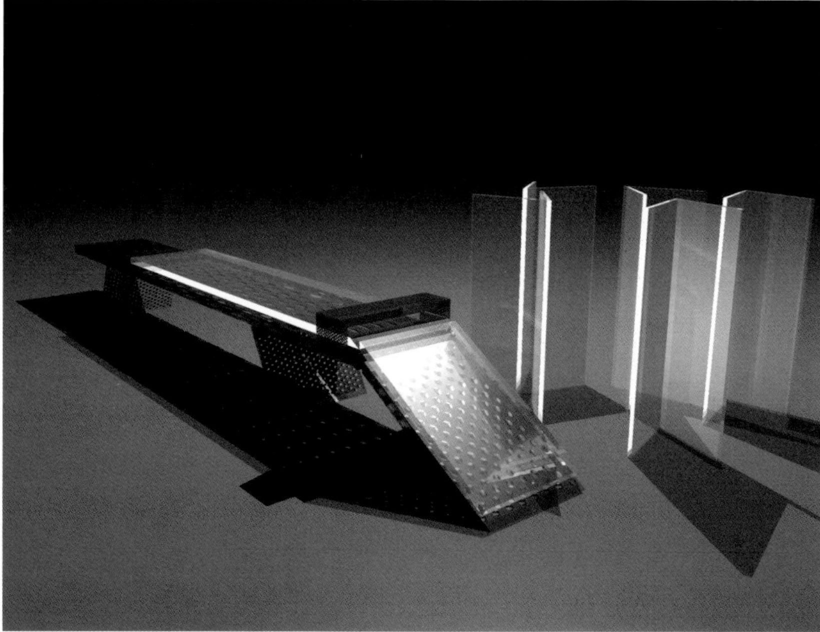

fig. 15 | A tool that heats up a line in a glass pane to make edged-glass construction possible

fig. 16 | Free-form or rectangular shapes forged out of monolithic glass

fig. 17 | Molded curved glass trimmed into exact shapes and welded together

fig. 18 | Diamand-tipped grinding tools for smoothing the seams to a highly transparent monolithic envelope

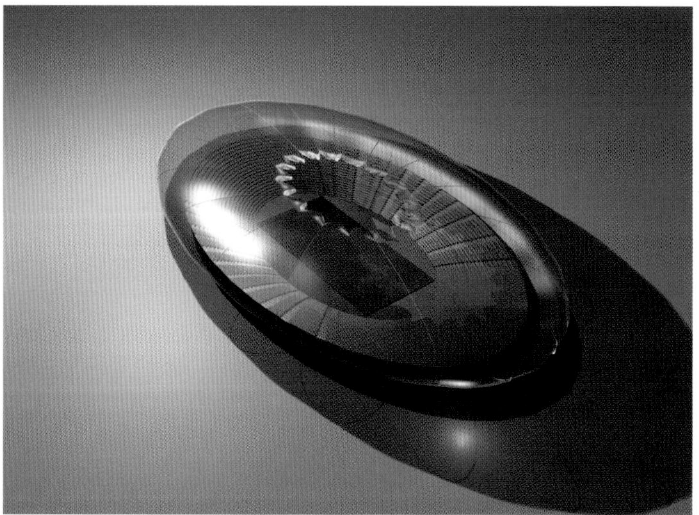

fig. 19 | Reinforcement of site glass, made possible with the use of glass textiles or knitted glass fibers and allowing for overall transparency

Glazing for Extreme Loadings

H. Scott Norville

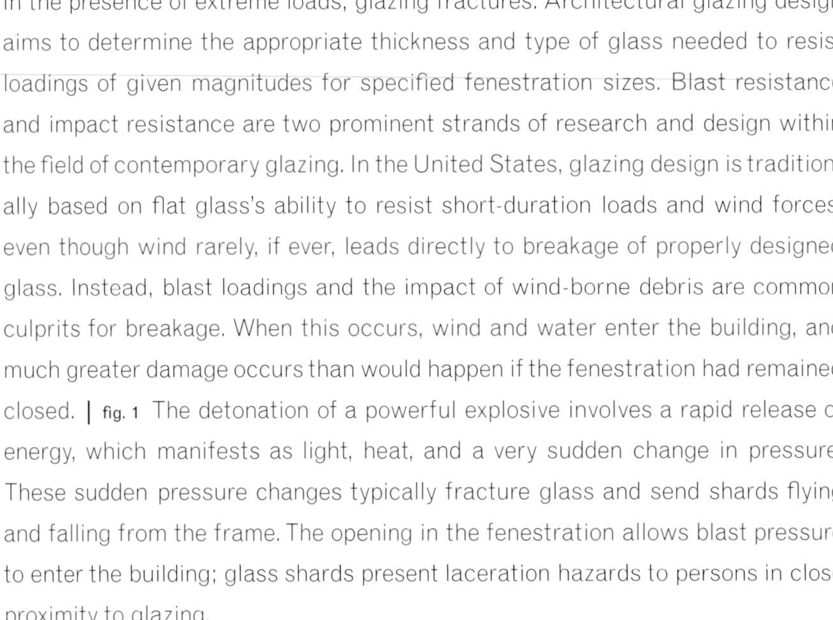

In the presence of extreme loads, glazing fractures. Architectural glazing design aims to determine the appropriate thickness and type of glass needed to resist loadings of given magnitudes for specified fenestration sizes. Blast resistance and impact resistance are two prominent strands of research and design within the field of contemporary glazing. In the United States, glazing design is traditionally based on flat glass's ability to resist short-duration loads and wind forces, even though wind rarely, if ever, leads directly to breakage of properly designed glass. Instead, blast loadings and the impact of wind-borne debris are common culprits for breakage. When this occurs, wind and water enter the building, and much greater damage occurs than would happen if the fenestration had remained closed. | **fig. 1** The detonation of a powerful explosive involves a rapid release of energy, which manifests as light, heat, and a very sudden change in pressure. These sudden pressure changes typically fracture glass and send shards flying and falling from the frame. The opening in the fenestration allows blast pressure to enter the building; glass shards present laceration hazards to persons in close proximity to glazing.

fig. 1 | Storefront glazing fracture in Oklahoma City bombing

Blast-resistant Glazing

Blast-resistant glazing must perform several functions. When an explosion occurs, it should fracture safely, meaning that it must prevent shards from flying and falling from the fenestration. Blast-resistant glazing should also maintain closure of the fenestration to prevent air-blast pressure from entering protected spaces within the building. Upon fracture, it should absorb the blast, not transfer it to the structure. Finally, since the vast majority of blast-resistant glazing will never need to serve these functions, it must also perform the functions of normal glazing without requiring excessive maintenance.

Many methods exist to facilitate blast-resistant glazing design. Those advanced by federal agencies tend to be costly. These include: ASTM F 2248 Standard Practice for specifying an equivalent three-second duration design-loading for blast resistant glazing fabricated with laminated glass; and ASTM E 1300 Standard Practice for determining load resistance of glass in buildings. When designed using this method, blast-resistant glazing performs all requisite functions, whether a blast occurs or not.

Impact-resistant Glazing

Similar to blast-resistant glazing, impact-resistant glazing must maintain closure of the fenestration following impact, but it need not absorb energy. Impact-resistant glazing design has not yet reached the level of sophistication of blast-resistant glazing; it continues to undergo trial designs and tests. Testing methods consist of impacting glazing systems and then subjecting the glazing spectrum to cyclic pressure. These include: ASTM F 1996 Standard Specification for performance of exterior windows, curtain walls, doors and impact-protective systems hit by windborne debris in hurricanes; and ASTM F 1886 Standard Test Method for performance of exterior windows, curtain walls, doors, and impact-protective systems affected by missiles and exposed to cyclic pressure differentials.

Designing blast- and impact-resistant glazing requires a consideration of postbreakage behavior. The ideal is glazing that remains in the frame, preventing shards from falling and flying from the fenestration. In this regard, the best and most cost-effective glazing is laminated glass because in the event of fracture, shards tend to adhere to the interlayer and its method of attachment to the supporting frame tends to maintain closure of the fenestration. These are key qualities for consideration when facilitating glazing designs for extreme loading conditions. | fig. 2

Adhesive Connections

Bernhard Weller, Silke Tasche, and Stefan Unnewehr

The transparent nature of glass challenges architects to use it as inconspicuously as possible. In the field of structural glazing, the panes are usually connected to one another or to the supporting structure through point fixings or clamping plates; however, typical boring point fixings are not ideal for handling glass. This is particularly true in the area around the boring, where peak tensions that cannot be plastically reduced occur. Therefore, when glass is used in construction, special attention must be paid to its brittleness.

The use of adhesives in glass construction is not only appropriate to the material, it allows for the creation of simple, inconspicuous details. With adhesive fixings, loads are transmitted over large areas. Joining glass members in this way offers great advantages, and the transmission of loads to the supporting component occurs evenly throughout the entire adhesive area.

For more than twenty years, adhesive joints in glass construction exclusively used one- and two-component silicones. The objective of Adhesive Bandages was to investigate alternative types of adhesives. Nearly 3,000 laboratory tests on load-bearing adhesive joints composed of glass and various metal surfaces bonded with UV- and light-curing acrylates were analyzed. The comprehensive examination of materials under laboratory conditions was supplemented by a number of tests on large-scale samples with load-bearing adhesive joints.

The use of UV- and light-curing acrylates in glass construction can potentially expand the variety of connections and details possible because of the inherent transparency of the adhesive, and could also offer production advantages and increased material strength. To initiate this development, it is essential to study the aging process of bonded connections between float glass and metal surfaces. Any such investigation should incorporate combinations of different types of materials utilized for brackets and surface treatments to examine punctual and linear adhesive joints.

Accelerated aging tests were carried out in accordance with the European guideline ETAG 002. The scope of the aging tests was reasonably extended in regard to intended use. Among other test scenarios, the samples were exposed to natural weathering for a period of several years. Interpretations of the test results focused on the quality of the bonded connection relative to the influence of a "tin side" or an "air side," along with other parameters for studying the effect of the adhesive layer's thickness or the glass surface treatment on improving the long-term stability of joints. The maximum load capacity and serviceability of adhesive connections using UV- and light-curing acrylates were tested in accordance with current regulations for glass structures. This examination included: glass units acting as barriers for preventing people from falling; glass louvers in facades; and overhead glazing and doors with bonded infill panels. The majority of tests were conducted on new building components, some of which had been exposed to natural weathering for a few years prior to testing. For the first time, this research verified the fundamental suitability of UV- and light-curing acrylates under specific limitations in glass construction. | figs. 1–8

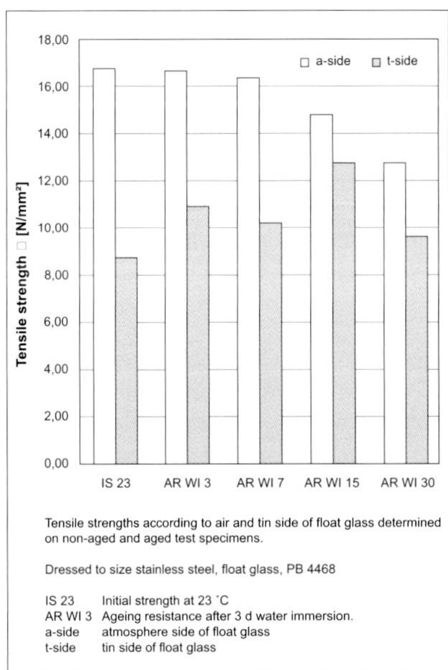

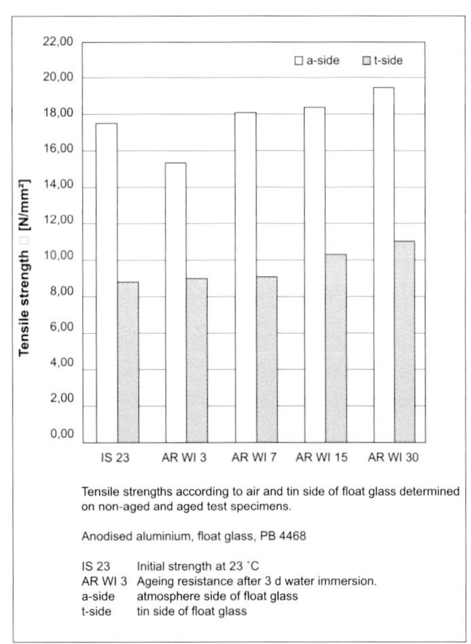

figs. 1 + 2 | Results of tensile strength tests for UV- and light-curing acrylates

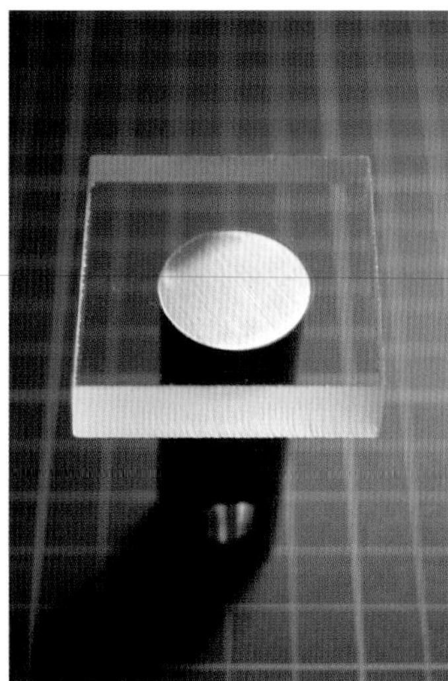

fig. 3 | Transparent adhesive bonding with UV- and light-curing acrylates

fig. 4 | Fittings of glass balustrades after impact tests, with adhesively bonded joints intact

figs. 5 + 6 | Test specimens exposed to natural weathering

fig. 7 | Metal samples with different surface qualities

fig. 8 | Specimens for tensile-strength tests

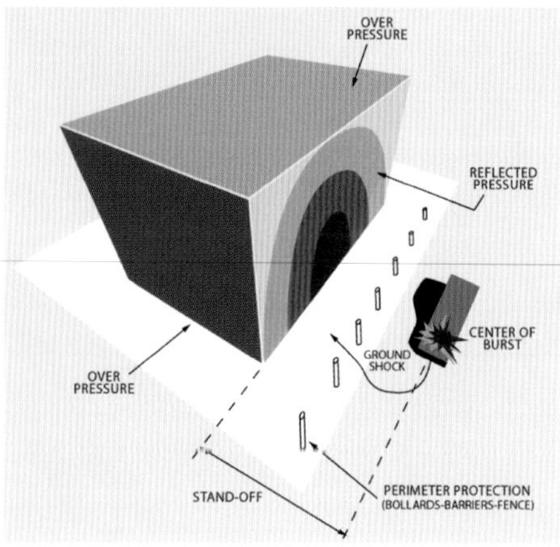

fig. 1 | Illustration of pressure distribution as the result of an explosion

Explosive Loadings and Flexible Facades

Bob Smilowitz

Revealing the protective potential of glazed envelopes in response to explosive loading requires a full understanding of blast wave propagation, the performance of facade materials, and the numerical solution of multidegree-of-freedom dynamic systems. The shock waves resulting from the detonation of explosive materials at grade level weaken as blast energy dissipates over an ever-expanding hemispherical surface. | **fig. 1** A shock wave is characterized by near-instantaneous peak pressure followed by exponential decay and then a subsequent longer duration (but lower intensity) negative suction phase. The intensity of the propagating shock wave is intensified as the pulse encounters a material whose density differs significantly from air. These reflection factors are greater for high-intensity pulses; they are greater for near normal angles of incidence. While the intensity of blast waves may overwhelm even the most robust glazed facade at short standoff distances, the effectiveness of protective facades becomes apparent as distance increases. Therefore, a hardened envelope may be best equipped to protect against the collateral effects of a detonation in the vicinity of the structure.

Glass is inherently brittle and fragile compared to other structural materials such as concrete and steel. Furthermore, glass exhibits greater statistical variation from sample to sample. As a result, any analysis of a glazed facade requires an understanding of the statistical likelihood of the material properties. Due to its brittleness, explosive testing of glass samples considers the potential of hazardous airborne debris. The use of laminated glass products and anti-shatter film limits the extent and velocity of airborne debris, therefore minimizing the potential for hazard. A sufficient depth of rebate is required to prevent laminated or filmed glass from exiting the frames, and a sufficiently robust mullion is required to resist both the flexural and membrane forces that may be tributary to the framing.

Explosive testing of full-scale curtain-wall systems are routinely conducted to demonstrate the effectiveness of glass, framing, connections, and anchorages. This testing demonstrates the benefits of flexible facade systems for dissipating considerable amounts of blast energy through controlled deformations. These tests are used to calibrate analytical methods for modeling the facade and determining its response to blast loading. Three-dimensional nonlinear explicit-dynamic finite-element analyses is the most accurate method for evaluating and designing blast-resistant curtain walls. Comparisons between physical test results and finite element calculations show the effectiveness of these solutions when attempting to predict the hazardous potential of flexible facade systems. | **figs. 2-4**

fig. 2 | Blast-resistant curtain wall that is engineered to take advantage of inherent flexibility and to withstand maximum loads transferred by the glazing

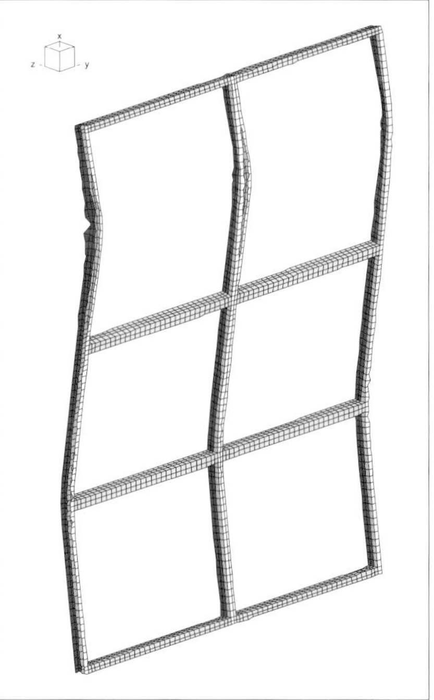

fig. 3 | All joints use pin connections; glazing is adhered using structural silicone sealant to transfer collected loads to frames

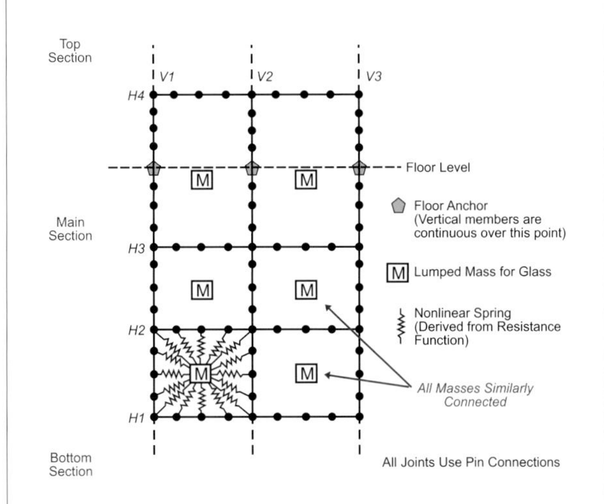

fig. 4 | Pin connections in joints maximize flexibility and minimize loss

Telecom Center, Munich, Germany

Delta-X GmbH, Engineering

Albrecht Burmeister

The twin towers and rotunda of the Telecom Center in Munich, Germany, are in danger of blast-loading due to their close proximity to the BFB building, where pure alcohol is stored. Not only are strain-rate dependent material laws required, but you must also describe potential broken-glass scenarios. Therefore, failure criteria for glass, its interlayer, and its bonding are required. | figs. 1 + 2

Due to the complexity of the problem, we decided to use a numerical simulation to deal with different types of facades. This type of numerical simulation allowed us to solve the wave propagation problem, resulting in different pressures for different surfaces. Due to the fact that glass and framing interact during impulsive pressure loads, we also used complex finite element models to describe parts of the structure. Using this type of procedure, it was possible to realize the architectural idea, keep the glass thickness as originally designed, and achieve an economical solution. | figs. 3–5

Theoretically, when dealing with impulsive loads, the use of flexible structures is recommended to reduce pressure on the structure. Postcritical membrane states are able to carry high-membrane forces if they can be sustained by the supporting structure. In our opinion, the development of these types of solutions should be based on numerical simulations. This is due to the scattering of shock-tube tests, as well as for economic reasons. As an important precondition, the numerical models used throughout the simulation have to be qualified. This is quite easy when dealing with unbroken glass.

It can be stated in summary that there are numerical solutions for describing broken glass. For real construction, we recommend dynamically optimizing the facade's load-bearing behavior. These concepts are not easy to apply, but they increase the capacity of current facade solutions. This enables architects and engineers to design transparent facades that are bomb- and blast-resistant.

References:

Burmeister, A., and H. Rahm, *Simulation explosionshemmender Fassadenkonstruktionen*, "Glas im Konstruktiven Ingenieurbau 4" seminar, Munich, Germany, Sept. 17, 2004.

Fenster, Türen and Abschlüsse, *Sprengwirkungshemmung, Anforderungen und Klassifizierung*, Teil 1: Stoßrohr.

Fraunhofer-Institut für Kurzzeitdynamik, Ernst-Mach-Institut Glas-Bruch-Verhalten im Stoßrohrversuch, 2003.

Kinney, G.F., and K.J. E. Graham, *Explosive Shocks in Air* (New York: Springer, 1985).

| **figs. 1 + 2** Telecom Center, designed by Kiessler + Partner Architekten, Munich, Germany, 2000

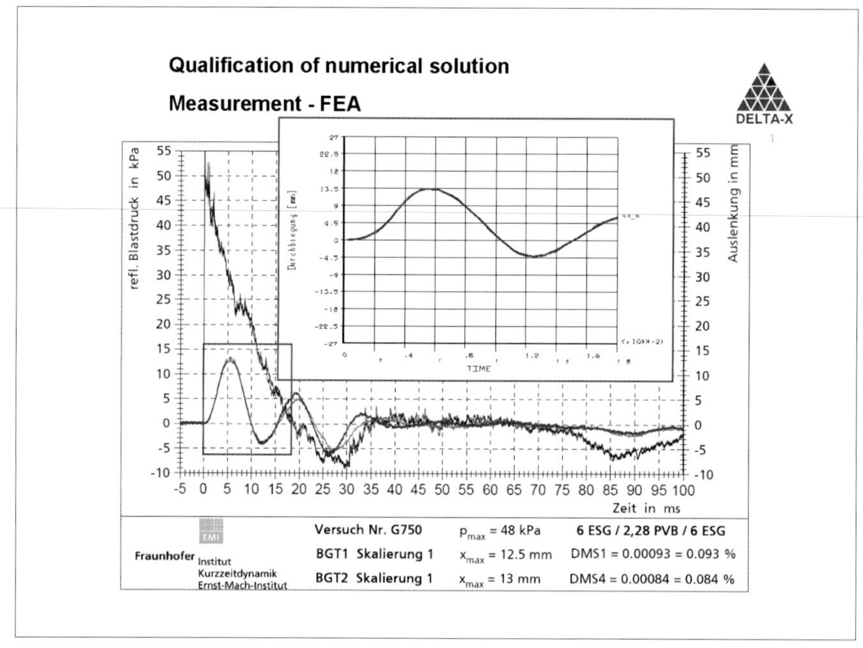

| **fig. 3** With our investigations, we try to activate the breakage of glass so that energy dissipates and we are able to take advantage of postcritical membrane states. A comparison of measured and calculated solutions shows that both are nearly the same.

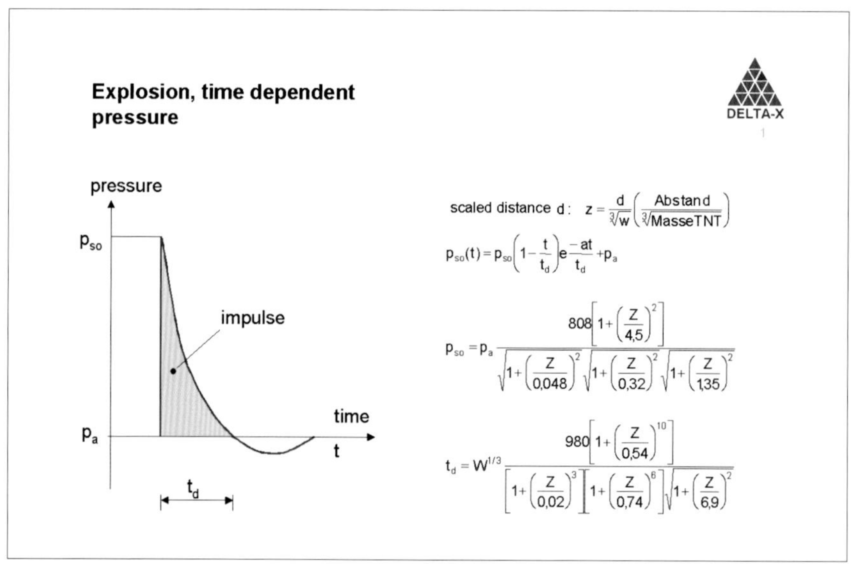

| **fig. 4** For typical explosive loads, describing the materials and structures is the main objective. This diagram shows the relationship between time and pressure in common explosions.

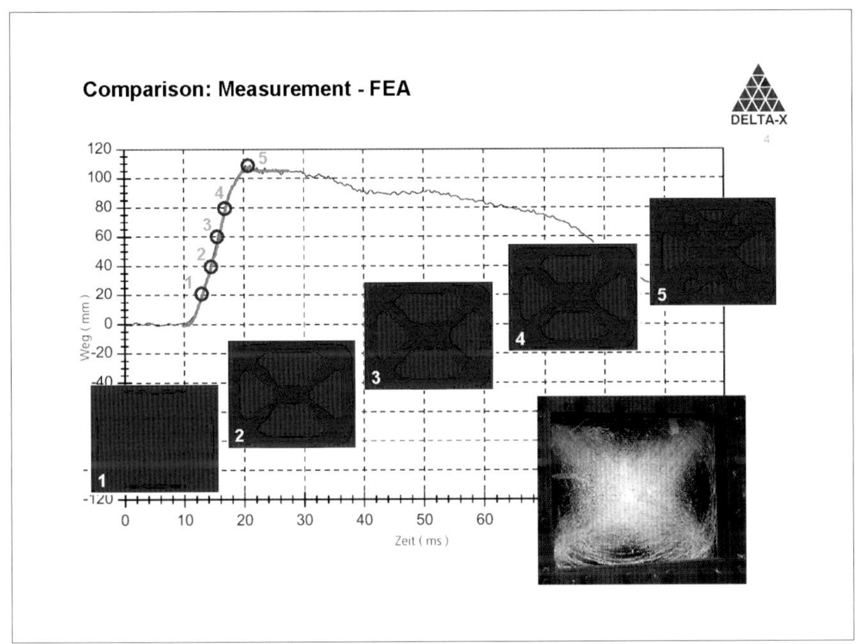

| **fig. 5** The results of a shock-tube test, in which glass was broken, show that observed behaviors are completely nonlinear and produce large deformations in the middle of the glass. To represent the glass numerically, we used identical shell elements. Shell 1 represents the unbroken glass, and Shell 2 represents the broken glass together with the appropriate stiffness and nonlinear material law. The green curve shows that calculated values were very close to measured ones. It also shows how the crack pattern develops over time. In the end, the crack pattern was very well represented in the numerical solution.

Visual and Spatial Effects

Inside Outside/Frame and Frameless

Laurie Hawkinson

The following images and text are a brief musing on the use of glass in architecture. The intention is to illuminate both the limitless possibilities and the precise effects that may be achieved given intent and specificity. Architectural details are presented as ways of seeing moments or events often thought to be invisible. Transparency in architecture is always associated with the window and the transmission of light from inside to outside. A window in architecture is always understood to be a binocular plane.

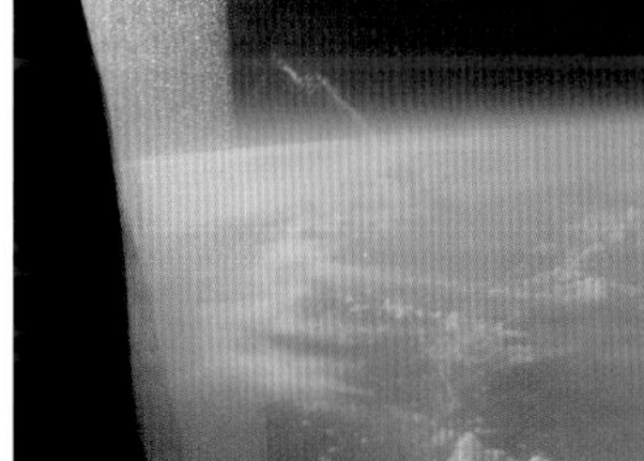

What are you looking at and how much do you see?

Where are you when you are looking out? The window becomes almost peripheral in a view from the interior of the space shuttle.

Do you want to see everything?

Bruno Reichlin, quoting from Le Corbusier's book *Precision,* suggests that architecture can also be told as a story of windows. In describing the revolutionary impact new developments in construction technology would have on architecture, Reichlin goes on to suggest that Le Corbusier employed the window as a metaphor for the history of architecture. In the case of Le Corbusier's strip window, the value of the threshold is diminished as the horizon is exposed and the exterior is allowed to enter the interior.

In the ribbon window, evoking Reichlin once again, "the landscape is there" in all of its immediacy, as if it were sticking to the window, because the transition between objects close at hand and those further away remains concealed. Through the ribbon window, perception of spatial depth is significantly diminished.

Following Reichlin further into his essay, "The Pros and Cons of the Horizontal Window: The Perret-Le Corbusier Controversy," we discover his suggestion that the horizontal window tears a hole in the "protective covering of the private person" and the outside world triumphs over the interior. Is this a seamless transition from inside to outside?

Is the window, which functions here as a literal threshold, still a window when visibility is controlled in one direction through the use of reflective or one-way mirrored glass?

Is the window still a window when it not only allows for the transmission of light but also provides security?

Is a window still a window when its primary role is as a protector from weather or as a shading device, depending on its operability? How big is the window? How large is the glass?

When glass is assembled in a larger frame, how does the frame relate to the proportions of the body? What is the relationship between the window frame and the body? How does the presence of that frame affect the experience of the viewer? Remove the frame and the modulation. Alter the proportion of the glass to create ambiguity at the threshold between inside and outside.

Transparency can be employed as a device for orientation, turning the building into a machine for viewing.

A corner of glass allows for a panoptic view. Above the horizontal strip, an exaggerated window exists only to let light in.

A translucent skin folds in on itself to form a continuous skylight.

A folded clerestory brings light from one interior space to another.

The building dematerializes through the reverse phenomenon of glass becoming perfectly opaque.

The dialectical nature of glass allows it to be simultaneously transmissive and opaque.

Glass forms an invisible barrier in a disappearing corner.

The wall appears to disappear.

The frameless detail of the glass creates an invisible plane, or it produces a view of the landscape through multiple layers of transparency.

How is such vast transparency produced? A seamless interior is created by separating the structure from the glass and articulating the exterior structure.

The relationship flips and the structure returns to the interior, extenuating the ambiguity of what is inside and what is outside.

The structure recedes from the corner while the ceiling plane extends beyond it, oblivious to the boundary it suggests.

The structure is expressed; the glass recedes.

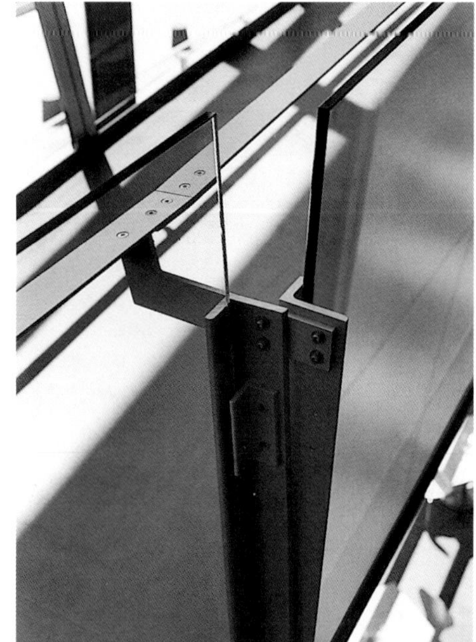

The relationship of the body to the components of the handrail is explored through the separation of glass from the vertical plane. One pane of glass moves away from perpendicular, changing the body's orientation to the view below. The frameless glass itself is structural, providing rigidity to the assembly and protection for the body.

Can glass, by itself, be a structural member or fitting? Here it takes on the role of invisible structural element, acting in both compression and tension.

The repetitive use of glass cord in a truss creates the effect of glowing translucency under the canopy while maintaining constant tension between the truss and what it supports.

A sense of destabilization is achieved by fracturing the view of the horizon.

Glass produces a watery grotto-like space through the phenomena of reflection and refraction.

The glass is made visible by setting it off from the perpendicular and intentionally inflecting the horizon.

Care is taken to expose the green edge of the glass, emphasizing its materiality by removing the frame and distancing the structure. At this threshold, the window is the door; the door is the wall; the wall is the material; the material is the structure; and the structure is the barrier that transmits and reflects glass. Is glass still glass?

Beyond Transparency

James Carpenter

Beyond providing a view and allowing light to penetrate interior spaces, glass can be seen as a membrane whose malleable properties give it the greatest potential to reveal the discrete information possessed by light. Many of our projects have been thresholds, because this is where the idea of what defines interior as separate from exterior is most apparent. Why assume, after all, that a piece of clear glass is adequate for defining that boundary condition? I think the boundary condition can be defined in many ways, both intellectually and materially. In our work with glass, transparency is one of a range of attributes that we consider.

Originally, I came to an understanding of glass as a substrate for light information through working with film projected onto glass and exploring glass as a medium for photographic imagery. As a result, I came to understand the cinematic potential of glass itself, as it interacts with light in the environment. Working with Corning over many years, we developed photosensitive glasses, three-dimensional photographic images in glass, and full-color images in glass, among other things. These technologies would later enable me to transform glass itself into film, using it as both the projector and the projection screen, as in the Structural Glass Prisms we designed for Edward Larrabee Barnes's Christian Theological Seminary in Indianapolis, Indiana. | **figs. 1–3**

fig. 1 | The cinematic potential of transparency, Structural Glass Prisms, Christian Theological Seminary, Indianapolis, Ind., 1985–1987

figs. 2 + 3 | Structural Glass Prisms, Christian Theological Seminary, Indianapolis, Ind., 1985–1987

Transparency is too glib a word to describe the variables that glass expresses. By balancing its properties of transparency, reflectivity, and translucency, glass can be designed to function simultaneously as a window or weather-membrane and as a medium for revealing light. In essence, we aim to invert the usual modernist idea of glass. This is the dichotomy of our work. We would like to see the structure become invisible, while the glass elements, usually invisible in the modernist sense, take on a visual presence, revealing the complexity of environmental and experiential information in and on the glass. We are challenging the conventional idea of glass in that, for us, structure is secondary visually to glass, which provides the content. I think that is one of our major contributions to glass practice in the last thirty years. | figs. 4–6

fig. 4 | An exploration of spatial compression, Retracting Screen, Dallas, Tex., 1993

figs. 5 + 6 | Retracting Screen, Dallas, Tex., 1993

The whole development of our technical vocabulary has been the result of the need for a clear and simple expression that supersedes the visual prominence of muscle-bound structures. The basis of our thinking, whether for a wall or bridge, is that the structure be sublimated. By understanding the structural properties of glass itself and by developing working relationships across many professions and areas of expertise, we have been able to avoid the conventional structure of deep beams, mullions, and metal-structure framing each glass panel; in other words, we have avoided all of the depth and robustness of structure associated with large-scale glass-wall structures. With a conventional structure, you squander the potential to reveal the qualities of transparency, reflectivity, and translucency; the view of the structure would otherwise dominate the viewers' perception, reducing the play of light to a field of pattern. By engaging structural solutions that support the underlying conceptual premise, the structure becomes less like a bookend to an idea. If the structural solution can't further the original idea, then the project is bound to fail. | **figs. 7–10**

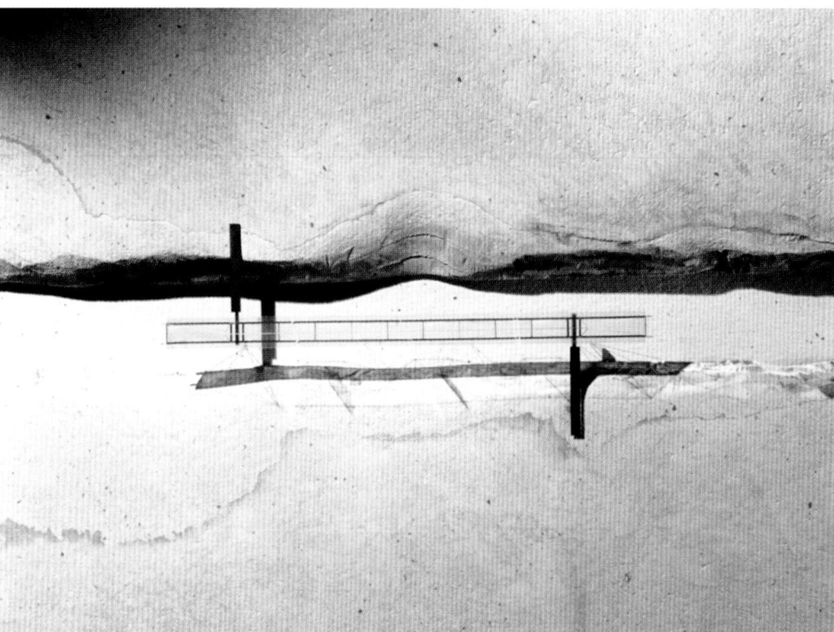

fig. 7 | Luminous Glass Bridge, Marin County, Calif., 1987

fig. 8 | At deck level, clear swiveling glass panels layer images of the surrounding landscape; as pedestrians cross the bridge, the panels spin on a central axis and the images rearrange over time.

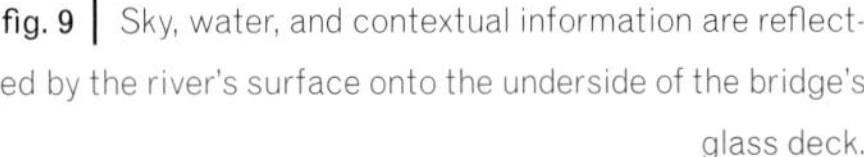

fig. 9 | Sky, water, and contextual information are reflected by the river's surface onto the underside of the bridge's glass deck.

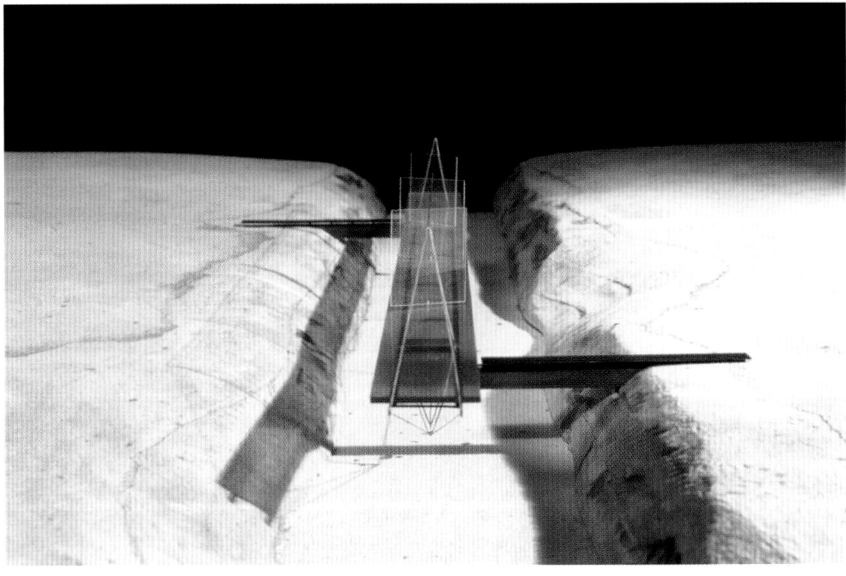

fig. 10 | Engineered with both vertical and horizontal surfaces, the bridge captures fragments of contextual information on two planes.

With the design of 7 World Trade Center each part of the building had a very specific role, and the design evolved within a specific context. David Childs of Skidmore, Owings & Merrill (SOM), who has been a very supportive collaborator on many of our projects, brought us in to participate on this project early on. At the time, there wasn't a complete idea about the tower, but SOM knew they wanted a solid base, defined by the transformers contained there, and that the base would somehow merge with the tower. They were looking at different conceptual ideas, such as a slinky, where the metal base would be very dense and get thinner and thinner as it stretched up the building. The broadest influence we brought to the project was to conceive the overall building as a structure that would be able to respond luminously to its immediate environment. Both the local urban conditions and the particular quality of downtown light would be the organizing principle of the design. From that point on, we worked on the principle of a volume of light, where the glass curtain wall would act as a reflector and a subtle reimaging device for its surroundings. When you look at the finished building, you're made more aware of the quality of light happening at that moment.

We did this both with an unconventional curtain wall and a unique skin for the base of the building. Instead of having the curtain wall interrupted at the floor plates, we allowed the glass unit to pass over the floor edge and terminate at the midpoint of the recessed spandrel, thereby defining the floors by revealing a void. Below the resulting floating portion of the insulated glazing unit (IGU), a reveal allows light to be inserted behind the curtain wall by means of a formed spandrel section. The spandrel section consists of an inclined blue reflector at the sill that reflects daylight up onto a vertically curved, specular metal panel, which in turn projects the light out and down through the backside of the floating section of the IGU. The result is that the tower's structure is embedded with light and merges with the sky. | figs. 11–14

Beyond transparency, our projects strive to make people aware of nature and to reveal nature's presence, despite our assumption that we are divorced from it. We conceive of ways to re-establish these connections, which inevitably are there but often overlooked. We understand glass as having the means to do this.

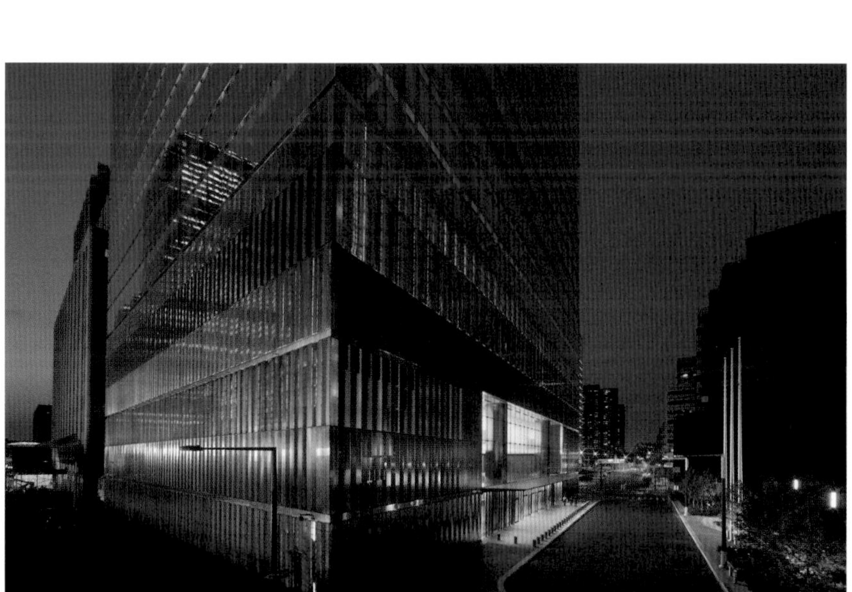

figs. 11 + 12 | Dematerializing structure and embodying nature, 7 World Trade Center, New York, N.Y., 2006

figs. 13 + 14 | 7 World Trade Center, New York, N.Y., 2006

Curtain Wall/Aberrant Masonry at 277 Mott Street

Stefan Röschert

Straight jacketed by building department and zoning requirements in New York's Little Italy, the Mott Street Town House, currently under construction, emerged as a pragmatic study of the monolithic ideals of architecture and the realities of contemporary curtain-wall construction at the studio of Diller Scofidio + Renfro.

Bound by the city's requirement to provide a predominantly masonry facade and by the physical constraints of a footprint measuring twenty by sixty feet, grand mineral curtains were created in a collaborative design process that sought to allow an influx of modulated light and air to penetrate the apartments, while adhering to the requirement to preserve the monolithic aspect of the neighborhood's hole-punched and windowed street elevations. | fig. 1

fig. 1 | Rendering, 277 Mott Street, Diller Scofidio + Renfro, New York, N.Y.

The eight-story construction is typologically prescribed by code and only expanded in that all of the apartments have floor-through open plans and are directly accessible by elevator. Due to their sectional tightness, the monolithic octroi for the outside are translated to the point of seamlessness through the use of monocoque construction, a technique in which the outer skin carries all or most of the stress. This frees the interiors so that all of the furniture can be built into a forty-foot-long wall, stretching and exaggerating the depth of the otherwise clutter-free rentals. Two floors of retail at and above street level are topped by a studio and two duplex apartments with a recessed terrace and roof-top and ground-floor gardens, all of which rests on top of a full-lot basement. | fig. 2

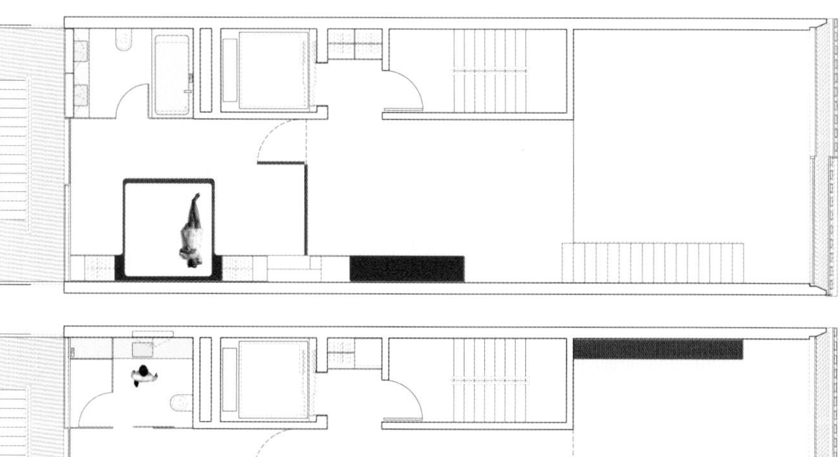

fig. 2 | First and second floorplans

The design for the town house is based on Gottfried Semper's Stoffwechsel theory, which suggests a change in matter in the construction of architectural enclosures while employing the same method of weaving of early-woven textile tents, from the pivotal Caribbean straw hut to nineteenth-century masonry-bound structural walls. Two phenomena lost in translation in this process were reintroduced into the contemporary understanding of the masonry curtain wall: flaccidity and the initial translucency of the textile.

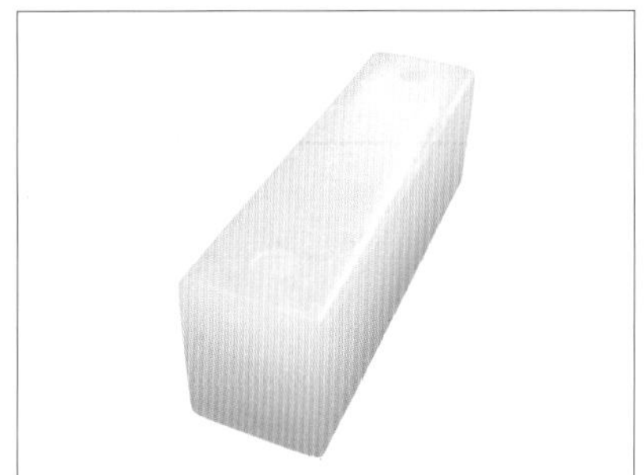

fig. 3 | Brick made of recycled optical borosilicate glass

Today's masonry walls are nonstructural skins designed to mimic traditional masonry walls. To enable these veneers to be suspended from buildings at any height, mortar has been replaced by high-performance silicones. On Mott Street, local code required mineral units bound by mortar, which we substituted with recycled and optical borosilicate-glass bricks that were handcrafted in Japan. | fig. 3 The compressive strength of these bricks is more than ten times that of traditional masonry. The bricks are shimmed using laser-cut, glass-fiber-filled polycarbonate plates in a prestressed assembly, with embedded duplex-alloy stainless rods woven into an expanded, masonry-bound translucent and flaccid curtain with an opening ratio of 40 percent. The resulting porosity allows for a variety of scenarios for modulating natural light and ventilation within the interior while maintaining a primarily masonry facade. | figs. 4 + 5

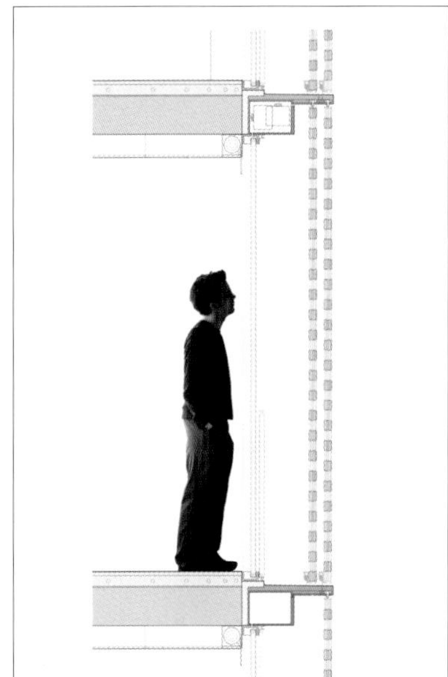

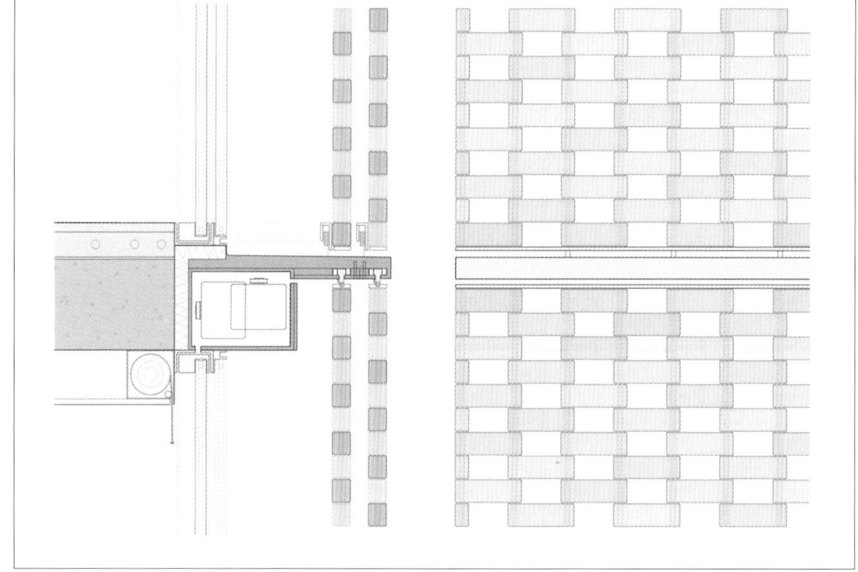

figs. 4 + 5 | Wall section and facade detail

Manufacturer Eddy Sykes of Cherson Prom was brought into the process during the project's design-development phase. Alan Burden of the engineering firm Structured Environment executed the calculations on miscellaneous metals for the assembly, while Bill Logan of IBA monitored the design process and oversaw testing as an outside consultant. As a result, engineer Will Laufs was able to run a model to concisely calculate the harmonics of the assembly and to optimize its performance. The building is scheduled for completion in spring 2009. | figs. 6–8

fig. 6 | Detail, mock-up of borosilicate brick curtain

fig. 7 | Testing configuration, mock-up of borosilicate brick curtain

Natural Frequency Mode	Mode type	Value Frequency in Hertz
First mode 1st	Sway in y-y (one bow)	f1 = 7.1 Hz > 2 Hz - ok
Second Mode 2nd	Sway in y-y (one bow)	f2 = 21.8 Hz > 2 Hz - ok
Third Mode 3rd	Torsional twist	f3 = 29.3 Hz > 2 Hz - ok

$$f_1 = 1/(2\pi) * \pi^2/L^2 * (EI/m)^{0.5} * (1+1/i^2 * P/P_{crit})^{0.5} = 6.8\ Hz$$

WernerSobekNewYork

fig. 8 | Facade deflection model

Energy and Comfort

Matthias Schuler

The purpose of climate engineering is to ensure the highest level of comfort for building occupants with the lowest possible impact on the environment. Transsolar accomplishes this by developing and validating innovative climate and energy concepts. The scope is to combine highly comfortable environments with minimum energy use while recognizing that environmental conditions are influenced by all aspects of design. Thermal comfort is a diffuse term. It depends not only on air temperature but on measurable factors that are strongly connected to the quality of the glazed envelope. Therefore, we work collaboratively from the start of the building-design process, considering each step from the standpoint of fundamental thermodynamics and physics. This generates a climate concept in which local conditions, form, material, and mechanical systems become synergistic components of a well-orchestrated climate control system.

Novartis WSJ 158, Basel, Switzerland

The intention of the architects was to provide a highly transparent building with a limited facade depth of seventeen feet, along with pure exterior and interior appearances. This created a conflict when trying to meet the low-energy commitment established by Novartis. The energy consumption for everything in the building including office equipment could not exceed 300 megajoules per square meter annually. A triple-glazed facade with an integrated shading device and a decentralized ventilation system, in combination with a slab cooling system, allowed us to minimize the ceiling depth by raising the floor fifteen centimeters. With an air-return system integrated into the structural shear walls and through the use of desk lights, all technical systems were merged so that the pure glass walls and a concrete ceiling could enclose the space. On sunny days, reflections from the outside transform the glass into an opaque surface, but on overcast days and at night the building shows its extreme transparency. | figs. 1–8

fig. 1 | Plexiglas model of Novartis Office Building, SANAA, 2004

fig. 2 | Exterior view, Novartis Office Building, SANAA

fig. 3 | Interior view, Novartis Office Building, SANAA

fig. 4 | View of variegated glazing, Novartis Office Building, SANAA

fig. 5 | Exterior, Novartis Office Building, SANAA

fig. 6 | Interior courtyard, Novartis Office Building, SANAA

fig. 7 | Reflection turns glass into an opaque surface, exterior view, Novartis Office Building, SANAA

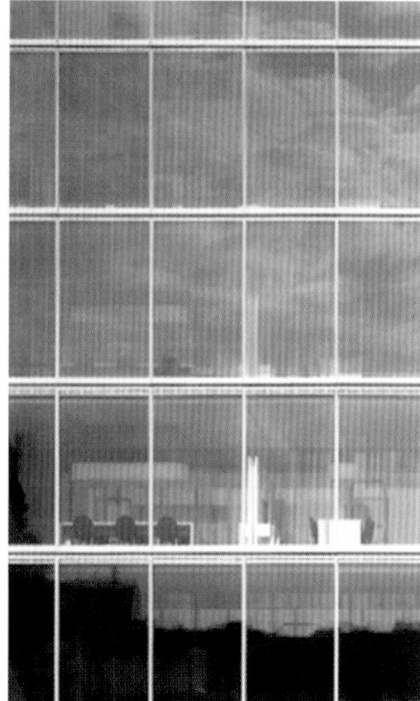

fig. 8 | Exterior view, Novartis Office Building, SANAA

S.R. Crown Hall, IIT School of Architecture, Chicago, IL

Our team assembled and analyzed a combination of modifications that, we believe, produced an enormous improvement in the quality of life for people in the building while also realizing a reduction in energy consumption and without affecting the aesthetics of the space or the status of the building as a twentieth-century icon. An overall improvement in the building's energy systems was achieved by reinstating trees; replacing lower glazing panels with low-E units, improving the building's airtightness; repairing and controlling ventilation flaps; increasing roof insulation to a thickness of three inches; replacing interior lights with T5 fluorescents to achieve seventy-five foot-candles; installing dimming and nighttime circuit controls and timers; and adding heat recovery to the ventiliation and floor cooling systems. It sounds like a long list, but it is worth noting that many of these elements were due for replacement. The net effect of these alterations are illustrated in the graphs and images that follow. | **figs. 9–14**

fig. 9 | Archival photo, night view, S.R. Crown Hall, IIT School of Architecture, Chicago, Ill.

fig. 10 | interior, existing conditions

fig. 11 | View of S.R. Crown Hall, IIT School of Architecture, Chicago, Ill.

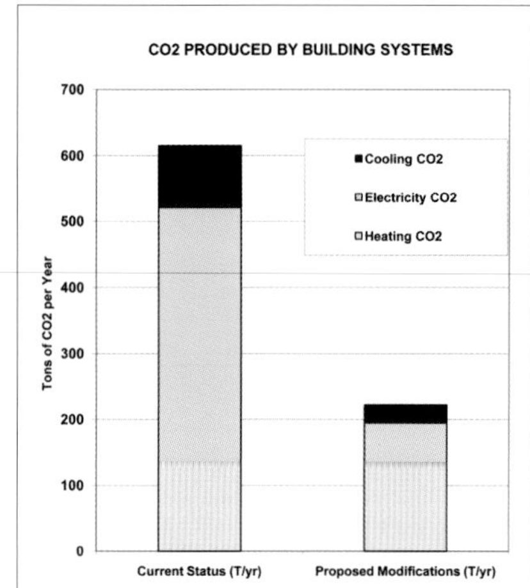

fig. 12 | Final refurbishment strategy based on approaches to the problem of conservation of energy

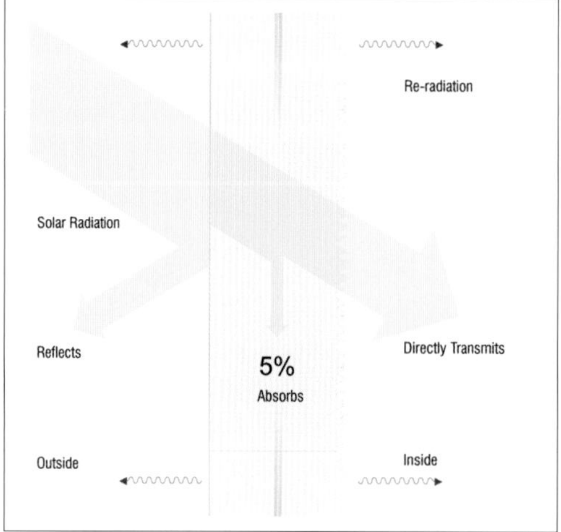

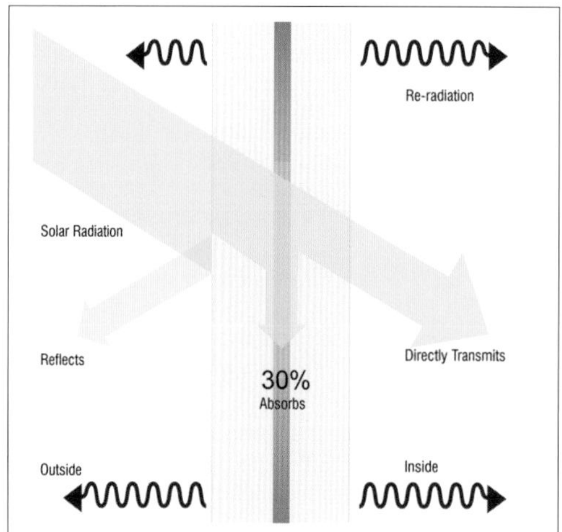

figs. 13 + 14 | Percentage of light transmitted through original (top) and refurbished (bottom) facade glass

Shadows and Light

François Roche

To use Jacques Lacan's metaphor, I refuse to look at myself in the mirror. In this way I reject the possibility of reassembling the multiple fragments—the multiple disorders—I have to rearticulate. The glass is definitively broken, and there's no pre-existing picture of this reflecting puzzle with which to reconstruct it. What's worse, the picture is on the floor in a multitude of images, disseminated as an *opus incertum* in multiples of fragments. Instead of reducing the existence of the unknown by limiting it to its own appearance, the glass remains fractal, a reflective reduction of reassembled reality. We could accept this non-self-representation as the first lost effect of the broken glass.

Glass is both a substance and an ideology. It's an apparatus that can be pulled and pushed in any direction. It helps us move from the mythology of transparency and technology described by Roland Barthes, with its positive overvaluing, to other strange boundaries—more ghostly, with blur refraction and lead anomalies altering perception like an illusionist membrane. To circle the topic without touching it, I would like to describe one of R&Sie(n)'s design protocols.

The Recycling "Bachelor Apparatus"

The commission was to renovate the FRAC (Fonds Regional d'Art Contemporain), a regional museum of contemporary art in the city of Orléans, in central France. It is also the venue for ArchiLab, a wild collection of radical and experimental architecture. You can imagine how deeply problematic it could be for an architect to design a contemporary architectural museum where his own work is a part of the collection. It's like digging your own grave in a frozen cemetery designed by you. More seriously, the main difficulty was defining a scenario for weaving together visitors and pieces in the collection. We wanted it to be the opposite of a graveyard; we thought it should be alive and breathing, like an organism able to swallow and digest the visitor: a museum as a nonpanoptic cabinet of curiosities, where people could lose themselves, when the users' manual itself is lost, on a permanent vacation or in permanent transformation, like "The House that Jack Built," an episode of the 1960s television series *The Avengers*.

Our heterotopic proposal involved dreaming up a *corps sans organe*, a body without an organ (BwO) in the sense of Antonin Artaud or Gilles Deleuze. We imagined a kind of a desiring machine for articulating substances and intensities, for slipping over surfaces and infiltrating flesh in a multitude of possible ways. This BwO was generated by smearing a model of the existing building with glue, sliming it to rediscover—in the massive depth of its viscosity—a way of embedding a multitude of accesses, walkways, and forked paths for revealing unlimited relationships by way of geographical detours and twists.

The disappearance of the building was a mechanism for reinjecting a new function and a new protocol. Like a heterotopic experiment, this labyrinth as museum would be a kind of a human trap. To predefine the emerging shape, we first dripped liquid sugar on an ugly model; then we parametrically reinterpreted this morphology through scripting. Stacked to a depth of three to six meters, the glass was produced via an endless process of accumulation—through a kind of Duchampian "bachelor machine." Our objective was to make the machine work randomly, as an agent of indeterminism. The software algorithm integrated latitudes of indeterminacy, thereby generating a loss of causality and control—as a speculation on the deficit of design, in anticipation of shape, and for lack of *gestaltung*. First the glass stack swallowed the building; then it swallowed the courtyard, turning it into a glass quarry, colonizing boundaries and vitrifying the city. In this way, the FRAC became an anthropophagous animal: a wild anomaly, an agent of contamination, a virus for infiltrating the conservative mind of its French neighborhood.

To reduce the cost of the apparatus, we worked with the bottle-recycling department at Saint-Gobain, one of the major manufacturers of glass in France. We needed two million glass sticks from double-quantity bottles. First we proposed to use 10 percent of the region's twenty-thousand annual tons of recycled glass; second, we proposed a longitudinal construction process spread over thirty years, like the building of Antoni Gaudí's Sagrada Família in Barcelona, Spain. Thus the redesigned FRAC would not make an iconic statement; it would be a dynamic apparatus, where the machine becomes a vector of indeterminate intensities. It is a twelve-meter-high robot, able to fully disappear by hiding itself in the substances it aggregates. It is a massive, nontransparent, green blur with a reflection-refraction effect, like the bottom of a bottle.

Thus we proposed to deprogram the existing shape through a step-by-step process of mutation, which depended on the variable impermanency of inputs such as desires, curating, and programming. In this labyrinth, we introduced a PDA-like technology to help visitors determine their own location via a Global Positioning System (GPS) and radio-frequency identification (RFID). This device remedies the lack of control and can be used to navigate or escape trajectories and to find a restroom or get beamed up—"Scotty, to the exit." At the same time, it creates the possibility for random, self-curatorial movement, where you might confuse your own paranoia with the unreality of your perception. | **figs. 1–14**

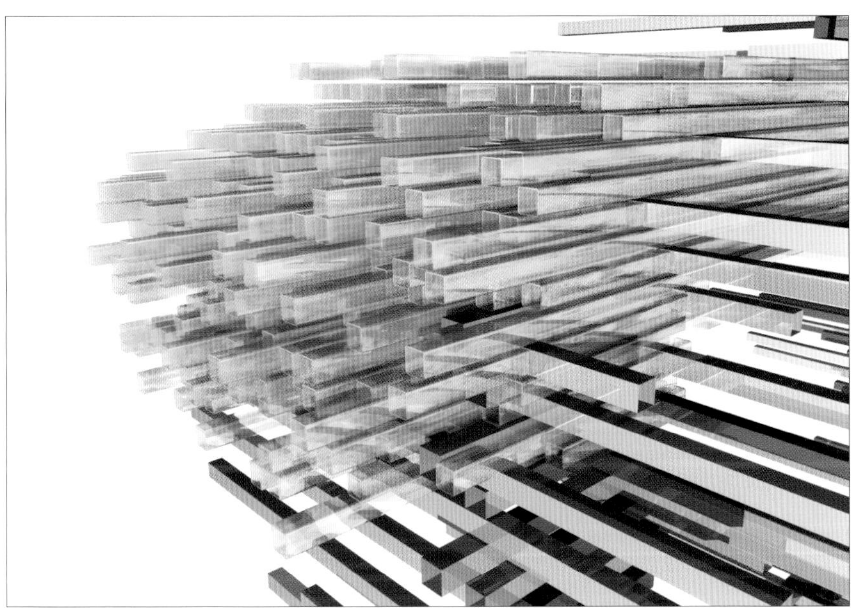

fig. 1 | Rendering of infrastructure, Fonds Regional d'Art Contemporain, Orléans, France

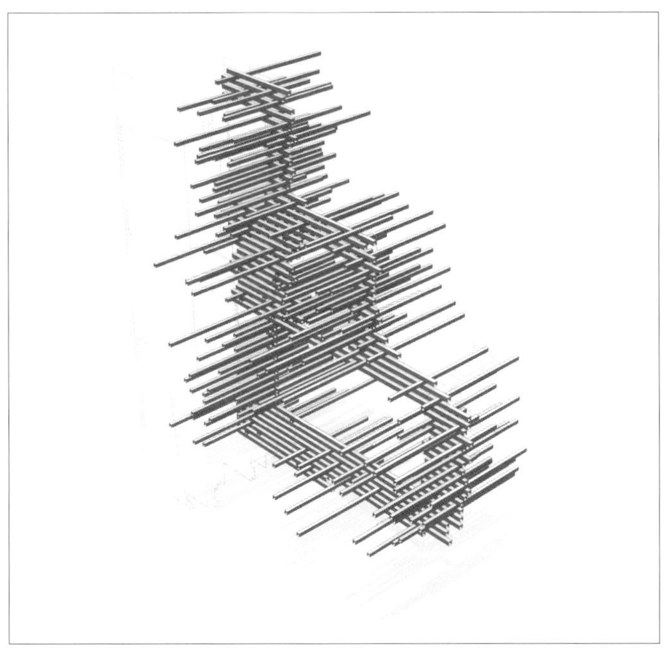

fig. 2 | Structural system

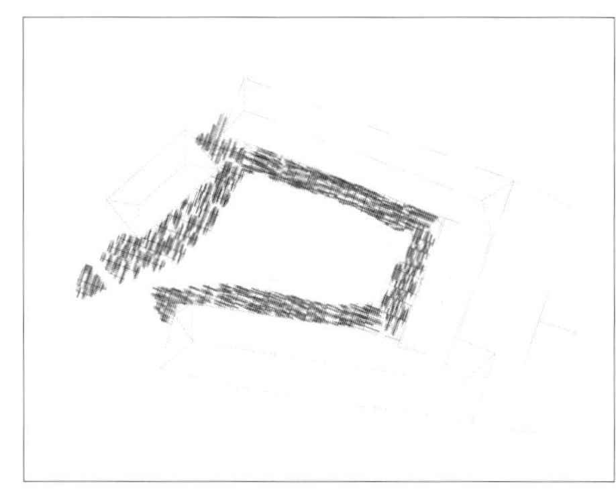

fig. 3 | Site plan

figs. 4 + 5 | Views of robot

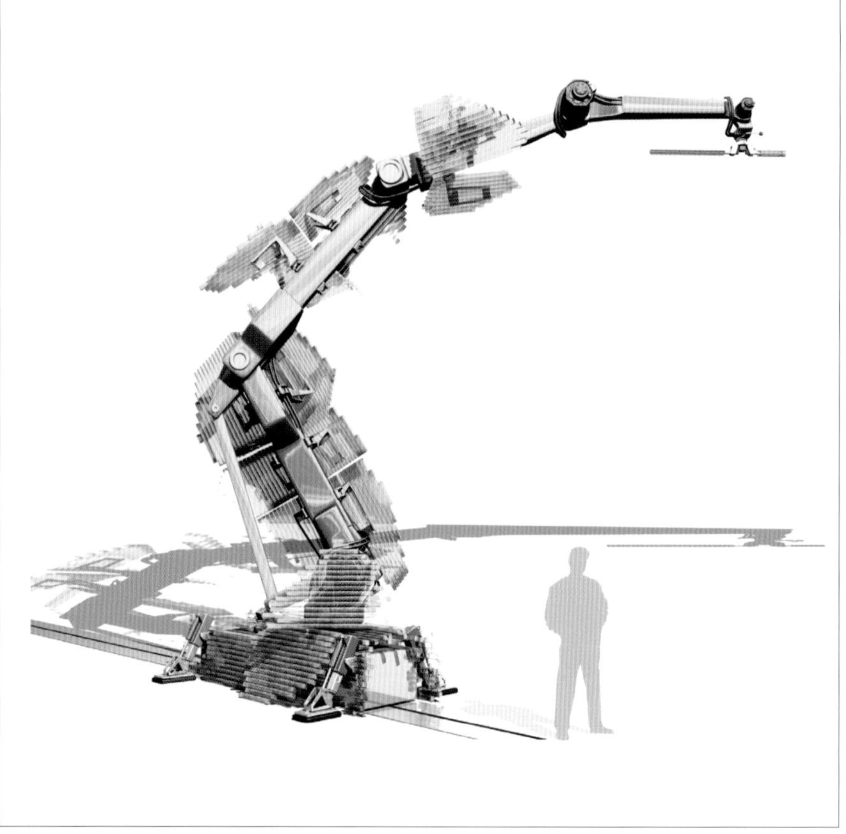

fig. 6 | View of robot with scale figure

fig. 7 | Recycling process

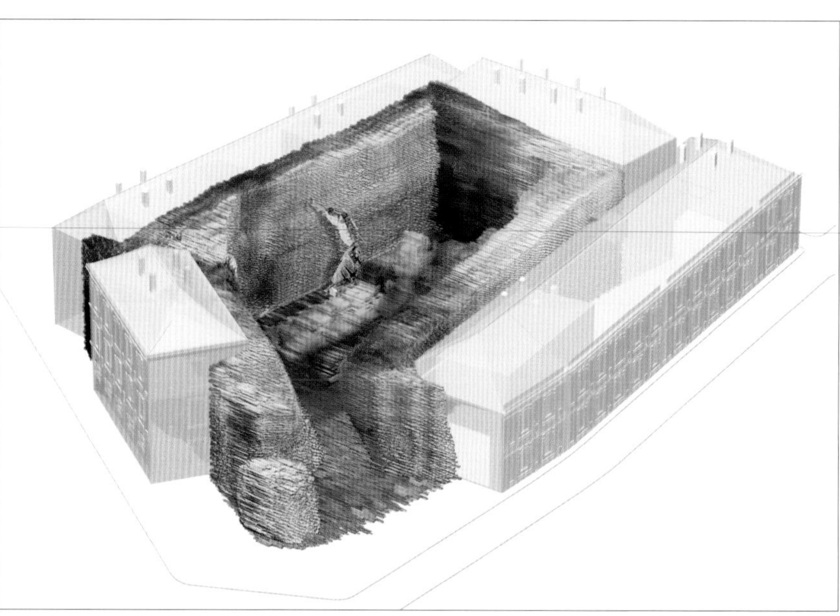

fig. 8 | Top view of bottle growth

fig. 9 | Rendering of robot in courtyard

fig. 10 | View from street

fig. 11 | Model test

fig. 12 | Model view

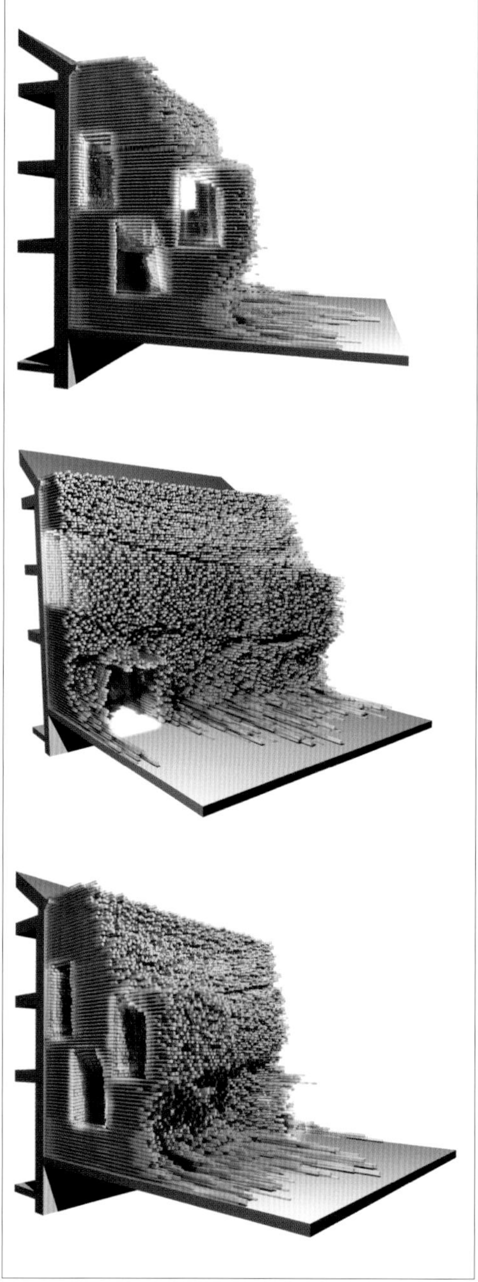

fig. 13 | Bottle aggregation

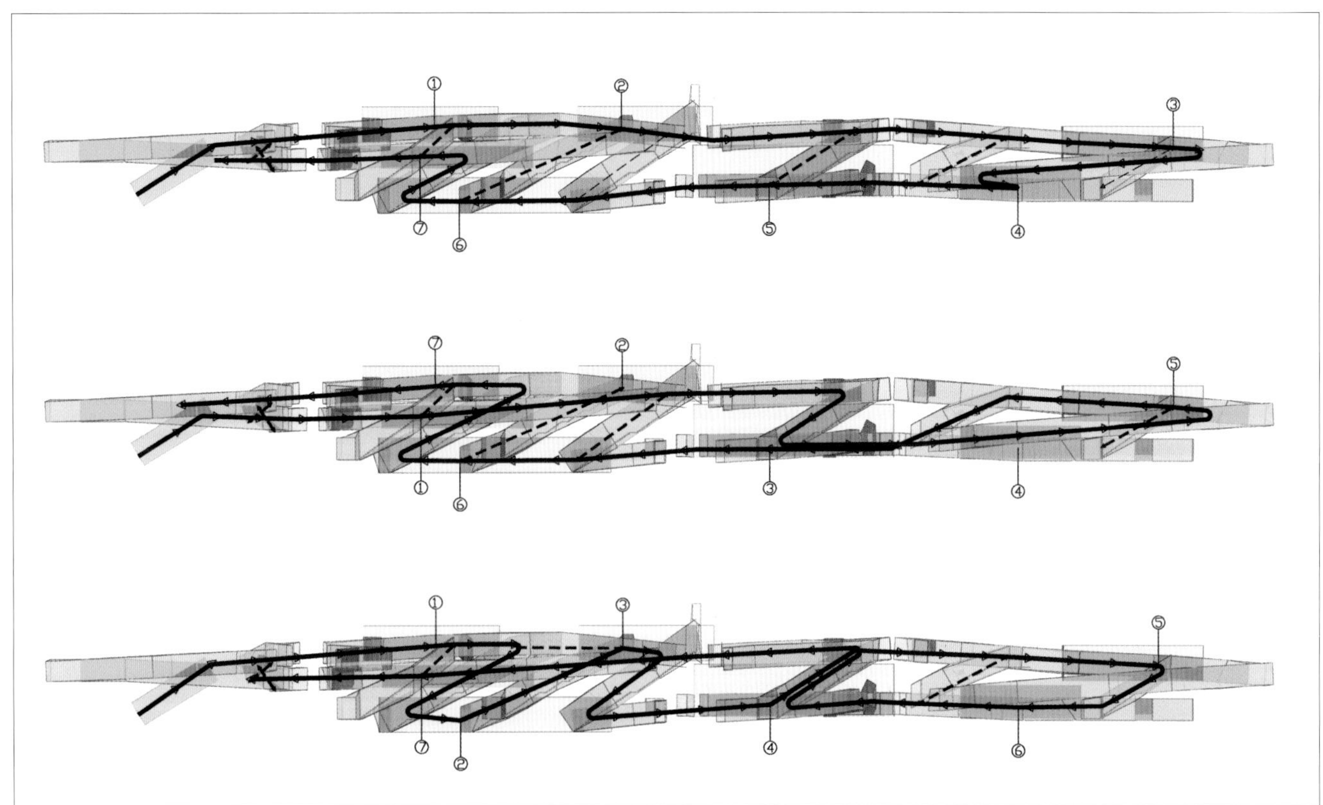

fig. 14 | Access routes

Phantom House: Sustaining the American Dream

Elizabeth Diller

Our studio has always been interested in the legacy of modernism and especially in the role glass has played. We look at the modernist project critically and generatively. The notion of democratized vision translates into broader research into visuality or the culture of vision. The brief for the Engineered Transparency conference asked, "In an era of ubiquitous and inexpensive global communications and increasingly expensive energy costs, what are the critical implications of glass in building in the next decade? Will energy issues force a major change in transparent architecture? Has the concept of transparency—so fully embedded in architectural theory and history—been dislocated? Has its genius moved out of architecture and into the mathematics of information transparency and its self-generated, self-navigated forms of media?" This formulation pits glass against electronic technologies in the most reductive way. I reject the notion that electronic media is replacing glass as the new transparency—a last gasp of twentieth-century rhetoric, already cliché—and assert that the modernist project is very much alive, and that contemporary materials, technologies, and environmental concerns are all part of its evolution.

"Phantom House: Sustaining the American Dream" was made in collaboration with Atelier Ten, at the invitation of the *New York Times*. It appeared in the *New York Times Magazine*'s eco-architecture issue in May 2007. The project—which makes a case for glass and sustainability as not mutually exclusive—comes out of a concern that while the current movement has focused public consciousness on the delicate and vulnerable state of the environment, green architecture has been hardening into a new orthodoxy calling for a lifestyle of guilt and sacrifice.

Green architecture is, in a sense, at odds with the American dream, which promises that a lifetime of hard work will be rewarded with prosperity and material comfort. This project asks whether we must accept a reversal of this promise to be good global citizens and whether it is realistic to base sustainable design, or at least a form of sustainable design characterized by asceticism, on a culture that thrives on excess. We believe that green architecture will only succeed by satisfying our quest for the good life while finding the means for paying for it.

Phantom House is a single-family home on an elevated two-acre lot overlooking a rapidly growing city in the southwestern United States. The house is a living, thinking organism, a sophisticated desert dweller that dynamically adapts to its harsh environment. It is a twin indoor/outdoor house with a physical component hovering over its phantom counterpart so that, function for function, these components mirror one another along a horizontal axis of shared services. The indoor living area floats over the external living area; wet functions stack one over the other, and this is also the case for dining, sleeping, and the rest of the house's components. The enclosed area represents only a modest footprint, yet a comparable amount of outdoor space is activated as usable living area. In the Phantom House, sustainability and pleasure converge. Glazing is plentiful, yet it is also responsive to heat gain. The pool provides refreshing respite for the body while being self-conserving. The environmental system responds to the microcomforts of its inhabitants, while maintaining overall reductions in energy and resource use.

There are four guiding principles for the house. First is redundancy as efficiency: the doubling of domestic functions allows use and location to be determined according to seasonal, daily, and hourly conditions, thus reducing the need for 24/7 climate control. Second is soft ownership: the private ownership model, which fosters obsolescence and waste, is replaced by a new green economy, connecting the home with larger economic and ecological systems in a production-consumption cycle. Third is comfort shadow: the environment is customized to the scale of the body, tracking its movements and anticipating its needs and preferences. And fourth is a feedback loop between body and house: the body and house are "aware" of one another; energy is salvaged from domestic activities and banked for other purposes.

This is a day in the life of Janis and Marley, the occupants of the Phantom House. They have been married for five years. They are childless and in their thirties. The children of aging hippies, they were named after counterculture icons. They are a professional couple: he's an engineer for a software development firm, and she's a consultant for an internet marketing company. The story is set in Phoenix, Arizona, on July 15, the hottest day of summer.

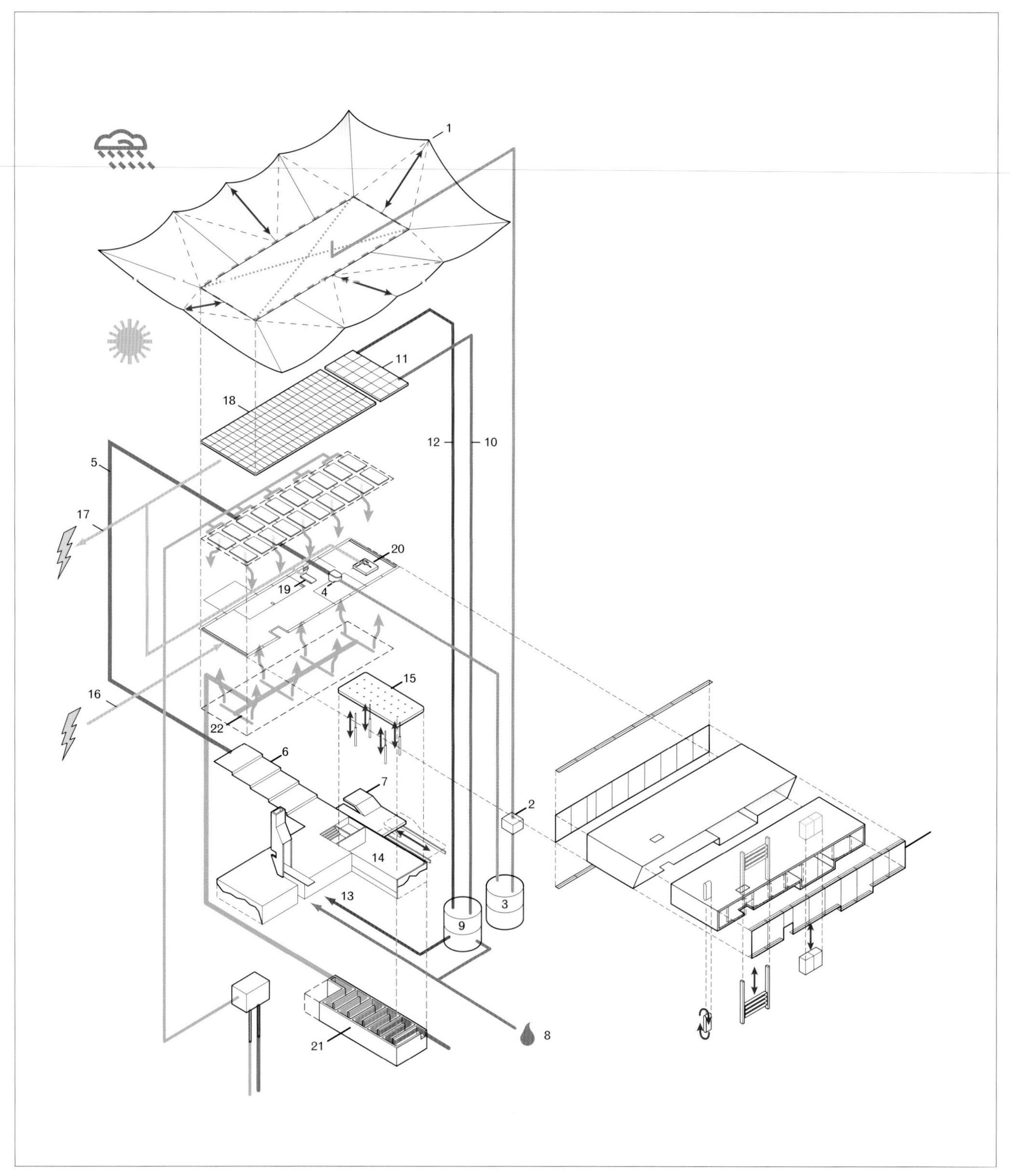
1
11
18
12
10
5
17
20
19
4
15
16
22
6
7
2
14
13
3
9
8
21

Key

1 | Ground-coupled heating and cooling uses the steady temperature of the earth (about 55 degrees) as a source of heat, sending the excess from the house back into the earth.

2 | OpaciView is a high-performance, double-layer, low-emissivity glass wall system. It's made up of a gasochromic outer layer with a porous film of tungsten oxide that lightens or darkens depending on the heat of the sun and whether anyone is home. An inner layer of liquid-crystal glass can be activated for privacy or used as a projection screen. A ventilated cavity between the layers is controlled by dampers that are opened during the day to remove heat buildup and closed at night for insulation.

3 | Rent-Your-Roof provides photovoltaic cells for rooftop surfaces. The cells are owned and operated by the local utility provider and leased to consumers. When energy generation exceeds domestic use, electricity is returned to the grid, so there's no need to store energy in an on-site battery. All development and operational risks are borne by the utility, and units can be easily upgraded.

4 | It takes thousands of trees to print a Sunday paper.

5 | RotoFridge is a highly insulated conveyor refrigerator that serves both the upper and lower kitchen areas. Food is displayed one-layer deep and can be delivered to and retrieved from a small opening. No energy is wasted hunting for items with the refrigerator door open.

6 | EasyShower uses a water-efficient showerhead that produces large water droplets without a wasteful waterfall.

7 | WorkOut Generator converts the energy residents expend exercising into 110-volt AC, which in turn feeds a storage battery in the house that can be hooked up to various devices.

8 | The chlorine-free EcoPool incorporates a water-bed lid on hydraulic legs to minimize evaporation when the pool is not in use and also create a lounge surface.

9 | LawnDrawer is a mobile turf surface that slides on a track and can be used as a front or back lawn, or for sunbathing or sitting in the shade the house, it acts as a reverse chimney: water sprayed on pads at the top evaporates, which cools the air and forces it down into the living space.

10 | CoolingBlanket uses presaturated, water-retaining fibers that allow body heat to escape through evaporation. It is stored in the RotoFridge.

11 | Fire-Ice-Place cools and warms ambient air. To cool the house, it acts as a reverse chimney: water sprayed on pads at the top evaporates, which cools the air and forces it down into the living space.

12 | DryerCloset is a convertible closet that shuttles among upper and lower open-air rest areas, where clothes can be line-dried.

13 | DomestiSleep regulates energy output. The house can be put into hibernation mode when no one is home.

14 | RapidCool uses a ventilation system supplied by a thermal mass labyrinth made of zigzagging corrugated concrete walls beneath the pool. Cool night air is stored within the labyrinth and quickly drawn into the house, as needed, via an under-floor system with the help of a fan. The cool end of the labyrinth doubles as a wine cellar.

15 | Home on the Go is an add-on service for cell phones and PDAs that communicates, through GPS, with the home's interactive control systems.

16 | Rent-a-Rug is one of several local leasing agencies that recycle home-flooring products, allowing the customer flexibility in flooring choices and the manufacturer to reuse or harvest materials, reducing demand on virgin resources.

17 | The house is built from recycled, remanufactured, and renewable materials. Wood species are selected from the nearest sustainably managed forest.

18 | RoofFunnel is a flexible roof membrane that is triggered by humidity and precipitation sensors, doubling the roof's surface-catchment areas. A cistern collects water that is funneled to the toilet and the irrigation system.

19 | EcoFlow Garden uses waste water filtered through natural treatment terraces; plant species are selected to thrive on available nutrients.

20 | Independent fixtures for each function ensure energy is used only as needed.

21 | NightFlush makes use of the desert's nocturnal drop in temperature to cool the labyrinth at night and the house during the day.

22 | PiezoSleeper incorporates transducers in the mattress to collect and convert excess human energy into electricity stored in the house's rechargeable battery.

Phantom House: Sustaining the American Dream

Elizabeth Diller

Timeline

05:00

Marley (M) is sound asleep. Janis (J) gets out of bed. She spent a restless night after their argument the previous evening. As M and J slept, a ground-coupled cooling system[1] adjusted the temperature of the bedroom to a comfortable 12 degrees lower than the air outside.

06:00

The alarm clock goes off. M hits the snooze button. In the bedroom, the OpaciView[2] facade is triggered by the alarm; it goes from opaque to 80 percent clear in three minutes. M begins to stir. The Rent-Your-Roof[3] system starts to harvest the energy the house needs for the day.

07:00

J is preparing breakfast in the upper kitchen. M passes through, kisses J on the forehead, and goes downstairs to retrieve the Sunday paper[4] and a bagel from the RotoFridge.[5] He spreads out at the lower dining table. J eats in the upper study while scanning the news online.

08:00

M hops into the EasyShower[6] then shaves and dresses for work. On his way out, he steps into the study to pick up his recharged handheld device. J abruptly clicks onto a homepage. She asks M to pick up fresh chilies and turmeric on his way home for tonight's dinner party.

09:00

J works at her laptop while nervously snacking from her top desk drawer.

10:00

Talking nonstop into a hands-free headset, J logs one hour on the WorkOut Generator:[7] twenty minutes each on the treadmill, stationary bicycle, and rowing machine. The glass in the gym dims to 30 percent transparency as the sun's intensity and J.'s body heat increase.

11:00

J cools off in the EcoPool.[8] Then she showers, extends the LawnDrawer,[9] and dries off in the sun. The pool returns to the evaporation-saver position. As the thermometer hits 99 degrees, J retreats to the shade and naps under a CoolingBlanket.[10]

12:00

With the temperature soaring, J goes upstairs, grabs an ice-cream bar and settles in front of the Fire-Ice-Place,[11] feverishly pounding the keys of her laptop with one hand.

13:00

J selects a sundress from the DryerCloset,[12] grabs her to-do list, unplugs her electric car, and drives to her first appointment. The DomestiSleep[13] system is triggered by the departure of the second car: glass facades are dimmed; the air-displacement system, RapidCool,[14] is shut down; and the cooling panels are set to 10 percent of their capacity.

14:00

The house hibernates.

15:00

As M's car comes within five miles of the house, the Home on the Go[15] unit triggers the DomestiSleep and RapidCool systems to awaken the house and begin to cool it down. M walks inside, throws off his jacket and prepares a martini. Realizing he has forgotten to pick up the chilies and turmeric, M leaves J a message and rushes out, overriding the DomestiSleep system.

16:00
J arrives in time to let in the Rent-a-Rug[16] installer, who is scheduled to exchange the living room carpet. She reads M's note as she sips his untouched martini. She changes into a swimsuit and brings her laptop to the lower living space.

17:00
The installer replaces an old rug with a recycled felt rug to cover the wood floor,[17] peering outside occasionally. J pulls off the CoolingBlanket and pretends to sleep. The glass transitions to 90 percent clear, as clouds hide the sun. The retractable RoofFunnel[18] senses rain and begins to deploy.

18:00
J plucks a few fresh tomatoes from the EcoFlow Garden[19] on her way upstairs and begins to prepare for dinner. Monsoon rain and winds bombard the house for 15 minutes; more than 6,500 gallons of water are collected.
M returns. He has forgotten the chilies.

19:00
J is agitated as she continues to cook. She changes into a new minidress, minutes before the guests arrive.
M retrieves several bottles of California red from the wine cellar, located in the RapidCool under the pool.

20:00
J shows their guests, Leonard and Casey, her new Paul McCarthy prints. M prepares the margaritas.

21:00
Dinner is served in the lower dining area. J apologizes for the blandness of the rasam, and a conversation ensues about travel in southern India.

22:00
The conversation turns from the Phoenix Suns to presidential candidates to cactus gardens.

23:00
After dessert, M and Casey take a dip.
J goes online in the upper study, then joins Leonard in front of the gas fire.

24:00
M dims the lights[20] and gives the house a NightFlush[21] to prepare for the next day and then climbs into the PiezoSleeper.[22]

Acknowledgments

Engineered Transparency began as an academic conference sponsored by the Graduate School of Architecture, Planning, and Preservation (GSAPP) in collaboration with the Fu Foundation School of Engineering and Applied Science at Columbia University and the Institute of Building Construction at the Technische Universität Dresden. The idea—for architecture and engineering schools to collaborate—was initiated by Mark Wigley, dean of the GSAPP; with Christian Meyer, chair of the Department of Civil Engineering; and Bernhard Weller, director of the Institute of Building Construction at Dresden. A partnership was formed with an interdisciplinary focus on glass. Initially, we examined the degree to which we could still, in fact, isolate glass in the broad context of building systems. We were questioning whether we could continue to refer to glass simply as glass. The fields of engineering and materials science were revealing new strains of what, historically, we had called glass architecture and engineering; this instigated a need for clarification on what constituted the state of the art in glass, today. It was not the glass itself, but its assembly in insulated glazing units (IGUs)—and the new processes of lamination and coatings, as well as the relationship between glazing and a building's structural, mechanical, and environmental systems—that were critical. These questions were not being asked in isolation; they were set deep within the minds of shared colleagues, and they were situated within contemporary projects constituting pre-existing collaborations between key engineers and architects. Engineered Transparency: Glass in Architecture and Structural Engineering explored these collaborations and placed the work in an academic context. The conference captured a moment when the professions of architecture and engineering—and the scholarship that surrounds and often propels them—were far more reflexive and intertwined than they had been since the early twentieth century. It was the right time to examine this shared work, in part because the work was revealing new directions.

Engineered Transparency, as a title, is a reflection of Robert Slutzky and Colin Rowe's canonical 1964 essay, "Transparency: Literal and Phenomenal." Yet it is meant to be absolutely current and direct. The transparency identified in new installations of glass architecture is thoroughly engineered, and this process was one that quite literally relied on a deep strain of analysis at the levels of material science, fabrication, and installation. The architects, engineers, and scholars who spoke at the conference and contributed to this book all mined this vein, and each was given a great deal of preliminary information on the overall organization and goals of the conference. Engineered Transparency did not intend to replace the early scholarship around transparency so much as to indicate a newly rich field of operations—between engineers, materials scientists, and architects—that was also increasingly transparent in how it exchanges information, as well as newly responsive and less distinct. This transparency was active both in building and as part of practice.

If we were to identify each person that gave shape to the conference, the list would be this book's table of contents. Almost everyone who participated stepped outside of their comfort zone. Those that took lead roles in shaping panels and exposing their longstanding work to new directions were Kenneth Frampton, Laurie Hawkinson, Reinhold Martin, Detlef Mertins, Joan Ockman, and Antoine Picon. Others generously allowed their work to be sited against new colleagues. Beatriz Colomina's conversation with Matthias Schuler, for example, was a highlight of the conference. Joan Ockman attempted to reframe environmental engineering against a history of glass architecture. Scott Marble took on translation of light (through glass) to energy. Roberto Bicchiarelli, Graham Dodd, Werner Sobek, and Guy Nordenson all engaged at the levels of art, political, and cultural history, forging a new level of communication with scholars and architects.

The conference benefited from the tremendous energy and intelligent work of Benjamin Prosky. The book was shaped with tremendous insight by my partner, Jeannie Kim, and our shared partners at Princeton Architectural Press, particularly Laurie Manfra and Jan Haux. The original graphic identity of the event was formed by Luke Bulman and his design firm, Thumb. Diana Darling and William Menking of the *Architect's Newspaper* were our media sponsors and helped situate the project's ambitions, early on. Jieun Yang was the conference's amazingly effective research assistant. The conference was accompanied by the exhibition, Through Glass, curated by Rosana Rubio-Hernandez, who also provided advice and insight on the conference structure. Special thanks also to Phillip Anzalone, Mehmet Bozatli, Anne Burt, Cory Clarke, Josh Draper, Lou Fernandez, John Ramahlo, Stephanie Salomon, Mark Taylor, and the GSAPP audiovisual crew, who ran the conference. Bernard Tschumi graciously provided a short documentary interview to discuss the GSAPP's technology program and courses. Special thanks also to Devon Ercolano Provan, director of the GSAPP Development Office; and Melissa Cowley Wolf of our Alumni Office. David Hinkle, associate dean, is at the center of any project at the GSAPP, and he helped guide this work. Eunjeong Seong helped shape the conference and book with a wealth of technical advice.

Engineered Transparency was generously supported by Oldcastle Glass, and in particular by Chief Executive Officer Edwin B. Hathaway. With his associates, Susan Trimble and Heather Hatch, we were able to reach a far wider professional audience and broaden the scope of the school's engagement with industry. This book and the accompanying documentary film were made possible by Oldcastle Glass, and their partnership creates a new engagement with industry that our professions and schools will increasingly rely on.

As a long-term project, the GSAPP has solidified the book and conference as a multiyear, ongoing project: the Columbia Conference on Architecture, Engineering, and Materials. The series will focus on a new material each year. Mark Wigley, dean of the GSAPP, has been tremendously inventive in opening the school to new opportunities and, in particular, in linking us to our colleagues. The conference and this book would not have been possible without his drive and momentum.

—Michael Bell

This book would not have been possible without the generosity of Oldcastle Glass and the support of Dean Mark Wigley at the Graduate School of Architecture, Planning, and Preservation at Columbia University. Thanks also to Gavin Browning for his editorial assistance, and Sharon Kim for her expert image editing. I would also like to sincerely thank Benjamin Prosky for his enthusiastic support during all phases of decision making and production. Thanks are also due to each contributor to this volume, with the acknowledgment that they met impossible deadlines and never complained about our near constant communiqués. Warmest thanks to my co-conspirator, Michael Bell, for his careful editorial eye and his wonderful ability to turn even the slightest conversation about this project into a larger discussion about the profession and discipline of architecture. Lastly, at Princeton Architectural Press, we are indebted to Laurie Manfra for her editorial acuity, to Nancy Eklund Later for inquiring about this project before we had even thought about it, and to Jan Haux for the elegant design of the book and his immediate understanding of its challenges.

—Jeannie Kim

Afterword

This book is a fairly unique experiment. It brings together a group of architects and engineers to discuss a topic of common interest: glass. Although it has been used for centuries, glass in architecture has changed dramatically in recent years. For the engineering community, the increasing use of glass as a structural material poses many challenges. Among them, ductility is one of the most fundamental requirements of modern structural engineering. If structures fail, they should do so in a ductile mode and with plenty of advance warning. For example, some time ago, the city of Chicago endured a severe winter, during which more than one thousand structures collapsed under the heavy loads of snow, many of them simple structures such as warehouses and garages. Not a single human life was lost, illustrating that the fundamental objective of structural engineering has always been to save lives.

As a brittle material with a tendency to fail suddenly and without inelastic deformations or any sign of impending failure, glass appears to be the least ideal option for a structural material. The disparity between its actual and desirable behaviors is the primary challenge that engineers face.

The various contributions collected in this volume—from a stellar group of engineers and architects—may serve as a reminder that the gap between architecture and engineering did not always exist. Previously, there was only one professional: the master builder who acted as both architect and engineer. The rise of modern science and technology forced an unfortunate specialization, and both professions continue to suffer the consequences. It is quite possible, however, that civil engineers, often known as bridge builders, can help fill this gap. What better way to begin such an endeavor than through this book.

—Christian Meyer, Chair and Professor, Fu Foundation School of Engineering and Applied Science, Department of Civil Engineering and Engineering Mechanics, Columbia University

Contributors

Michelle Addington
An associate professor at Yale School of Architecture, Michelle Addington also taught at Harvard University's Graduate School of Design for ten years and prior to that at Temple University and Philadelphia University. Her background includes work at the NASA Goddard Space Flight Center, where she developed structural data for composite materials and designed components for an unmanned spacecraft. She conducts research on discrete systems and technology transfer and serves as an adviser on energy and sustainability for many organizations, including the U.S. Department of Energy and the American Institute of Architects. Her writings on energy, environmental systems, lighting, and materials have appeared in many books and journals; she is the coauthor of *Smart Materials and Technologies in Architecture* (Architectural Press, 2004).

Michael Bell
Michael Bell is a professor at Columbia University's Graduate School of Architecture, Planning, and Preservation, where he directs the core design studios. He is the founder of Michael Bell Architecture, based in New York City, and has received four Progressive Architecture Awards. He has authored several books published by the Monacelli Press, including *16 Houses: Designing the Public's Private House* (2000); *Michael Bell: Space Replaces Us; Essays and Projects on the City* (2004); and he coauthored *Slow Space* (2000). He has taught at the University of California, Berkeley; Rice University; and Harvard University's Graduate School of Design. In 2000, he led a team of architects providing research, planning, and design for 2,100 units of housing on a 100-acre parcel of oceanfront land owned by the City of New York. Bell also founded 16 Houses, a low-income housing design program in Houston, Texas.

Albrecht Burmeister
Since 1988, Albrecht Burmeister has been a partner and managing director of Delta-X GmbH, an engineering firm based in Stuttgart, Germany, specializing in lightweight steel structures, structural glazing, structural dynamics, and the finite element method (FEM) in the engineering design process. He is also on the engineering faculty of the University of Applied Sciences Rosenheim. Burmeister is a member of the standardization committee that oversees design and application regulations for the use of glass in buildings and civil engineering projects, and he directs the working group, Bomb Blast-Resistant Design (Fachverband Konstruktiver Glasbau).

James Carpenter
A leading architect in the development of new and emerging glass and material technologies, James Carpenter heads James Carpenter Design Associates, which has advanced architectural design by focusing on the integration of natural light into the structure and design of large buildings. The firm specializes in enclosure systems, glass structures, skylights, and building skins for major projects, which have included World Trade Center Tower 7, the Time Warner Jazz at Lincoln Center, and the new MTA Transit Center at Fulton Street, all in New York City, as well as Gucci Tokyo.

Beatriz Colomina
A professor at Princeton University School of Architecture and the founding director of the Program in Media and Modernity, Beatriz Colomina is the author of *Domesticity at War* (MIT Press, 2007); *Doble exposición: Arquitectura a través del arte* (Akal, 2006); and *Privacy and Publicity: Modern Architecture as Mass Media* (MIT Press, 1994); the editor of *Architecture Production* (Princeton

Architectural Press, 1988); and *Sexuality and Space* (Princeton Architectural Press, 1992); and coauthor of *Cold War Hot Houses: Inventing Postwar Culture from Cockpit to Playboy* (Princeton Architectural Press, 2004). Colomina is currently working on her next research project, "X-Ray Architecture: Illness as Metaphor."

Elizabeth Diller

Architect Elizabeth Diller is a principal in the collaborative design studio of Diller Scofidio + Renfro, based in New York City. Among the firm's current projects are the Juilliard School, Alice Tully Hall, and the School of American Ballet, for Lincoln Center; a park situated on the High Line, an obsolete railway running through the Chelsea neighborhood; and the Kopp Townhouse, a private residence in the Nolita neighborhood of New York City. Diller Scofidio + Renfro's new building for the Institute of Contemporary Art (ICA), in Boston, opened in December 2006.

Graham Dodd

As a mechanical and facade engineer at Arup, based in London, Graham Dodd specializes in the design, manufacture, and construction of structural glass and facade systems. He has led teams of facade engineers involved in all aspects of glazing design and contracting for projects in Europe, Asia, and North America. His expertise has developed the firm's knowledge of the structural use of glass, and Dodd has contributed his specialist skills to numerous innovative projects for Arup. His early experience with varied industries has resulted in knowledge of a wide range of materials, manufacturing, and product design processes. Dodd has worked in the field of glass structures and design since 1988.

Miguel Jaenicke Fontao

Miguel Jaenicke Fontao is a principal at FAM Arquitectura y Urbanismo S.L., based in Madrid, Spain. The studio was established in 2002 after winning a series of prizes that allowed for the creation of an office. While the office has been characterized by singular projects, it has also been engaged in the construction of small-scale residences in distinct parts of Spain, as well as unique projects that straddle the disciplines of architecture, urban design, and planning.

Kenneth Frampton

The Ware Professor of Architecture at the Graduate School of Architecture, Planning, and Preservation at Columbia University, Kenneth Frampton trained as an architect at the Architectural Association School of Architecture, in London, and has worked as an architect and architectural historian and critic in England, Israel, and the United States. He is the author of numerous distinguished books, including: *Modern Architecture: a Critical History* (Thames and Hudson, 1980); *Modern Architecture and the Critical Present* (St. Martin's Press, 1982); *Studies in Tectonic Culture: the Poetics of Construction in Nineteenth and Twentieth Century Architecture* (MIT Press, 1995); *American Masterworks: Houses of the Twentieth and Twenty-First Centuries* (Rizzoli, 1995); *Le Corbusier: Architect of the Twentieth Century* (Harry N. Abrams, 2002); and *Labor, Work and Architecture: Critical Essays, 1968–1988* (Rizzoli, 1995). An updated and expanded fourth edition of *Modern Architecture: A Critical History,* released in 2007.

Laurie Hawkinson

Laurie Hawkinson is a partner of Smith-Miller + Hawkinson Architects, a New York City–based architecture and urban planning firm. The firm's projects include the expansion of the Corning

Museum of Glass, in Corning, New York; the Wall Street Ferry Terminal at Pier 11 in New York City; and the outdoor cinema and amphitheater at the North Carolina Museum of Art, in Raleigh. The firm was a finalist for the Olympic Village Design Competition sponsored by the NYC2012 Olympic Committee. Its current projects include the U.S. Land Port of Entry at Champlain and at Massena, both in New York, for the General Services Administration. Hawkinson is a professor at Columbia University's Graduate School of Architecture, Planning, and Preservation.

Robert Heintges
Robert Heintges is the principal of Heintges & Associates, an international consulting firm that provides a wide range of services to architects and building owners for the design and implementation of curtain wall, cladding, and specialty glazing. Since its inception in 1989, the firm has consulted on more than thirty-million square feet of facades throughout the world, including many high-profile and award-winning projects. Heintges is an adjunct professor at the Graduate School of Architecture, Planning, and Preservation at Columbia University, where he has taught since 1990. He currently teaches an advanced seminar and technical studio on curtain walls.

Steven Holl
Steven Holl has realized cultural, civic, university, and residential projects in the United States and internationally. In 1976, he founded Steven Holl Architects, which currently operates offices in New York and Beijing. The firm has been recognized around the world with numerous awards and accolades, and its work has been widely published and exhibited. In June 2007, Steven Holl Architects opened the highly acclaimed Nelson-Atkins Museum of Art, in Kansas City, Missouri. Currently under construction are Linked Hybrid, a mixed-use complex in Beijing, China; the Nanjing Museum of Art and Architecture, in Nanjing, China; the Vanke Center, in Shenzhen, China; the Herning Center of Arts, in Herning, Denmark; and facilities for New York University's Department of Philosophy, in New York City. An accomplished author, he is also a professor at Columbia University's Graduate School of Architecture, Planning, and Preservation.

Ulrich Knaack
Ulrich Knaack completed his architecture studies at Rheinisch-Westfaelische Technische Hochschule at Aachen University, in Germany. His thesis was awarded the 1998 Friedrich Wilhelm Prize. He went on to lecture in structural design and glass construction at the university. In 2000, he joined the architectural firm RKW Architektur und Städtebau, based in Düsseldorf, where he was responsible for the design and planning of numerous large scale, fast-track projects. He has taught at the University of Applied Sciences, in Detmold, Germany. In 2005, he was appointed professor of structural design at the School of Architecture/TU (Technical University) Delft. Knaack's main areas of focus and research are facades, new materials, and industrial building methods.

Scott Marble
Scott Marble is a founding partner of Marble Fairbanks, based in in New York City, and an adjunct assistant professor at Columbia University's Graduate School of Architecture, Planning, and Preservation, where he directs the Avery Digital Fabrication Lab. The work of Marble Fairbanks has been published and exhibited around the world and is in the permanent collection of The Museum of Modern Art, in New York; and the Nara Prefectural Museum, in Nara, Japan. The firm has won numerous AIA Design Awards, American Architecture Awards, a Progressive

Architecture Award, and an I.D. Magazine Award. *Marble Fairbanks: Bootstrapping*, featuring recent projects and critical essays on the firm's work, was published in 2006 by the University of Michigan Press.

Reinhold Martin

Reinhold Martin is an associate professor at Columbia University's Graduate School of Architecture, Planning, and Preservation, where he directs the PhD program in architecture and the MS program in advanced architectural design. He is a founding coeditor of the journal *Grey Room*; a partner in the firm of Martin/Baxi Architects, in New York City; and has published widely on the history and theory of modern and contemporary architecture. Martin is the author of *The Organizational Complex: Architecture, Media, and Corporate Space* (MIT Press, 2003) and the coauthor of *Entropia* (Black Dog, 2001) and *Multi-National City: Architectural Itineraries* (Actar, 2007). He is currently working on a book that re-theorizes postmodernism.

Detlef Mertins

Detlef Mertins is a professor and chair of the Department of Architecture at the University of Pennsylvania. From 1991 to 2003, he taught at the University of Toronto, where he held a Canada Research Chair and directed the graduate program. He has authored numerous books, including: *Mies in America* (Canadian Centre for Architecture, 2001); *Mies in Berlin* (Museum of Modern Art, 2001); and the English edition of Walter Curt Behrendt's *The Victory of the New Building Style* (Getty Trust Publications, 2000); and he is a contributing author of *Zaha Hadid* (Guggenheim Museum, 2006). His publications related to glass and transparency include *The Presence of Mies* (Princeton Architectural Press, 1994); "Transparencies Yet to Come: Sigfried Giedion and the Prehistory of Architectural Modernity," his PhD dissertation; "The Enticing and Threatening Face of Prehistory: Walter Benjamin and the Utopia of Glass," published in *Assemblage* 29 (1996); "Walter Benjamin and the Tectonic Unconscious," published in *ANY* 14 (1996); and "Transparency: Autonomy and Relationality," published in *AA Files* 32 (1997).

Christian Meyer

Christian Meyer is a professor of civil engineering at Columbia University. His areas of research include analysis and design of concrete structures, concrete material science and technology, structural engineering, earthquake engineering and structural dynamics, and computer analysis of structures. Meyer has consulted for numerous organizations, including the California Department of Transportation; Stone and Webster Engineering Corporation, in Boston; Weidlinger Associates, in New York; Auton Computing Corporation, in Edison, New Jersey; the U.S. Army Armament Research and Development Command, in Dover, New Jersey; the New York City Department of Environmental Protection; and the MTA Bridges and Tunnels in New York City. Meyer received a Vordiplom from the Technische Universität Berlin, and MS and PhD degrees from the University of California, Berkeley. He is a registered professional engineer in Massachusetts, New Jersey, and New York.

Guy Nordenson

Guy Nordenson is a structural engineer and professor of structural engineering at Princeton University School of Architecture, where he is also a faculty associate at the University Center for Human Values. After studying at MIT and the University of California, Berkeley, he began his career in 1976 as a draftsman in the joint studio of R. Buckminster Fuller and Isamu Noguchi, in Long Island City. Nordenson has worked as a structural engineer in San Francisco and New York.

He established the New York office of Ove Arup & Partners in 1987, where he was director for ten years. In 1997, he began his own practice, Guy Nordenson and Associates Structural Engineers. In 2003, he was the first recipient of the American Academy of Arts and Letters' Academy Award in architecture for contributions by a nonarchitect. In 2006, Mayor Michael Bloomberg and the New York City Council appointed him Commissioner of the New York City Art Commission; he is the first engineer to be appointed to the Art Commission since it establishment in 1898.

H. Scott Norville

A registered professional engineer in the state of Texas, H. Scott Norville serves as professor and chair in the Department of Civil Engineering at Texas Tech University, where he has been teaching since 1981. In 1974, he received his BS degree in civil engineering from the University of Toledo, in Ohio; he received his MS and PhD degrees from Purdue University in 1976 and 1981, respectively. Shortly after arriving at Texas Tech, he began conducting research on the strength of architectural glass and its behavior under extreme loadings. In conjunction with his research, he spearheaded the use of rational approaches in determining reasonable design load-resistance values for laminated architectural glass. Norville currently serves as cochair of the ASTM Task Group E06.51.13 on glass strength, chair of ASTM Task Group F12.15 on blast-resistant glazing, and as a member of several other committees related to glass design.

Joan Ockman

Joan Ockman is the director of the Temple Hoyne Buell Center for the Study of American Architecture at Columbia University's Graduate School of Architecture, Planning, and Preservation, where she has taught architectural history, theory, and design since 1985. This year, she also held guest teaching appointments at the Berlage Institute, in Rotterdam, where she taught a master class as part of the Rotterdam Biennale; and the State University of New York, Buffalo, where she was the Clarkson Visiting Chair. Among the publications she has edited, her award-winning book *Architecture Culture 1943–1968: A Documentary Anthology,* originally published by Rizzoli in 1993, is in its fourth edition. More recently, she coauthored *Architourism: Authentic, Exotic, Escapist, Spectacular* (Prestel Publishing, 2005). In 2003, she was honored by the American Institute of Architects for distinguished achievement. She holds a professional degree in architecture from the Cooper Union School of Architecture, and she has worked in the architectural offices of Richard Meier and Partners and Eisenman Architects.

Toshihiro Oki

Toshihiro Oki is a licensed architect who worked in New York City for seven years before joining the firm SANAA, in Tokyo, Japan, in 2003. Currently based in New York, he oversaw the completion of the Glass Pavilion at the Toledo Museum of Art in 2006 and the New Museum of Contemporary Art in New York in 2007. Oki received a BArch degree from Carnegie Mellon University.

Antoine Picon

Antoine Picon is a professor of the history of architecture and technology at Harvard University's Graduate School of Design, where he also serves as director of doctoral programs. He has published extensively on the relationships between architecture, urban design, science, and technology, with a special focus on construction history and theory. Among his publications, he is the author of the English translation of *French Architects and Engineers in the Age of the Enlightenment* (Cambridge University Press, 1992); *Claude Perrault (1613–1688) ou la curiosité d'un classique*

(Picard, 1988); *L'Invention de l'ingénieur moderne* (Presses de l'Ecole Nationale des Ponts et Chaussées,1992); *La ville territoire des cyborgs* (Editions de l'imprimeur, 1998); and *Les Saint-Simoniens: Raison, Imaginaire et Utopie* (Belin, 2003). He recently completed a monograph on the work of architect and engineer Marc Mimram.

Nina Rappaport

Nina Rappaport is an architectural critic, curator, and educator. She is the publications director at Yale School of Architecture and editor of the biannual publication *Constructs*, as well as a series of books on studio work at Yale. She is the author of *Support and Resist: Structural Engineers and Design Innovation* (Monacelli Press, 2007). She has contributed articles and essays to *Architecture, Architectural Record, Praxis, Future Anterior*, and *Tec21*. She has taught seminars on the postindustrial factory and on innovative engineers at City College and Yale. She is currently an adjunct professor at Parsons School of Design. She was a Design Trust for Public Space Fellow and coauthor of *Long Island City: Connecting the Arts* (Episode Books, 2006).

Susanne Rexroth

Prior to training in architecture, Susanne Rexroth completed MA studies in German literature, history, and European ethnicity at Albert-Ludwigs-Universität Freiburg, in Germany. After receiving an architecture degree from the Technische Universität Berlin, Rexroth worked as an architect in the planning offices of Löhnert & Ludewig and Langeheinecke & Claussen, both in Berlin. She served as a researcher in the School of Architecture and Design at the Universität der Künste, in Berlin, where she also earned a doctorate for her work on the design potential of solar panels, with a focus on historic buildings. She currently teaches at the Institute of Building Construction, Technische Universität Dresden.

Thomas J. Richardson

Thomas J. Richardson earned a BS degree in chemical physics at Michigan State University and a PhD in inorganic chemistry at the University of California, Berkeley. He leads a materials research team for the Windows and Daylighting Group, Building Technologies, in the Department of Environmental Energy Technologies Division at Lawrence Berkeley National Laboratory, at the University of California, Berkeley. He heads a group of chemists developing lithium batteries for the U.S. Department of Energy's Batteries for Advanced Transportation Technologies (BATT) program, and he is also pursuing lightweight hydrogen storage solutions for fuel cell cars. His work in the field of electrochromic windows won an R&D 100 Award in 2004.

François Roche

François Roche is a licensed architect (DPLG) in France. In 1989, he founded R&Sie(n) with Stéphanie Lavaux and Jean Navarro, based in Paris. The organic, oppositional architectural projects of the firm explore the bond between building, context, and human relations. R&Sie(n) considers architectural identity to be an unstable concept, defined through temporary forms in which the vegetal and biological combine into a dynamic element. The firm is currently undertaking a critical experiment with new warping technologies to prompt architectural scenarios of cartographic distortion, substitution, and genetic territorial mutations. He is currently a visiting assistant professor at Columbia University's Graduate School of Architecture, Planning, and Preservation, where he teaches an advanced studio.

Stefan Röschert

Born in Geneva, Stefan Röschert worked with Ateliers Jean Nouvel, in Paris, and Skidmore, Owings & Merrill, in New York, before joining the architectural firm Diller Scofidio + Renfro. He has worked extensively as a brand strategist, consultant, and designer for several New York- and Paris-based companies. In 1999, he founded his own firm, urbanautics, in Berlin (with subsequent offices in Tokyo and New York), conceived with a broad focus on private clients in architecture, consulting, and design, as well as on European competitions and theory. Röschert received his Diplom-Ingenieur in architecture with distinction from the Technische Universität Berlin. He earned his MS degree in architecture at Columbia University's Graduate School of Architecture, Planning, and Preservation in 2001.

Jens Schneider

Jens Schneider is a structural engineering consultant at Goldschmidt Fischer und Partner, in Heusenstamm, Germany. He was previously an engineering consultant at Schlaich Bergermann und Partner in Stuttgart, Germany, specializing in glass structures; and a scientific assistant at Darmstadt University of Technology, Institute for Structural Analysis, in the Department of Civil Engineering. He holds a PhD in structural engineering from Darmstadt University of Technology and is the author of more than 30 publications on glass. He is a professor of engineering at the University of Applied Sciences, in Frankfurt, Germany, where he has lectured on steel structures at the Institute for Structural Engineering and Structural Mechanics.

Matthias Schuler

Matthias Schuler is a managing director of Transsolar Energietechnik, in Stuttgart, Germany. Trained as a mechanical engineer at the University of Stuttgart, he worked as a scientific assistant at the university, where he participated in international research projects on low-energy commercial buildings. Based on this work, he founded the company Transsolar, a climate-engineering consulting firm, in 1992. The company's aim is to ensure that buildings achieve the highest possible level of comfort at the lowest possible environmental impact. The firm has offices in Stuttgart, Munich, and New York. Schuler has worked on national and international projects with architects such as Kazuyo Sejima, Frank O. Gehry, Steven Holl, Ben van Berkel, and Helmut Jahn.

Kazuyo Sejima

In 1995, Kazuyo Sejima founded the architectural firm SANAA, with Ryue Nishizawa, in Tokyo, Japan. Sejima holds an MArch degree from Japan Women's University and worked for Toyo Ito & Associates. Among SANAA's recently completed projects are the theater for the Almere Cultural Arts Center, in the Netherlands; the Glass Pavilion at the Toledo Museum of Art, in Ohio; the Zollverein School of Management and Design, in Essen, Germany; the Novartis Campus Building, in Basel, Switzerland; the Naoshima Ferry Terminal, in Japan; and the New Museum of Contemporary Art, in New York. Her current projects include the Louvre-Lens project, in Lens, France; the EPFL Rolex Learning Center, in Lausanne, Switzerland; the Vitra Factory Building, in Weil am Rhein, Germany; a house for the China International Practical Exhibition of Architecture, in Nanjing, China; and the expansion of the Institut Valencià d'Art Modern (IVAM), in Spain.

Robert Smilowitz

Robert Smilowitz is a principal in the Applied Sciences Division of Weidlinger Associates, based in New York. He is also an adjunct professor of engineering at Cooper Union, in New York. He earned a PhD degree from the University of Illinois at Champaign-Urbana. Smilowitz has more than thirty years of experience participating in protective design and vulnerability studies of numerous federal courthouses, federal office buildings, embassy structures, airline terminals, and commercial properties. He has participated in the explosive testing of full-scale curtain-wall systems, and he is a principal developer of analysis software for evaluating curtain-wall response to an explosive terrorist threat. He is a General Services Administration National Peer Professional and a registered professional engineer in New York and California.

Werner Sobek
Trained as an architect and structural engineer, Werner Sobek has been a professor at the University of Stuttgart, in Germany, since 1995. He has been the head of the university's Institute for Lightweight Structures and Conceptual Design since 2000, succeeding Frei Otto. He is also the founder of Werner Sobek Engineering and Design, one of the leading engineering consultancies worldwide. The firm, established in 1992, currently has offices in Stuttgart, Frankfurt, Moscow, and New York. Sobek holds a PhD in structural engineering from the University of Stuttgart and previously worked at Schlaich Bergermann und Partner, in Stuttgart. In 2004, his work was the subject of the exhibition, Show Me the Future, held at the Pinakothek der Moderne, in Munich.

Silke Tasche
Silke Tasche received her diploma in structural engineering from the Technische Universität Dresden, where she specialized in building construction. As a scientific assistant, she led a research project on adhesive bonding in glass construction. Silke has authored numerous relevant papers on glass engineering and adhesive bonding. She is currently a senior researcher at the Institute of Building Construction, Technische Universität Dresden.

Richard L. Tomasetti
Richard Tomasetti is chairman of Thornton Tomasetti, an international engineering firm that has provided structural engineering for the world's two tallest buildings: the Petronas Towers, in Kuala Lumpur; and Taipei 101, in Taiwan. Based in New York, his firm recently completed the New York Times Building in New York City. Many of the firm's projects include innovative uses of glass for aquariums, winter gardens, atriums, curtain walls, and protective design. Among his numerous honors and awards are election to the National Academy of Engineering, the 2006 AIA NY Chapter Award, and the New York Association of Consulting Engineers' 2002 Engineer of the Year Award. Tomasetti is an adjunct professor in the departments of Civil Engineering and Engineering Mechanics at Columbia University and New York University.

Stefan Unnewehr
Stefan Unnewehr studied architecture at the Rheinisch-Westfaelische Technische Hochschule at Aachen University. During his studies, he developed an interest in structural design and building construction. Having received several awards and recognitions, he was hired by Foster + Partners in London, where he worked on a number of significant building projects. He became a registered Architect in 2007 and currently forms part of an interdisciplinary team of scientists researching innovative glass connections.

Bernhard Weller

Bernhard Weller is a professor of civil engineering and director of the Institute of Building Construction at the Technische Universität Dresden, in Germany. With expertise in the design, testing, and use of glass, his research focuses on the appropriate material design of glass and glass bonding. Weller studied civil engineering at Rheinisch-Westfaelische Technische Hochschule at Aachen University, in Germany, and continued there as a scientific assistant at the Institute of Concrete Structures. Previously, he worked as an engineering consultant, with an emphasis on structural design, after which he was appointed professor of building construction at the Technische Universität Dresden.

Mark Wigley

Since 2004, Mark Wigley has served as dean of Columbia University's Graduate School of Architecture, Planning, and Preservation. Prior to joining Columbia, in 2000, as director of advanced studios, Wigley taught for ten years at Princeton University School of Architecture. He received both his BArch and PhD degrees from the University of Auckland, in New Zealand. He has served as guest curator for exhibitions at the Museum of Modern Art, in New York; the Drawing Center, in New York; the Canadian Centre for Architecture, in Montreal; and the Witte de With Center for Contemporary Art, in Rotterdam. An accomplished scholar and design teacher, he has written extensively on architectural theory and practice. He is the author of *The Architecture of Deconstruction: Derrida's Haunt* (MIT Press, 1995); *White Walls, Designer Dresses: The Fashioning of Modern Architecture* (MIT Press, 1996); and *Constant's New Babylon: The Hyper-Architecture of Desire* (Uitgeverij 010, 1998). In addition to publishing numerous essays on art and architecture, he coedited *The Activist Drawing: Situationist Architectures From Constant's New Babylon to Beyond* (MIT Press, 2001) and is one of the founding editors of *Volume*, a quarterly magazine published by Columbia University's Graduate School of Architecture, Planning, and Preservation with Archis and OMA*AMO.

Credits

Project credits

7 World Trade Center

Architect: Skidmore, Owings & Merrill
Civil and Transportation Engineer: Philip Habib & Associates
Client: Silverstein Properties
Curtain Wall Design: James Carpenter Design Associates
Daylight Consultant: Carpenter/Norris Consulting
Energy Analysis: Transsolar
Geotechnical Engineer: Mueser Rutledge Consulting Engineers
MEP Engineer: Jaros Baum & Bolles
Structural Engineer: WSP Cantor Seinuk

11 March Memorial, Atocha Train Station

Architect: FAM Arquitectura y Urbanismo S.L.
Client: Madrid City Council and RENFE.
General Contractor: Dragados S.A.
Installation Engineer: Urculo Ingenieros. Comacal.
Structural Engineer: Schlaich, Bergermann and Partner

Gefter-Press House

Architect: Michael Bell Architecture
Architect of Record: Stephen O'Dell
Contractors: Mitchell Rabideau and Cav Ark Builders
Glass Supplier: Rochester Insulated Glass
Lighting Design: David Singer
Mechanical Engineer: Altieri Sebor Wieber
Project Team: Thomas Long, Stephen O'Dell, and Eunjeong Seong
Structural Engineer: Nat Oppenheimer

Glass Pavilion, Toledo Museum of Art

Acoustical Consultant: Harvey Marshall Berling Associates
Architect of Record: Kendall/Heaton Associates
Architect: SANAA
Civil Engineer: Mannik & Smith Group
Client: Toledo Museum of Art
Climate Engineer: Transsolar
Engineer of Record: Guy Nordenson and Associates
Facade/Glass Consultant: Front Inc.
Geotechnical Engineer: Bowser-Morner
MEP Engineer: Cosentini Associates
Project Manager: Paratus Group
Project Team: Kazuyo Sejima, Ryue Nishizawa, and Toshihiro Oki
Structural Engineer: SAPS/Sasaki and Partners

IAC/InterActiveCorp

Architect: Gehry Partners, LLP
Audiovisual: McCann Systems
Construction Management: Turner Construction Company
Curtain Wall/Glass Consultant: Israel Berger & Associates
Curtain Wall Manufacturer: Permasteelisa
Development Partner: Georgetown Company
Executive Architect: Adamson Associates Architects
Geotechnical Engineer: Langan Engineering & Environmental Services
Interior Architect: STUDIOS architecture
IT and Security Consultant: TM Technology Partners
MEP Engineer: Cosentini Associates
Project Team: Frank O. Gehry, Craig Webb, and John Bowers
Structural Engineer: DeSimone Consulting Engineers

Nelson-Atkins Museum of Art

Architect: Steven Holl Architects
Client: Nelson-Atkins Museum of Art
Glass Consultant: R.A. Heintges & Associates
Landscape Architect: Gould Evans Goodman Associates
Lighting Consultant: Renfro Design Group
Local Architect: Berkebile Nelson Immenschuh McDowell Architects
Mechanical Engineers: Ove Arup & Partners and W.L. Cassell & Associates
Design Architects: Steven Holl and Chris McVoy,
Project Architects: Martin Cox and Richard Tobias,
Structural Engineers: Guy Nordenson and Associates and Structural Engineering Associates

277 Mott Street

Architect: Diller Scofidio + Renfro
Client: Karl Kopp
Facade Consultants: Israel Berger & Associates, Miscellaneous Metals, and Structured Environment (Alan Burden)
Facade Manufacturer: ChersonProm
Glass Bricks: Nippon Electric Glass
Harmonics Engineer: Werner Sobek Engineering
Project Team: Ric Scofidio, Stefan Röeschert, and Simon Arnold
SMEP Engineers: Arup (New York)
US Distributor: TGP (Technical Glass Products)

Image credits

Portfolio

pp.17–31: all images courtesy of SANAA

Essays

pp. 33–38: fig. 1, reprinted with permission from Bruno Taut, *Alpine Architektur* (Hagen inWest: Erschienenim Folkwang-Verlag G.m.b.H., 1919); figs. 2 and 4, courtesy of Graphische Sammlung, Staatsgalerie Stuttgart, Germany; fig. 3, courtesy of Wenzel-Hablik-Stiftung; fig. 5, reprinted with permission from László Moholy-Nagy, *Von Material zu Architektur* (Munich: A. Langen, c1929); fig. 6, courtesy of the Canadian Centre for Architecture; fig. 7, courtesy of the Russian State Archive for Literature and Art; fig. 8, courtesy of the State Tretyakov Gallery in Moscow.

pp. 39–44: fig. 1, photograph by Cervin Robinson; fig. 2, photograph by Tim Street-Porter; fig. 3, photograph by Kenneth Kirkwood; figs. 4 and 5, courtesy of Philip Johnson Alan Ritchie Architects; fig. 6, courtesy of InterActiveCorp.

pp. 45–54: figs. 1, 2, and 4, courtesy of the Victoria and Albert Museum; figs. 3 and 5, reprinted with permission from Konrad Wachsmann, *The Turning Point of Building: Structure and Design*, trans. Thomas E. Burton (New York: Reinhold Pub. Corp., 1961); figs. 6 and 8, reprinted from Sigfried Giedion, *Befreites Wohnen* (Zürich; Leipzig: Orell Füssli Verlag, 1929); fig. 7, courtesy of Fondation Le Corbusier/Artists Rights Society New York (ARSNY); figs. 9–12, reprinted from Arthur Korn, *Glas im Bau und als Gebrauchsgegenstand*, (London: Barrie & Rockliff, 1968); fig. 13, reprinted from Erich Mendelsohn, *Amerkia: Bilderbuch eines Architekten* (Braunschweig : Friedr. Vieweg & Sohn Verlagsgesellschaft, 1991); fig. 14, photograph by Norman McGrath; fig. 15: courtesy of Artists Rights Society New York (ARSNY)/ADAGP, Paris/estate of Marcel Duchamp; fig. 16: courtesy of the Buckminster Fuller Institute; fig. 17: courtesy of Artists Rights Society, New York (ARSNY)/estate of Reyner Banham.

pp. 55–64: figs. 1 and 2, courtesy of Albert Kahn Associates, Inc.; fig. 3, photograph by Richard Steiff; fig. 4, photograph by Ezra Stoller; figs. 5 and 6, courtesy of Peter Rice; fig. 7, courtesy of Dewhurst Macfarlane; fig. 8, courtesy of REX; figs. 9 and 10, courtesy of Schlaich Bergermann.

pp. 65–68: figs. 1 and 2, courtesy of Weiss/Manfredi; fig. 3, photograph by Marc Moundry.

pp. 72–77: figs. 1, 2, 4, 6, and 7, courtesy of Guy Nordenson and Associates; fig. 3, photograph by Tim Hursley; figs. 8 and 9, courtesy of Paul Warchol.

pp. 78–87: fig. 1, reprinted from Bruno Reichlin, "The Pros and Cons of the Horizontal Window," *Daidalos: Berlin Architectural Journal*, no. 13 (September 1984): 64–78; fig. 2, photograph by Charles Eames; fig. 3, reprinted from the *Saturday Evening Post*, April 26, 1958; figs. 4 and 14, courtesy of SANAA; figs. 5 and 10, courtesy of Edward Duckett; fig. 6, film still reprinted from James Sibley Watson Jr., *Highlights and Shadows*, 1937; fig. 7, film still reprinted from Pierre Chenal, *Bâtir*, 1928; fig. 8, reprinted from William Pars Graatsma, *Glaspaleis Schunck* (Heerlen: Nederland, 1935); fig. 9, photograph by Hedrich-Blessing, Inc.; fig. 11, photograph by Arnold Newman; figs. 12 and 13, the Museum of Modern Art/licensed by SCALA/Art Resource, NY (ART166252); figs. 15, 16, and 17, courtesy of the United States Customs Department; fig. 18, photograph by Chris Greenberg; fig. 19, photograph by Todd Pitman.

pp. 90–95: figs. 1, 2, and 3, courtesy of Michael Bell; figs. 4 and 5, John Hejduk Foundation; fig. 6, courtesy Michael Bell and Guy Vinson, fig. 7, film still reprinted from Hans Namuth, *Painting on Glass*, 1950; fig. 8, R.C. Dove, *Experimental Stress Analysis and Motion* (Columbus, OH: Charles E. Merrill, 1964).

Projects

pp. 97–106: photographs by Andy Ryan; all other images courtesy of Steven Holl Architects.

pp. 107–18: pp.108–110, 111 left, and 113–115, photographs by Bilyana Dimitrova; pp. 111 right, 112, and 118, photographs by Richard Barnes; all other images courtesy Michael Bell Architecture.

pp. 119–30: p. 128 top right, courtesy of Guy Nordenson and Associates; pp. 128 bottom and 129 bottom, courtesy of Transsolar; p. 129 top, courtesy of ARUP Lighting; all other images courtesy of SANAA.

pp. 129–36: All images courtesy of thomasmayerarchive.com.

pp. 137–44: p. 137, photograph by Verena von Holtum, p. 138, photograph by Andreas Keller; pp. 139–41, photographs by David Sundberg; pp.142–144, all images courtesy of James Carpenter Design Associates.

pp. 145–51: photographs by Esau Acosta; all other images courtesy of FAM Arquitectura r Urbanismo S.L.

Technical Innovations: Material and Light

pp. 153–55: all images courtesy of Thomas J. Richardson.
pp. 156–57: both images courtesy of Marble Fairbanks.
pp. 158–60: figs. 1–4, courtesy of Graham Dodd; figs. 5–7, photographs by Nikolas Weinstein.
pp. 161–63: figs. 1 and 2, courtesy of Wuerth Solar GmbH & Co., KG, Germany; fig. 3, photograph by Wolfgang Pulfer; figs. 4 and 5, courtesy of SCHOTT AG, Mainz, Germany.
pp. 164–67: fig. 1, courtesy of Adriana Lira; fig. 2, courtesy of Naree Phinyawatan; figs. 4, and 5, courtesy of Nasser Abulhasan.

Technical Innovations: Structure and Glass

pp. 169–82: figs. 1 and 5, courtesy of Roland Halbe; figs. 2 and 10, courtesy of Zooey Braun, fig. 3, courtesy of Johannes Marburg; figs. 4 and 6, courtesy of H.G. Esch, Hennef, Germany; fig. 7, courtesy of LIN, Berlin, Germany; figs. 8 and 9, courtesy of Werner Sobek.
pp. 183–88: fig. 2, courtesy of T.A. Michalske; figs. 10–13, courtesy of 3deluxe; figs. 1 and 3–9, courtesy of Jens Schneider.
pp. 189–92: fig. 1, courtesy of the Victoria and Albert Museum; fig. 2, courtesy of Kevin Roche John Dinkeloo and Associates; fig. 3, courtesy of Rafael Viñoly Architects; figs. 4, 5, and 6, courtesy of William Nicholas Bodouva + Associates; figs. 7 and 8, courtesy of Lohan Caprile Goettsch Architects; figs. 9 and 10, courtesy of Pelli Clarke Pelli Architects.
pp. 193–201: figs. 1 and 2, courtesy of Dennis Schlepper; figs. 3 and 4, courtesy of Jürgen Heinzel; fig. 5, courtesy of Tillmann Klein, Marcel Bilow, and Harry Buskes; fig. 6, courtesy of Marcel Bilow and Tillmann Klein; figs. 7 and 8, courtesy of Marcel Bilow; figs. 9–11, courtesy of Ulrich Knaack, Marcel Bilow, and Tillman Klein; figs. 12, 13, and 17, courtesy of Ulrich Knaack and Marcel Bilow; figs. 14–16, 18, and 19, courtesy of Torben Inderhees.
pp. 202–203: all images courtesy of H. Scott Norville.
pp. 204–207: all images courtesy of the Institute of Building Construction, Technische Universität Dresden.
pp. 208–209: all images courtesy of Weidlinger Associates.
pp. 210–213: all images courtesy of Delta-X GmbH, Engineering.

Visual and Spatial Effects

pp. 215–223: p. 215, center two photographs courtesy of NASA; p. 216 top image, courtesy of Fondation Le Corbusier/Artists Rights Society, New York (ARSNY); p. 220, middle photograph by Michael Moran; p. 221 second photograph from top, p. 222 top two photographs, and p. 223 top two photographs, all by Judith Turner; all other images, all pages, courtesy of Smith-Miller + Hawkinson Architects.
pp. 224–32: figs. 1 and 11–13, photographs by David Sundberg; fig. 2, photograph by Balthazar Korab; fig. 3, photograph by James Carpenter; figs. 4–6, photographs by Brian Gulick; figs. 7–10, courtesy James Carpenter Design Associates; fig. 14, photograph by Andreas Keller.
pp. 233–35: figs. 1–7, courtesy of Diller Scofidio + Renfro; fig. 8, courtesy of Werner Sobek Engineering & Design.
pp. 236–40: figs. 1, 2, and 4–6, courtesy of SANAA; figs. 3 and 7–14, courtesy of TRANSSOLAR.
pp. 241–49: figs. 1–14, courtesy of François Roche and Stéphanie Lavaux of R&Sie(n).
pp. 250–55: all images courtesy of Diller Scofidio + Renfro.

This book was made possible by the generous sponsorship of Oldcastle Glass®, the leading North American supplier of architectural glass and aluminum glazing systems, including custom-engineered curtain and window walls, architectural windows, storefront systems, doors, and skylights.